DATE DUE

African American Biographies

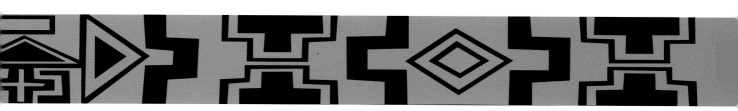

Volume 10

Tyson, Mike—Zollar, Doris

GROLIER

an imprint of

◣SCHOLASTIC

www.scholastic.com/librarypublishing

First published 2006 by Grolier,
an imprint of Scholastic Library Publishing,
Old Sherman Turnpike
Danbury, Connecticut 06816

Set ISBN 978-0-7172-6090-4
Volume ISBN 978-0-7172-6100-0

Library of Congress Cataloging-in-Publication Data
African American biographies.
     p. cm.
   Includes index.
   Contents: v.1. Aaliyah–Blyden, Edward W.—v.2. Bond, Horace
Mann–Clarke, John Henrik—v.3. Cleaver, Eldridge–Edmonds, Kenneth
"Babyface"—v.4. Edwards, Herman–Greener, Richard —v.5. Greenfield,
Elizabeth–Jacobs, Harriet—v.6. Jakes, T. D.–Loury, Glenn C.—v.7. Love,
Nat–Oliver, Joe "King"—v.8. O'Neal, Shaquille–Satcher, David—v.9.
Savage, Augusta–Tyson, Cicely—v.10. Tyson, Mike–Zollar, Doris
   ISBN 978-0-7172-6090-4
   I. African Americans—Biography—Juvenile literature. I.
     Scholastic Library Publishing

E185.96.A439 2006
920'.009296073–dc22
[B]

                    2005050391

For information address the publisher:
Grolier, Scholastic Library Publishing,
Old Sherman Turnpike,
Danbury, Connecticut 06816

FOR THE BROWN REFERENCE GROUP PLC

Project Editors:	Sally MacEachern, Aruna Vasudevan
Design:	Q2A Solutions
Picture Researchers:	Laila Torsun, Sharon Southren
Index:	Kay Ollerenshaw
Design Manager:	Lynne Ross
Production Director:	Alastair Gourlay
Senior Managing Editor:	Tim Cooke
Editorial Director:	Lindsey Lowe

Academic consultants:

     Molefi Kete Asante, Professor,
        Department of African American
        Studies, Temple University
     Mario J. Azevedo, Chair and Frank Porter
        Graham Professor, Department of Africana
        Studies, University of North Carolina at
        Charlotte
     Scott M. Lacy, University of California Faculty
        Fellow, Department of Black Studies,
        University of California
     Mawusi Renee Simmons, Development
        Consultant and Museum Docent, University
        of Pennsylvania Museum Philadelphia,
        Pennsylvania

Printed and bound in Singapore

ABOUT THIS SET

This is one of a set of 10 books about the African Americans who have helped shape the past of the United States and who play a vital part in the nation's life today. Some were leaders of the abolitionist movement against slavery in the latter half of the 19th century; others excelled in their fields despite being born into slavery themselves. The abolition of slavery after the Civil War (1861–1865) did not mark the end of the prejudice that prevented most black Americans from fulfilling their potential, however. During the first half of the 20th century the African Americans who made their names in the arts, entertainment, sports, academia, or business remained exceptions who reached prominence as the result of a determined struggle to overcome discrimination and disadvantage.

The civil rights advances of the 1950s and 1960s removed legal and institutional barriers to African American achievement, but pioneers in many fields still faced greater difficulties than their white peers. By the start of the 21st century, however, black Americans had become prominent in all fields of endeavor, from space exploration to government.

This set contains biographies of more than a thousand of the many African Americans who have made a mark. Some are household names; others are largely—and unjustly—overlooked or forgotten. Their entries explain not only what they achieved, but also why it was important. Every entry has a box of key dates for quick reference. Longer entries also include boxes on the people who inspired great African Americans or people they themselves have influenced in turn. Most entries have a "See also" feature that refers you to related articles elsewhere in the set. If you want to find out more about an individual there are suggested books and Web sites. Addresses may change, however, and the accuracy of information on sites may vary.

Throughout the set are a number of guidepost articles. They provide an overview of particular aspects of African American experience, such as the civil rights movement or the Harlem Renaissance of the 1920s, and help place the individuals featured in the biographies in a wider context.

The biographies are arranged alphabetically, mostly by last name but also by stage name. Each volume contains an index that covers the whole set and will help you locate entries easily.

CONTENTS

TYSON, Mike
Boxer

Mike Tyson made a rapid ascent to the top of world boxing. Known as "Kid Dynamite," Tyson won his first world heavyweight title at age 20. For over three years he was at the top of his sport, but after losing his title in 1990 Tyson entered a long period of decline, the low point of which was a period spent in jail as the result of a conviction for rape.

Early life

Born on June 30, 1966, in Brooklyn, New York City, Michael Gerald Tyson was the son of Lorna Tyson and Jimmy Kirkpatrick. Tyson's parents split up before he was born and he was brought up by his mother in the city's poverty-stricken Brownsville area. Tyson drifted into a life of petty crime. Frequent brushes with the law led to his being sent, at age 12, to the Tryon School for Boys in Johnstown, New York, where he took up boxing.

The world of boxing

Bobby Stewart, the school's boxing coach, spotted the young Tyson's potential and introduced him to Cus D'Amato, a veteran trainer who lived in the Catskill Mountains. D'Amato had trained boxing champion Floyd Patterson in the 1950s; he became Tyson's mentor and in 1982 his guardian, following the death of Tyson's mother. Tyson later said: "Cus was my backbone.... He did everything for my best interest."

Under D'Amato's tutelage, Tyson developed into a highly skillful boxer. After a brief but successful amateur career, Tyson turned professional; his first fight was a first-round knockout victory against Hector Mercedes on March 6, 1985. The fight set the tone for Tyson's early career: Few opponents managed to last longer than two rounds, and word of Tyson's destructive power spread. Tyson suffered a huge set back when D'Amato died in 1985; some people believe that his death contributed to Tyson's later troubles.

Tyson had a shot at the world title against World Boxing Council (WBC) heavyweight champion Trevor Berbick on November 22, 1986. A decisive second-round victory made Tyson the youngest heavyweight champion in history. He also won the World Boxing Association

▼ **On March 7, 1987, Mike Tyson (right) acquired the World Boxing Association belt when he defeated James "Bonecrusher" Smith.**

INFLUENCES AND INSPIRATION

Of all the great black American boxers who won world championships, Mike Tyson identified most with Sonny Liston, who held the heavyweight title in the early 1960s.

There were several parallels between the two fighters. Like Tyson, Liston grew up in poverty and was in trouble with the law at a young age. Both Tyson and Liston were portrayed as inhuman monsters by the media. Liston played up to his bad boy image and Tyson often attributed his own bad behavior to a need he felt to live up to his media-created public image.

Both boxers were seen as unbeatable until they lost their titles to underdog challengers—Tyson was knocked out by James "Buster" Douglas, Liston lost to Muhammad Ali after he failed to answer the bell in the seventh round. Neither Liston nor Tyson's careers recovered.

(WBA) title on March 7, 1987, after he defeated James Smith and added the International Boxing Federation (IBF) title on August 1 when he defeated Tony Tucker. By this time Tyson was one the most recognizable athletes in the world and a popular subject with the press. His 1988 marriage to black actor Robin Givens and their subsequent divorce less than a year later amid accusations of Tyson's physical abuse kept the boxer in the news. His association with controversial boxing promoter Don King also made headlines.

After 37 consecutive wins Tyson fought James "Buster" Douglas in Tokyo, Japan, on February 11, 1990. Tyson was regarded by many boxing fans as an unstoppable force and few people gave Douglas any chance of winning the heavyweight championship. In one of the greatest upsets in boxing history, he knocked Tyson out in the 10th round.

Controversy

After losing his title Tyson won a handful more fights, but his comeback was halted in July 1991, when he was accused of rape by a Miss Black America beauty contestant who had met Tyson at a pageant rehearsal. Tyson denied the charges, but when the case went to trial in 1992 the jury found him guilty. Tyson was sentenced to 10 years in prison, with four suspended: He served just three years of his sentence and was released in March 1995.

Resuming his fighting career a few months later, Tyson beat Pete McNeely in just 89 seconds. In 1996 he regained two of his world championship belts by beating British fighter Frank Bruno and American Bruce Seldon. He lost the WBA heavyweight title to Evander Holyfield in November 1996. The rematch against Holyfield in June 1997 was one of the most controversial heavyweight fights in history. Enraged by what he believed to be an intentional headbutt, Tyson twice bit Holyfield's ear, tearing a chunk out of it. The incident led to a disgraced Tyson having his boxing license withdrawn. He was not able to box for 18 months.

To add to his troubles, Tyson also suffered severe mental health problems and was taking antidepressants. Although his license was renewed in October 1998, after just one comeback fight Tyson was jailed for a year for assaulting two motorists. He resumed his boxing career on his release, beating a handful of low-quality opponents before challenging Lennox Lewis for the WBC and IBF heavyweight titles. The buildup to the fight was marred by a brawl between the two fighters at a press conference. The fight itself, which took place on June 8, 2002, was one-sided, with Lewis outclassing the challenger.

Tyson was a shadow of his former self, but he fought on, a decision prompted by his now desperate financial situation. After a solitary victory in 2003, he lost two fights against opponents he was expected to beat easily, after which he announced his retirement. In 2003 Tyson was placed 16th in *Ring* magazine's all-time best punchers list.

KEY DATES

1966	Born in Brooklyn, New York City, on June 30.
1986	Becomes youngest ever world heavyweight champion when he defeats Trevor Berbick for the WBC title.
1992	Found guilty of rape.
1997	Loses world title fight to Evander Holyfield.
2002	Knocked out by champion Lennox Lewis in the eighth round of the world title fight.

See also: Ali, Muhammad; Holyfield, Evander; King, Don; Liston, Sonny

Further reading: O'Connor, Daniel (ed.). *Iron Mike: A Mike Tyson Reader.* New York, NY: Thunder's Mouth Press, 2002. www.boxrec.com/boxer_display.php?boxer_id=000474 (Record).

TYUS, Wyomia
Athlete

Wyomia Tyus was a highly successful American runner during the 1960s. She won three Olympic gold medals and became the first woman to retain the Olympic title in the 100 meters (1964 and 1968).

Olympic Gold

Born in Griffin, Georgia, on August 29, 1945, Tyus exceled as an athlete from a young age. Her speed and agility as a runner made her stand out in high school. Tyus went on to Tennessee State University, where she was put forward for the Olympic trials.

In 1964 Tyus took part in the Summer Olympics in Tokyo, Japan, at age 19. She won the 100-meter race, beating fellow American Edith McGuire by two-tenths of a second. She also won a silver medal as part of the U.S. 4 x 100-meter relay team, which finished behind Poland. Later that year Tyus also won the 100 meters in the Amateur Athletic Union (AAU) championship meet.

Other achievements

In the next few years Tyus's reputation strengthened. She was an AAU champion at 100 yards (1965–1966) and 220 yards. In addition she became a three-time winner of the 60-yard dash (1965–1967), setting world records in the event in 1965 and 1966.

Tyus continued to excel as an athlete. She won numerous national championships in sprint events, and a gold medal in the 200 meters at the Pan-American Games in 1967. The following year saw Tyus return to the Olympics, this time held in Mexico City, to defend her title in the 100 meters. During the final Tyus set a new world record of 11.08 seconds and became the first woman to retain the Olympic 100-meter title. She also qualified for the 200-meter final, but only finished sixth. Taking part

▲ *Wyomia Tyus wipes away tears as she accepts a gold medal at the Mexico City Olympics in 1968.*

in the final leg of the 4 x 100-meter relay, Tyus won her third gold medal and helped set a new world record. At the victory ceremony the team dedicated their medal to the 200-meter gold and bronze medalists, Tommie Smith and John Carlos respectively, who had been suspended from the U.S. team for giving the Black Power salute at their victory ceremony.

Tyus retired from competing after the 1968 Olympics. She went on to instruct at dozens of sports clinics both in the United States and abroad, as well as lecturing on the role of sports in culture. She also made several TV appearances on such shows such as *ABC Superstars, Challenge of the Sexes*, and *The Merv Griffin Show.* Tyus was also a commentator for ABC's coverage of the Olympic Games in Montreal, Canada, in 1976. She was inducted into the U.S. Olympic Hall of Fame in 1985.

See also: Smith, Tommie

Further reading: http://www.womenssportsfoundation.org/ cgi-bin/iowa/athletes/record.html?record=305 (Short biography at the Women's Sports Foundation site).

KEY DATES

1945   Born in Griffin, Georgia, on August 29.

1964   Wins a gold medal for the 100 meters and a silver medal for the 4 x 100-meter relay at the Olympic Games in Tokyo, Japan.

1968   Becomes the first woman to retain the Olympic 100-meter title, and wins a third gold.

1985   Inducted into the U.S. Olympic Hall of Fame.

UPSHAW, Gene
Football Player

After a hugely successful career as a left guard with the Oakland Raiders, Gene Upshaw was made executive director of the National Football League Players Association (NFLPA) in 1983. Since then Upshaw has worked diligently at enhancing, protecting, and defending the individual rights of professional football players throughout the National Football League (NFL) as chairman of National Football League Players Incorporated, a for-profit corporation for player group licensing. Upshaw was elected to the Pro Football Hall of Fame in 1987, his first year of eligibility.

The road to success

Born in Robstown, Texas, on August 15, 1945, Eugene "Gene" Thurman Upshaw, Jr., was an outstanding athlete. He played college football at Texas A & I University (now Texas A & M–Kingsville), graduating with a BS in 1967. Following graduation he was drafted to the NFL Oakland Raiders, where he played offensive guard for 16 years. He

▼ **Gene Upshaw is the only player in NFL history to have played in Super Bowls in three different decades.**

KEY DATES	
1945	Born in Robstown, Texas, on August 15.
1967	Begins playing for Oakland Raiders (until 1981).
1983	Elected director of the NFL Players Association.
1987	Inducted into the Pro Football Hall of Fame.

played in 217 league games and appeared in six Pro Bowls. Named the AFC's Lineman of the Year in 1973 and 1974, Upshaw was also voted top lineman in the NFL (1977) and runner-up for the honor (1980).

Upshaw was a team captain and also served as an NFLPA player representative and officer for 13 years. He served as player representative for the Raiders from 1970 to 1976 and was a member of the NFLPA executive committee from 1976 through 1980, when he was elected president of the NFLPA, a post that he held until 1983. In the post Upshaw took part in all negotiations resulting in the 1977, 1982, and 1993 Collective Bargaining Agreements (CBA) between the NFLPA and the NFL, and extensions of the CBA in 1996, 1998, and 2001. Upshaw is also on the executive board of the American Federation of Labor and Congress of Industrial Organizations.

Honors

The recipient of many awards and honors, Upshaw was given the prestigious Byron "Whizzer" White Humanitarian Award for his outstanding contribution to "team, community, and country" in 1980. Two years later he was honored with the A. Philip Randolph Award for significant accomplishments as one of the outstanding black leaders in the United States. In 1993 he was listed 13th of the top 100 most powerful people in sports in the annual list compiled by the *Sporting News*. In 2004 the Manheim Touchdown Club announced a new football award, the Gene Upshaw Division II Lineman of the Year Award for outstanding offensive or defensive lineman.

See also: Randolph, A. Philip

Further reading: http://football.about.com/cs/legends/p/geneupshaw.htm (Biography).

USHER
Musician

Usher Raymond, IV, better known to fans as Usher, is an award-winning musician. Spotted at age 14 and signed to the LaFace label of Kenneth "Babyface" Edmonds and Antonio "L. A." Reid, Usher released his first album, *Usher*, to critical acclaim. Like many contemporary musicians, Usher has also ventured into movies, appearing in such films as *Texas Rangers*, starring Ashton Kutcher.

Early life
Born in Chattanooga, Tennessee, on October 14, 1978, Usher was raised by his single mother, Jonnetta Patton. He grew up singing in church choirs. At age 12, Usher moved with his mother to Atlanta, Georgia, home to super group TLC, LaFace Records, and So So Def, producer Jermaine DuPri's record label.

In junior high school Usher began entering local talent shows. At age 14 he was performing at a *Star Search* competition when he was discovered by an A&R (Artists and Repertoire) rep from LaFace Records, who arranged an audition. Reid immediately signed Usher.

In late 1993, when Usher was one month short of his 15th birthday, his debut LaFace single, "Call Me a Mack," from the soundtrack of John Singleton's movie *Poetic Justice* debuted on the charts. A year later he released his debut album, *Usher*. Coexecutive produced by Sean Combs, it rose to No. 25 on the rhythm-and-blues (R&B) chart. The hit single, "Think of You," came from the album.

Usher's follow-up multiplatinum album, *My Way,* was released after he graduated from high school in 1997. It was coexecutive produced by Reid, Edmonds, and DuPri,

▲ **As well as being a successful musician, Usher has appeared in several movies, making his debut performance in The Faculty (1998), Robert Rodriguez's high school homage to the cult movie Invasion of the Body Snatchers.**

and featured the hit song "You Make Me Wanna," which earned Usher his first Grammy Award nomination for Best Male R&B Vocal Performance. Usher's fourth album, *8701*, was released on August 7, 2001. Because of Grammy deadline peculiarities, "U Remind Me" was able to win the Best Male R&B Vocal award two years running, making Usher the only artist besides Luther Vandross and Stevie Wonder to win the award in consecutive years.

The album *Confessions* (2004) has sold more than 11 million copies worldwide. It spawned three No.1 pop and R&B hit singles, "Yeah!," featuring rappers Lil Jon & Ludacris, "Burn," and "Confessions Part II." In 2005 Usher won three Grammy Awards for best contemporary R&B Album, Best Rap/Song Collaboration, and Best Contemporary Album of the Year.

See also: Combs, Sean; Edmonds, Kenneth "Babyface"; Lil Jon; Wonder, Stevie

Further reading: http://www.ushersite.com/biography.html (Official site).

KEY DATES

1978	Born in Chattanooga, Tennessee, on October 14.
1992	Spotted by a rep for LaFace Records; signed to LaFace after an audition with L. A. Reid.
1994	Releases debut album, *Usher,* coexecutive produced by Sean Combs.
1997	Releases *My Way;* "You Make Me Wanna" tops the R&B charts for eight weeks and is No.1 on the pop charts.
2001	Releases *8701*.
2004	Releases *Confessions;* garners many awards, including a Grammy in 2005.

VANDERZEE, James
Photographer

James VanDerZee (sometimes written Van Der Zee or Van DerZee) ran a flourishing portrait studio in Harlem, New York City, from the late 1910s. His photographs provide a unique pictorial record of the lives of African Americans during the vibrant years of the Harlem Renaissance.

Early life
Born in Lenox, Massachusetts, on June 29, 1886, VanDerZee was the second of six children of John VanDerZee and Susan Elizabeth Egberts. VanDerZee's parents and their extended family worked for the local rich white community. VanDerZee grew up close to his siblings and cousins. He was given his first camera in 1900, the year in which he left school. He learned his art by taking photographs of his friends and family.

Harlem
In 1905 VanDerZee moved to Harlem. Working as an elevator operator, he met and married Kate Brown. VanDerZee also worked as a musician, playing the violin and piano with the Harlem Orchestra; in his spare time VanDerZee developed his interest in photography.

In 1915 VanDerZee took a job as a darkroom assistant in a photographic studio in Newark, New Jersey. A year later he set up his own portrait studio, Guarantee Photo Studio (later the GGG Photo Studio), on West 135th Street in Harlem. His clients included middle-class African Americans who were eager to have their status, achievements, and wealth recorded in stylish, fashionable photographs. VanDerZee's marriage ended in divorce at about this time and he married a German–Spanish woman named Gaynella Greenlee.

A career in photography
By the 1920s VanDerZee had established himself as the leading photographer in Harlem. His photographs showed the beauty, dignity, and pride of his subjects through carefully constructed pictures. He paid great attention to the pose of his sitters, used elaborate props, and retouched and embellished the negatives to enhance the beauty and glamour of his subjects. His subjects included soldiers returning from fighting in World War I (1914–1918), families, and couples; sports teams and church groups; celebrities such as dancer Bill "Bojangles" Robinson, singers Florence Mills and Mamie Smith, and heavyweight-

KEY DATES	
1886	Born in Lenox, Massachusetts, on June 29.
1915	Gets job in a portrait studio in Newark, New Jersey.
1916	Opens the Guarantee Photo Studio in Harlem.
1969	His work is included in the *Harlem on My Mind* exhibition at the Metropolitan Museum of Art.
1983	Dies in Washington, D.C., on May 15.

boxing champion Jack Johnson; and many of the leading figures in the Harlem Renaissance. He also took memorial pictures of people who had died, which was a common custom of the time. As well as taking portraits, VanDerZee recorded community events such as marches and rallies, and acted as official photographer to many organizations, including the Universal Negro Improvement Association (UNIA), founded by Marcus Garvey.

Professional decline and rediscovery
The Great Depression of the 1930s led to falling incomes in the United States, and many people did not have the disposable income to pay a photographer to take official photographs. A simultaneous increase in the availability of cheaper personal cameras also had an adverse effect on VanDerZee's business and by the mid 1940s he was struggling to earn a living.

In the late 1960s VanDerZee's work was rediscovered by Reginald McGhee, a researcher working on the Metropolitan Museum of Art's exhibition *Harlem on My Mind* (1969). VanDerZee, in his eighties, became a popular photographer again, taking portraits of such celebrities as comedian Bill Cosby, boxer Muhammad Ali, and musician Miles Davis. He died in 1983, at age 97.

See also: Ali, Muhammad; Cosby, Bill; Davis, Miles; Garvey, Marcus; Harlem Renaissance; Johnson, Jack; Mills, Florence; Robinson, Bill; Smith, Mamie

Further reading: Willis-Braithwaite, Deborah. *VanDerZee: Photographer, 1886–1983*. New York, NY: Harry N. Abrams, 1998.
http://multirace.org/firstday/stamp78.htm (Biography).

VAN PEEBLES, Mario
Director, Actor

Director and actor Mario Van Peebles is a member of Hollywood's black royalty. The son of the acclaimed blaxploitation director Melvin Van Peebles, Mario starred alongside his father in the classic 1971 movie *Sweet Sweetback's Baadasssss Song.* Van Peebles has collaborated with his father on many projects over the years and in 2003 he directed and starred in *Baadasssss*, a documentary about *Sweetback.*

Early life
Born in Mexico City, Mexico, on January 15, 1957, Van Peebles was the oldest child of Melvin Van Peebles and photographer Maria Marx. Van Peebles grew up in Europe, where his father lived and worked for many years, and San Francisco, California. Raised around the film industry, Van Peebles appeared in his father's breakthrough movie *Sweet Sweetback's Baadasssss Song* as the young Sweetback. The movie was one of the highest earning independent films of the time and launched a whole new genre of blaxploitation movies.

Melvin Van Peebles instilled in his children a belief that education was the key to success and Van Peebles went on to study at Columbia University, graduating in economics in 1978. He worked for a year as a budget analyst in New York City's Department of Environmental Protection before leaving to pursue a career in acting.

Making a mark
A very handsome man, Van Peebles began modeling for the Ford and Elite agencies while acting in Off-Broadway plays. He started to get parts on television, appearing in such long-running shows as *One Life to Live, The Cosby Show,* and *LA Law.* He was also cast in movies such as *The Cotton Club* (1984), *Children of the Night* (1985), and

▲ **Mario Van Peebles attends the Berlin Film Festival in Germany, on February 9, 2004.**

Heartbreak Ridge (1986). Van Peebles also directed music videos for stars such as Kid Creole and the Coconuts, and episodes of TV shows such as *21 Jump Street.*

In 1991 Van Peebles received critical acclaim as the director of *New Jack City,* starring Wesley Snipes. In 1993 Van Peebles directed and starred in *Posse,* a movie set during the Spanish–American War (1898) about a black unit of soldiers; his father also appeared in the movie.

Van Peebles has directed other acclaimed films, often dealing with black American subjects. They include *Panther* (1995), which looked at the Black Panther Party, and *Sally Hemings: An American Scandal* (2000), about the relationship between President Thomas Jefferson and his black slave Sally Hemings.

See also: Hemings, Sally; Snipes, Wesley; Van Peebles, Melvin

Further reading: Van Peebles, Melvin. *No Identity Crisis: A Father and Son's Story of Working Together.* New York, NY: Simon & Schuster, 1990.
www.imdb.com/name/nm0005522/ (Biography and filmography).

KEY DATES	
1957	Born in Mexico City, Mexico, on January 15.
1971	Acts in father's film *Sweet Sweetback's Baadasssss Song.*
1991	Directs *New Jack City.*
2000	Directs *Sally Hemings: An American Scandal.*
2005	Directs and stars in *Baadasssss.*

VAN PEEBLES, Melvin
Director, Actor, Writer

Icon of African American cinema, Melvin Van Peebles is a man of many talents. A playwright, novelist, musician, actor, producer, director, composer, and editor, Peebles is probably best known for his movie *Sweet Sweetback's Baadasssss Song* (1971), which launched the blaxploitation genre. Van Peebles is also the father of the actor and director Mario Van Peebles.

Early life
Born in Chicago, Illinois, on August 21, 1932, Melvin Peebles added the "Van" to his name while studying in Holland in the 1950s. He went to school in Phoenix, Illinois, graduating in 1949. After studying briefly at West Virginia State College, he transferred to Ohio Wesleyan University. Van Peebles graduated in 1953 with a BA in literature, after which he joined the Air Force. He married photographer Maria Marx in 1955. After leaving the Air Force in 1956, he moved to Mexico and then to San Francisco, California, where he took a variety of jobs, including operating a streetcar, while painting, writing, and making short films, including *Sunlight* (1957).

▼ **Melvin Van Peebles, photographed here at the 2004 Berlin Film Festival, had an established film career in Europe before making his name in the United States.**

KEY DATES	
1932	Born in Chicago, Illinois, on August 21.
1967	Makes *La Permission* (*The Story of a Three-Day Pass*).
1971	Directs and stars in *Sweet Sweetback's Baadasssss Song*.
2001	Awarded France's Légion d'Honneur.
2003	Mario Van Peebles makes *Baadasssss*.

Movies
In 1959 Van Peebles enrolled at the University of Amsterdam, Holland. His marriage failed and Maria took their children back to the United States. Van Peebles joined the Dutch National Theater, acting while he continued to make short films. After moving to France, Van Peebles wrote, acted in, and made films, including the 1967 *La Permission* (*The Story of a Three-Day Pass*), based on his novel of the same name. The film, which examines the interracial romance between a black soldier and a white woman, brought Van Peebles to the attention of Hollywood. In 1970 he made his directorial debut there with the racial comedy *Watermelon Man*, using his earnings to fund the independent movie *Sweet Sweetback's Baadasssss Song*. Cofinanced by comedian Bill Cosby, the film focused on a black man's fight against white authority. Van Peebles promoted the film himself and when it opened it was a box-office success. *Sweetback* went on to gross $4.1 million.

Van Peebles went on to produce two Broadway musicals, which won several awards. He also continued to produce, direct, and act, as well as delving into the stock market in the 1980s, becoming the first black options trader on the American Stock Exchange. Van Peebles has collaborated successfully on several projects with his son Mario, including a film adaptation of his own book, *Panther*.

See also: Cosby, Bill; Van Peebles, Mario

Further reading: Van Peebles, Melvin. *No Identity Crisis: A Father and Son's Story of Working Together.* New York, NY: Simon & Schuster, 1990.
www.imdb.com/name/nm0887708 (Biography).

VANZANT, Iyanla
Writer, Therapist

Inspirational therapist, writer, and minister Iyanla Vanzant is one of the most familiar faces on television. Born Rhonda Harris, Vanzant changed her name to Iyanla, meaning "great mother," after she became a Yoruba priestess. A regular guest of talk-show host Oprah Winfrey, Vanzant has helped millions of people through her books and lecture tours, which often draw on her personal experiences of abuse and neglect. Vanzant has said: "My greatest desire is for people to know who they are from the inside out and to use that knowledge as a tool of empowerment and love."

Early life
Born in the back of a taxi cab in Brooklyn, New York, in 1953, Vanzant was sent, at age two, to live with her grandmother following her mother's death. After a vicious beating by her grandmother, Vanzant was shuffled around her various relatives, living with her father and stepmother before being sent to live with an aunt whose husband continually raped her. Although Vanzant tried to tell people about her trauma, she found that no one was prepared to listen. Her traumatic childhood was followed by teen pregnancy, two abusive marriages, and a nervous breakdown. Her life changed when she decided to walk away from the abuse, taking her three children with her.

Changing lanes
Vanzant enrolled at Medgar Evers College in New York, graduating with a BS in 1983. Determined to help people, she went on to study law at Queens College, graduating in 1988. Vanzant worked as a public defender in Philadelphia, Pennsylvania, for four years. She began to write lectures

▲ *Vanzant raised her three children by herself after she left an abusive marriage. Following her own daughter's death, she is raising her grandchild.*

to help women change their lives, expanding them into a book, *Tapping The Power Within: A Path To Empowerment For Black Women* (1992), which contained basic spiritual principles, self-affirmations, and personal rituals. It became a national bestseller.

Vanzant found herself in demand as a motivational guest on TV and radio, appearing on talk shows such as the *Oprah Winfrey Show*; she also had her own show, *Iyanla* (2001–2002). Vanzant has since written many award-winning books, including *The Value in the Valley* (1995 BlackBoard Book of the Year) and *Faith in the Valley* (1996 BlackBoard Book of the Year). She established the Inner Visions Spiritual Life Maintenance Center and Bookstore in Silver Spring, Maryland, where she conducts personal growth classes and weekend workshops for men and women. Vanzant also lectures all over the world.

See also: Winfrey, Oprah

Further reading: Vanzant, Iyanla. *Yesterday I Cried*. New York, NY: Pocket Books, 2000.
http://www.annonline.com/interviews/980213/ (Biography).

KEY DATES	
1953	Born in Brooklyn, New York City.
1969	Has the first of three children, at age 16.
1983	Earns a BS from Medgar Evers College, New York.
1988	Awarded a law degree from Queens College.
1992	Publishes *Tapping the Power Within: A Path to Empowerment for Black Women*.
1999	Publishes the autobiographical *Yesterday I Cried*.

VAN SERTIMA, Ivan
Academic, Anthropologist, Writer

An anthropologist, linguist, and literary critic, Ivan Van Sertima has dedicated his life to revising and understanding the role of Africans in the history of world civilizations. He said: "We have come to reclaim the house of history. We are dedicated to the revision of the role of the African in the world's great civilizations."

Early life
Born in Kitty Village, Guyana, South America, on January 26, 1935, Van Sertima began his academic career in earnest when he attended the School of Oriental and African Studies (SOAS), University of London, England. After graduating with honors in 1957, Van Sertima worked as a press and broadcasting officer for the Guyana Information Services. As part of his job he made weekly broadcasts to Africa and the Caribbean from London.

Interest in Africa
As a young man Van Sertima traveled extensively, exploring Africa and learning about African civilization and culture both past and present. In 1967, during some fieldwork in Tanzania, Van Sertima compiled the *Swahili Dictionary of Legal Terms*. Three years later he relocated to the United States to attend graduate school at Rutgers University, New Jersey. Although skilled as a broadcaster and linguist, Van Sertima's primary research interest was much more expansive: He investigated recent archaeological, linguistic, and cultural discoveries to challenge prevailing myths about Africa as a place without history or scientific achievement.

KEY DATES

1935   Born in Kitty Village, Guyana, on January 26.

1977   Publishes *They Came Before Columbus: The African Presence in Ancient America.*

1979   Founds the *Journal of African Civilizations*

1987   Appears before a congressional committee to argue that it was a myth that Columbus discovered America.

1991   Addresses the Smithsonian Institution to defend his lifelong research.

1998   Publishes *Early America Revisited.*

Challenging Columbus
In 1972 Van Sertima started a distinguished teaching career at Rutgers University. Not long afterward he published his hallmark work, *They Came Before Columbus: The African Presence in Ancient America* (1977). In the book Van Sertima asserted that archaeological records, oral traditions, linguistics, botanical data, and cultural studies provide sufficient evidence to hypothesize that Africans navigated their way to the Americas prior to 1492. He remarked: "The African presence in America before Columbus is of importance not only to African and American history, but to the history of world civilizations." Other scholars hotly contested Van Sertima's controversial theory, however.

Academic career
In 1979 Van Sertima attracted a new audience and new scholars when he founded the *Journal of African Civilizations*. The journal became respected in the fields of anthropology, history, and African studies. Some academics believe that it has been key to the research and development of pan-African scholarship. Demand for many of the journal's popular issues led to Van Sertima republishing the material in a series of anthologies, including *Blacks in Science, Black Women in Antiquity*, and *Great African Thinkers*.

Van Sertima's theories continued to draw criticism. In 1987 he appeared before a congressional committee to defend his theory that it was a myth that Columbus discovered the Americas. In 1991 he further defended his theory at the Smithsonian Institution.

In 2005 Van Sertima was professor of African studies in the department of Africana studies at Rutgers University, and he is acknowledged as one of the world's leading scholars on African civilizations and their rightful place in the history of humankind. He has received many honors and awards, including the Clarence L. Holt prize, awarded for work about the cultural heritage of Africa and the African diaspora.

Further reading: Van Sertima, Ivan. *They Came Before Columbus: The African Presence in Ancient America.* New York, NY: Random House, 2003. http://caribbean.halloffame.tripod.com/ Ivan_Van_Sertima.html (Biography).

VAUGHAN, Sarah
Singer

During her almost 50-year career, legendary singer Sarah Vaughan worked with most of the leading names in music, playing and recording with such stars as Duke Ellington, Quincy Jones, and Lester Young. Known as "Sassy" and the "Divine One" (a name given to her by TV presenter Dave Garroway), Vaughan became famous as a jazz artist and with more popular hits such as "Lover Boy" and a cover of Nat King Cole's "Nature Boy." Ella Fitzgerald called Vaughan "the world's greatest singing talent."

The making of a star

Born in Newark, New Jersey, on March 27, 1924, Vaughan was the daughter of Asbury and Asa Vaughan. Although her father earned his living as a carpenter, he was also an accomplished guitarist, and Vaughan's mother sang in the Mount Zion Baptist choir and gave Vaughan piano lessons from age seven. Vaughan also sang in the church choir and became known for her extraordinary voice. Her big break came when a friend dared her to enter the amateur talent contest held each week at the Apollo Theater in Harlem, New York City. Vaughan won and was spotted by the popular black musician Billy Eckstine who got her a spot with Earl Hines's band, along with Charlie Parker and Dizzy Gillespie.

In 1944 Eckstine left Hines's band to form his own bebop orchestra, taking Vaughan with him. She made her debut recording "I'll Wait and Pray" with the band later that year. Two years later Vaughan married trumpeter George Treadwell, the first of four husbands, who became her manager. Treadwell groomed Vaughan, turning her into glamorous star. Vaughan recorded with the Musicraft label

▲ *Sarah Vaughan sings in a New York City nightclub in 1949.*

and had hits with songs such as "Nature Boy," which reached No. 9 on the charts. She moved to Columbia and had more chart hits such as "My Tormented Heart." In 1954 she signed a dual deal with the pop label Mercury and its jazz subsidiary, EmArcy. At Mercury Vaughan recorded such classics as "Misty," and "Broken Hearted Melody;" at EmArcy she worked with Clifford Brown, Count Basie, and Cannonball Adderley, producing what some music critics argue is her finest music with such tracks as "Lullaby of Birdland."

After her marriage to Treadwell ended, Vaughan moved to the Roulette label, where she performed with the Count Basie Orchestra. She returned to Mercury briefly, where she collaborated with Quincy Jones. After leaving the label in 1966, Vaughan took a five-year break from recording. In the 1970s and 1980s she toured extensively and had success with such albums as the Grammy-winning *Gershwin Live* (1982). Vaughan smoked heavily and was diagnosed with lung cancer in 1989, the year she won a Grammy for Lifetime Achievement. She died in 1990.

See also: Adderley, Cannonball; Basie, Count; Brown, Clifford; Davis, Miles; Ellington, Duke; Fitzgerald, Ella; Gillespie, Dizzy; Jones, Quincy; Parker, Charlie; Young, Lester

Further reading: Gourse, Leslie. *Sassy: The Life of Sarah Vaughan.* New York, NY: Da Capo Press, 1994.
http://www.pbs.org/jazz/biography/artist_id_vaughan_sarah.htm (Biography).

KEY DATES	
1924	Born in Newark, New Jersey, on March 27.
1942	Wins talent competition at Apollo Theater, New York.
1944	Makes debut record, "I'll Wait and Pray."
1945	Records "Lover" with Charlie Parker and Dizzy Gillespie.
1989	Awarded a Grammy for Lifetime Achievement.
1990	Dies at Hidden Hills, California, on April 3.

VAUGHN, Mo
Baseball Player

Through 11 seasons in the major leagues—the first eight with the Boston Red Sox—first baseman Mo Vaughn gained a reputation as one of the most feared hitters in baseball. His lifetime batting average of .293 and slugging average of .523 place Vaughn among the most productive hitters of the 1990s.

Early life
Born in Norwalk, Connecticut, on December 15, 1967, Maurice Samuel Vaughn was the son of school teachers. His mother taught him to swing a bat at age two. Vaughn excelled in football as well as baseball, and many people thought that his 6 foot 1 inch (1.86m), 260-pound (117.93-kg) frame was more suited to football. However, Vaughn decided to concentrate on baseball. After graduating from high school, he enrolled at Seton Hall University, New Jersey, where he set several school batting records. His teammates called him "Hit Dog."

A baseball star
Drafted by the Boston Red Sox as the 23rd pick in the first round of the 1989 amateur draft, Vaughn was called up to the majors midway through the 1991 season. After a less-than-spectacular 18 months of play, in 1993 Vaughn started catching the baseball world's attention when he posted a .297 batting average and a slugging percentage of .525, notching 29 home runs and 101 runs batted in. Over the next five years of playing with the Red Sox, Vaughn never hit below .300; he made the All-Star team three of those years and earned the American League's Most Valuable Player honor in 1995.

After becoming a free agent at the end of the 1998 season, Vaughn left the Red Sox following disagreements with general manager Dan Duquette. Vaughn signed a six-

▲ **As well as being a respected baseball player, Vaughn set up the Mo Vaughn Youth Development Program in Dorchester, Massachusetts, which gives about $450,000 a year to youth programs.**

year deal worth $70 million with the Anaheim Angels. He missed several games after an opening-day injury, and his performance, while still solid, was not what it had been in Boston. Vaughn's batting average began to slide; after five straight seasons above .300, he never reached that plateau again. His poor conditioning led to increasing errors in the field; he had always been among league leaders in fewest errors at first base.

After missing the entire 2001 season because of an injury to his left arm, Vaughn was traded to the New York Mets, where his numbers continued to decline. A serious injury to his knee forced Vaughn to retire from baseball in May 2003. Known for his generosity and community spirit, Vaughn supported many local charities, including the Food Bank and Boys and Girls Clubs, and set up the Mo Vaughn Youth Development Program.

KEY DATES	
1967	Born in Norwalk, Connecticut, on December 15.
1989	Drafted by the Boston Red Sox.
1991	Makes major league debut with the Boston Red Sox on June 27.
1995	Named the American League's Most Valuable Player.
2003	Retires from baseball.

Further reading: http://www.baseballlibrary.com/ baseballlibrary/ballplayers/V/Vaughn_Mo.stm (Biography).

VERRETT, Shirley
Opera Singer

Shirley Verrett was one of the great divas of her generation. She sang first as a mezzo-soprano and later as a soprano, but she always referred to herself just as a singer. Verrett achieved international acclaim and performed at all the major opera houses.

An operatic star

Born in New Orleans, Louisiana, on May 31, 1931, Verrett grew up in Oxnard, California. Her parents, Leon Solomon and Elvira Harris Verrett, were devoted members of the Seventh Day Adventist Church. Verrett sang from age five in the church choir. Although the quality of her voice had been recognized at an early age, Verrett did not initially pursue a musical career. She worked in real estate for four years before she formally started to study voice.

On winning a television talent scouts' contest singing a contralto aria from Camille Saint Saens's opera *Samson and Delilah*, Verrett entered the Julliard School of Music, New York City, in 1956. Before she graduated in 1961 Verrett had made her professional operatic debut with

▼ **Shirley Verrett and Jon Vickers play the lead roles in Samson and Delila in 1983.**

Benjamin Britten's *The Rape of Lucretia* at Yellow Spring, Ohio, in 1957, and performed Manuel de Falla's *El amor brujo* (Love, the Magician) with Leopold Stokowski and the Philadelphia Orchestra (1960).

Verrett came to international acclaim with Georges Bizet's *Carmen* at the 1962 Spoleto Festival in Italy. She made her debut at the Metropolitan Opera House, New York, with *Carmen* in 1968. She made opera history in 1973 when she sang the two leading roles of Cassandra and Dido in Hector Berlioz's *Les Troyens* (The Trojans). From then on Verrett concentrated on singing soprano roles; her celebrated performances included the leading roles in Giuseppe Verdi's *Macbeth* (1976), Gaetano Donizetti's *La Favorita* (The Favorite, 1978), Giovanni Bellini's *Norma* (1979), and Giacomo Puccini's *Tosca* (1980). At the inauguration of the new Opéra Bastille in Paris, France, in 1990, Verrett sang in *Les Troyens*.

During the 1990s Verrett reduced her operatic appearances, dedicating more attention to theater performances, including Rodgers and Hammerstein's musical *Carousel* at the Lincoln Center (1994) and an Off-Broadway revival of *In Dahomey* (1999) at the New Federal Theater in New York. Verrett has received many awards, including the Marian Anderson Award and honorary doctorates from Julliard and Northeastern University. She has also taught at such places as the University of Michigan School of Music.

Further reading: Verrett, Shirley, with Christopher Brooks. *Never Walked Alone: The Autobiography of an American Singer.* Hoboken, NJ: John Wiley & Sons, 2003.
http://www.shirleyverrett.com (Official site).
http://www.juilliard.edu/update/journal480journal_substory_0205.asp (Julliard biography).

VESEY, Denmark
Rebel Leader

Denmark Vesey was a freed black man who fought to free his race from slavery in an abortive rebellion in 1822. Although Vesey was unsuccessful he had a powerful influence on many abolitionists, including David Walker (*see box on p. 18*). Soldiers in the first black regiment during the Civil War (1861–1865) reportedly used "Remember Denmark Vesey of Charleston" as their battle cry. Overlooked by many historians, at the end of the 20th century there was renewed interest in Vesey and his influence.

Early life
Thought to have been born in about 1767 in Africa or the Caribbean, Vesey most probably grew up in the Danish colony of St. Thomas (now part of the U.S. Virgin Islands). An enslaved youth thought to have been named Telemaque, who was described as beautiful in appearance, was in a cargo of slaves transported from the Danish Virgin Islands to St. Dominigue (now Haiti). At about age 14 he was bought by the slave merchant Joseph Vesey, who soon sold him. Enslaved for three months on the island, Vesey is reported to have suffered from epilepsy and was returned to Joseph Vesey as unsound goods. The slave master kept Vesey, making him his personal servant.

A free man
Vesey traveled extensively with his owner, seeing at first hand the miseries of slavery over the next two years. He also educated himself. Following Joseph Vesey's retirement, the two men settled in Charleston, South Carolina. In 1799 Vesey bet on number 1884 in a local lottery and won $1,500. He used $600 of the sum to purchase his freedom.

Working as a carpenter, Vesey became quite wealthy and purchased a house just a few blocks from where the governor and mayor of Charleston lived. Vesey became a respected member of the black community. In 1816 he and a group of other free blacks established an African Methodist Episcopal (AME) Church.

Vesey, who believed that slavery should end, used the pulpit to drum up support among the congregation. Particularly influenced by the Old Testament, Vesey argued that white slave owners were denying black people rights given to them by God. Vesey was aware of Toussaint L'Ouverture's successful rebellion of 1801 in Haiti and he

▲ *Dorothy B. Wright's 20th-century painting* **Vesey Talking to His People** *shows him from behind because there are no records of what he looked like.*

began to question whether the same thing could happen in Charleston. The AME Church became so popular that the local white authorities became increasingly intolerant of the large black congregation and worried about the possibility of a slave revolt. They harassed church members in police raids and mass arrests. Eventually the church was dispersed and its property destroyed, outraging the membership, especially Vesey.

A rebel leader
In spite of the degree of financial ease that Vesey very likely enjoyed, he did not flee the South as many free blacks did. Vesey was determined to see what he could do to help blacks who were enslaved. By virtue of his background Vesey could speak French, English, Creole, and Spanish. All these languages proved useful when he was recruiting people to support his protest against slavery. Charleston had the largest population of free and enslaved black people of any U.S. city, as well as the

INFLUENCES AND INSPIRATION

Some commentators believe that Denmark Vesey was influenced as he grew up by the rhetoric of the American Revolution (1775–1783) and the discrepancy between its principles of freedom and the institution of slavery. As a literate black man who had recently purchased his own freedom, he must also have been aware of other slave rebellions. In 1800 in Virginia Gabriel Prosser had attempted to capture Governor James Monroe, execute town leaders, and hold others for ransom in order to gain freedom and to obtain property. Prosser was betrayed by a fellow slave. Many of Vesey's recruits were refugees from Haiti, where Toussaint L'Ouverture had led a successful slave army, but had later been betrayed by the French who offered to make peace but then arrested him instead.

Vesey's plans influenced other activists. Although unsuccessful, he became a martyr among radical and militant black abolitionists. In 1828 David Walker, a free black man who also belonged to the AME Church in Charleston, South Carolina, and was, like Vesey, strongly influenced by AME founder Richard Allen, published *David Walker's Appeal to the Colored Citizen's of the World*. In it Walker urged black people to rebel against slavery and predicted the destruction of America if slavery did not end. In 1831, just nine years after Vesey planned his great revolt, slave Nat Turner led an insurrection in Virginia that took the lives of at least 55 whites. Turner was executed, along with 21 other rebels.

largest population of enslaved black people, who were imported there directly from Africa. There was also a group of so-called French Negroes, enslaved black people who were the property of white people who had fled Haiti during the revolution. This group was especially valuable to Vesey's efforts because they were the largest group of black people to have seen a successful insurrection; many were also skilled blacksmiths who could help in making weapons.

Vesey capitalized on his facility with languages and his connections with the AME and Presbyterian churches, and with enslaved and free blacks to create a wide series of alliances. None of his coconspirators were free men, however, and he had an extreme mistrust of mixed-race blacks, feeling that they were more likely to betray him. He also avoided recruiting house slaves, believing that they were more likely to be loyal to their slave masters. One of his recruits was a slave named Gullah Jack, who was revered and feared as a religious man in the Obeah, the African folk religion, and who brought to the rebellion a force of coastal island slaves. Some historians believe that Vesey might also have had ties with Muslims, who made up about 10 percent of the city's blacks.

Vesey recruited potential rebels from 1818 until 1822. The rebels planned to seize the treasury, put every white person they encountered to death, and burn Charleston to the ground before fleeing to Haiti. The conspirators decided that they would revolt on July 14, 1822, a Sunday and a day on which black people could legally congregate. On May 15, however, a house slave told his owner about the rebellion. The authorities were put on alert. Vesey brought the date of the insurrection forward to June, but he and several hundred other conspirators were captured. Vesey was hanged on July 2. Between 6,000 and 9,000 black people were believed to have been involved in the rebellion at some level.

KEY DATES

1767   Born in about this year, in Africa or the Dutch Colony of St. Thomas (now in the U.S. Virgin Islands).

1799   Purchases freedom after winning a lottery.

1816   Helps establish an AME Church in Charleston, South Carolina.

1822   Plans a rebellion to assassinate the mayor, burn the city, take the arsenal, kill whites, and flee to Haiti; is betrayed and executed on July 2.

1831   Nat Turner's rebellion occurs; Turner and 21 rebels are executed.

See also: Allen, Richard; Gabriel; Slavery; Turner, Nat; Walker, David

Further reading: Robertson, David. *Denmark Vesey: The Buried Story of America's Largest Slave Rebellion and the Man Who Led It.* New York, NY: Alfred A. Knopf, 1999.
http://www.africawithin.com/bios/denmark_vesey.htm (Article on Vesey and the rebellion).

WADDLES, Charleszetta "Mother"
Social Activist

Charleszetta Waddles was the founder of the Perpetual Mission for Saving Souls of All Nations, a charity that provides a range of social services to low-income citizens in Detroit, Michigan. Better known simply as "Mother Waddles," she became a household name across the state and was revered for her compassion, warmth, and energy.

Early life

Charleszetta Lina Campbell was born in St. Louis, Missouri, on October 7, 1912, one of seven children of Henry and Ella Brown Campbell. When her father, a barber, lost his living, he was shunned by his church community and died soon afterward in 1924. To help support her brothers and sisters, Waddles had to leave school and find full-time work. She married at age 14 and began to raise her own family, but ended up bringing up her children by herself.

In 1936 Waddles, moved with husband Leroy Wash to Detroit, Michigan, in search of a new life. Many of Detroit's black and immigrant communities lived in extreme poverty and hardship, even during the growing prosperity of the decades following World War II (1939–1945). A deeply religious woman, Waddles was determined to do something for her neighbors. She said, "One day I had a vision. The Lord told me to feed the hungry and clothe the naked." In 1957, with the support of her third husband, Payton Waddles, she established the Perpetual Mission for Saving Souls of All Nations.

A Perpetual Mission

Beginning as little more than a soup kitchen, the Perpetual Mission rapidly expanded to include such services as job training and placement, a restaurant, an emergency helpline, and a cooking school. Waddles obtained a large warehouse that housed hard-to-afford products from lawnmowers to mattresses that had been donated to those in need.

KEY DATES	
1912	Born in St Louis, Missouri, on October 7.
1957	Founds the Perpetual Mission in Detroit, Michigan.
2001	Dies in Detroit on July 12.

▲ *Mother Waddles once remarked "You can't give people pride but you can provide the kind of understanding that makes people look to their inner strengths and find their own sense of pride."*

Over the years the Mission, which was funded only by private donations, often had money troubles, and was forced to move premises or temporarily close its doors. Mother Waddles, however, strove tirelessly to keep her project afloat, working 12 hours a day and on call around the clock, even when she was well into her eighties. She was always willing to try new ideas. In the late 1960s, for example, she wrote and produced *Mother Waddles' Soulfood Cookbook* as one way of raising funds. After a long illness Waddles died on July 12, 2001, at age 88. Her funeral service was attended by more than 1,000 Detroit citizens, and the Detroit police honored her with a 12-gun salute.

Today the Perpetual Mission, now under the presidency of Mother Waddles's son Leroy, continues to serve the Detroit community. The Perpetual Mission helps more than 100,000 people every year.

Further reading: Henry, Donna. "Mother Waddles: One Woman's War on Poverty." *Essence*, October 1, 1990. www.motherwaddles.com (Perpetual Mission site).

WALCOTT, Jersey Joe
Boxer

Jersey Joe Walcott became the heavyweight champion of the world at age 37, defeating Ezzard Charles on July 18, 1951. At the time he was the oldest man to become world champion. Born Arnold Raymond Cream, Walcott adopted the name of his father's favorite boxer, welterweight, Joe Walcott of Barbados.

Early life
Born in Merchantville, New Jersey, in 1914, Walcott was the son of Joseph Cream, who moved to the United States from the Caribbean island of Barbados. In 1928, after his father's death, Walcott traveled to Jack Blackburn's Gym in Philadelphia, Pennsylvania, to fulfill his father's dream that he become a boxer. Blackburn took the boy under his wing, working with him to refine his technique.

Walcott's first recorded professional bout took place on September 9, 1930; he knocked out Cowboy Wallace in the first round. When Blackburn was asked to train an amateur champion in Chicago, he agreed, provided Walcott was part of the deal. Poised on the edge of his big break, Walcott came down with typhoid. It took a year for him to recover. Meanwhile Blackburn had met the young Joe Louis. Later Walcott said "If I hadn't gotten sick and been able to meet that man in Chicago, who knows, I could have been the champion before Joe Louis."

During the Great Depression of the 1930s Walcott had to support his mother and siblings and took a series of menial jobs in order to make ends meet. He fought only two inconsequential fights between 1941 and 1945. Many

▲ *Jersey Joe Walcott photographed in 1951, when he was heavyweight champion.*

of his peers thought that Walcott's boxing career was over.

The emergence of a star
After the end of World War II (1939–1945), boxers heavier than 175 pounds (79.3kg) were in short supply, and Walcott began to fight more. On December 5, 1947, Walcott fought Joe Louis, knocking him down twice at Madison Square Garden, but Walcott lost a 15-round decision. A year later Walcott lost to Louis again; he also lost his first two title fights against Charles, but he won the title in 1951 in his third fight against the champion. He retained the belt in a fourth fight against Charles in 1952, but lost it in an epic fight against Rocky Marciano in Philadelphia later that year. In his last professional fight, on May 15, 1953, Walcott lost again to Marciano.

After his retirement Walcott worked as a boxing and wrestling referee. In the early 1980s he was appointed chair of the New York State Athletic Commission; he retired in 1984. After his death in 1994, trainer Eddie Futch called him "one of the finest technicians in heavyweight boxing."

See also: Louis, Joe

Further reading: Roberts, James. *The Boxing Register.* McBooks Press, 2002.
http://www.ibhof.com/walcott.htm (Biography).

KEY DATES

1914   Born in Merchantville, New Jersey, on January 31.

1930   Makes his pro debut, knocking out Cowboy Wallace in the first round on September 9.

1947   Loses his first heavyweight title fight against Joe Louis on December 5.

1951   Wins the heavyweight title fighting Ezzard Charles on July 18.

1952   Loses heavyweight title to Rocky Marciano on September 23.

1953   Is knocked out by Marciano in his final fight.

1994   Dies in Camden, New Jersey, on February 25.

WALKER, Alice
Writer, Activist

Pulitzer prize-winning author Alice Walker has written several highly successful books, including *The Color Purple* (1982), which in 1985 was turned into a Hollywood movie by Steven Spielberg, starring Oprah Winfrey. Walker's literature explores African American life, race, violence, and poverty; it celebrates the lives of remarkable independent black women. Walker is also a well-known activist, who has campaigned on such issues as the U.S. boycott of Cuba and female genital mutilation.

Early life
Born in Eatonton, Georgia, on February 9, 1944, Alice Malsenior Walker was the youngest child of sharecroppers Willie Lee Walker and Minnie Tallulah Grant. When Walker was eight, her brother accidentally shot her in the eye with a pellet from a toy gun while they were playing cowboys and indians, blinding her right eye and scarring her for life. Walker was a shy and introspective child. She was close to her family, especially her female relations; Walker draws on them in her literature, celebrating their independence and spirit, often in the face of great adversity.

As a child Walker showed great intelligence and excelled at her studies. In 1961 she received a scholarship to study at the prestigious Spelman College, where she became involved in the civil rights movement. She traveled to Finland in 1962, attending the Youth World Peace Festival, and later went to the home of Martin Luther King, Jr., to meet the civil rights leader. She left Spelman in

▲ *Alice Walker calls herself a womanist, saying "Womanist is to feminist as purple is to lavender."*

1963, transferring to Sarah Lawrence College in New York. In 1964 Walker spent the summer in Africa, but found on her return home that she was pregnant. She eventually had an abortion, but struggled with depression and suicidal thoughts, feelings that she wrote about in her poetry.

Moving on
In 1965, after graduating with a BA, Walker began working for the New York City welfare department. Two years later she married Jewish civil rights lawyer Mel Leventhal, with whom she moved to Jackson, Mississippi. Both Walker and Leventhal worked for the rights organization Head Start; Walker also took part in the voter registration program. Living in the South, Leventhal and Walker were heavily

KEY DATES

1944   Born in Eatonton, Georgia, on February 9.

1961   Awarded a scholarship to Spelman College; transfers to Sarah Lawrence College two years later.

1967   Marries Jewish civil rights lawyer Mel Leventhal; marriage ends 10 years later.

1970   Publishes the novel, *The Third Life of Grange Copeland.*

1979   Publishes *I Love Myself When I Am Laughing ... And Then Again When I Am Looking Mean and Impressive: A Zora Neale Hurston Reader.*

1982   Publishes *The Color Purple*; wins a Pulitzer Prize.

2000   Publishes *The Way Forward Is with a Broken Heart.*

INFLUENCES AND INSPIRATION

Alice Walker has been influenced by several writers, including Harlem Renaissance writer Jean Toomer, poet Gwendolyn Brooks, South African novelist Bessie Head, and the white Southern writer Flannery O'Connor. In the 1970s Walker came across the work of Zora Neale Hurston, a black writer and anthropologist who had died in obscurity. Walker published the groundbreaking anthology *I Love Myself When I Am Laughing … And Then Again When I Am Looking Mean and Impressive: A Zora Neale Hurston Reader* (1979), which helped put Hurston's work back in print.

Walker, who is an ardent feminist, also developed the concept of "womanism," or black feminism, which she introduced in her 1983 collection *In Search of Our Mothers' Gardens: Womanist Prose*. Walker herself explained that she came up with the word because she liked the "sound, the feel, the fit of it; because I cherish the spirit of the women the word calls to mind, and because I share the old ethnic-American habit of offering society a new word when the old word it is using fails to describe behavior and change that only a new word can help it more fully see."

criticized for their interracial relationship, about which Walker later wrote in a piece entitled "To My Husband" (2000). Although very busy, Walker managed to find the time to write. Her short story "To Hell with Dying" was published by the poet Langston Hughes in his anthology *The Best Short Stories by Negro Writers* (1967). A year later Walker published the poetry collection *Once*.

The emergence of a writer

In 1970 Walker finished her first novel, *The Third Life of Grange Copeland*, with the help of a McDowell Fellowship, named after librarian George D. McDowell, which helps fund research. The book explores male violence in three generations of a black Southern family, the Brownfields. Some people criticized Walker's depiction of black men as violent, but Walker justified it by saying that she knew too many Brownfields in real life. Walker continued to explore such themes, along with others linked with racism and sexism, in her short story collection *In Love and Trouble: Stories of Black Women* (1973) and in the 1976 novel *Meridian*, which was set in the civil rights era. Critically well received, the book helped establish Walker's reputation as a formidable writer.

Moving on

In 1977 Walker's marriage ended. She moved to California and accepted a teaching position at Wellesley College, where she taught the first black women's writing course. It was during this time that she discovered a forgotten black writer, Zora Neale Hurston (*see box*); Walker later published a book on Hurston's work.

After being awarded both a Guggenheim Fellowship and a National Endowment for the Arts Fellowship Walker was able to concentrate on writing her next work. In 1982 she published what is probably her best-known novel, *The Color Purple*. Centering on Celie, a Southern black woman, the book is written as a series of letters and is a gritty representation of violence, abuse, and love. After being raped repeatedly by her stepfather and married off to an older man, Celie finds love and happiness through her relationships with women. Written in simple but poetic language, the book was a huge success and earned Walker a Pulitzer Prize and the National Book Award in 1983. Walker received further acclaim when the book was turned into a successful Academy Award-nominated film by Steven Spielberg in 1985. She linked characters in her later books to those featured in *The Color Purple*. *The Temple of My Familiar* (1989) features Celie's granddaughter Fannie, and Celie's daughter-in-law appears in *Possessing the Secret of Joy* (1992).

Other pursuits

A well-known rights activist, Walker highlighted the issue of female genital mutilation in the documentary and accompanying book *Warrior Marks* (1993). The recipient of many awards, she has taught at several universities, including the University of Massachusetts and Yale. Walker also cofounded Wild Trees Press in 1974.

See also: Brooks, Gwendolyn; Hughes, Langston; Hurston, Zora Neale; Toomer, Jean; Winfrey, Oprah

---

Further reading: Walker, Alice. *Anything We Love Can Be Saved: A Writer's Activism.* New York, NY: Random House, 1997.
http://www.library.csi.cuny.edu/dept/history/lavender/walker.html (Links to various articles on Walker).

WALKER, C. J. "Madam"

Entrepreneur, Philanthropist

Madam C. J. Walker's life is a story of the American Dream come true. Born into abject poverty Walker, who was born Sarah Breedlove but later took the name of her third husband, Charles Joseph Walker, rose to become the head of a million-dollar hair and beauty empire. She was a successful businesswoman at a time when many women, irrespective of their color, were denied basic rights. Walker, who was a great philanthropist, helped empower black women by supplying them with wider vocational and educational choices.

Early life

Born in Delta, Louisiana, on December 23, 1867, Walker was the daughter of sharecroppers Owen Breedlove and Minerva Anderson. Walker and her siblings lived in extreme poverty. In 1873 Walker's mother died, followed two years later by her father. Sent to live with her sister Louvenia and her abusive husband Jesse Powell, in 1891 Walker married Moses McWilliams to escape her brother-in-law's cruelty. Later she spoke of the marriage as strictly a practical rather than a romantic decision. In 1894 Walker gave birth to a daughter, Lelia, but by age 20 she was a widow struggling to bring up a young child. Walker moved to St. Louis, Missouri, where she earned a living as a washerwoman.

A hair revolution

Life in St. Louis was not initially much easier for Walker. She moved often, sometimes living with her brothers for short periods of time. In 1894 Walker married John Davis, but he drank a lot and had affairs and their relationship was not a happy one. In addition to her other problems Walker found herself losing her hair as a result of her poor diet and daily exposure to the chemicals in the laundries where she worked. She began to experiment with different products to stop the hair loss, mixing up remedies in her washtub and giving them to friends and family to use. Walker realized that there was a gap in the market for specialized black hair products.

In 1903 Walker joined the sales team of Annie T. Malone, who sold scalp and hair treatments. Walker moved to Denver, Colorado, and worked as a cook while selling Malone's products. In 1905, however, she began to sell her own treatments, including the Wonderful Hair Grower and Glossine Hair Oil. In the following year she married

▲ *Walker once said about her business, "I want the great masses of my people to take a greater pride in their appearance."*

journalist Charles Joseph Walker, who helped her market and advertise her products. Selling her goods door to door, Walker soon had a flourishing business in Denver. She marketed a new steel version of the hot comb and developed the Walker System for removing the kinks from black hair. Walker began to travel in the South and East, marketing her goods and giving lectures and demonstrations in black communities. She also trained agents to sell her goods.

Giving back to the community

In 1910 Walker moved her center of operations to Indianapolis, Indiana, where she set up a factory, a training center, and research laboratories. As she continued to travel Walker became skilled in sales and business. She surrounded herself with able advisers, and she used her daughter Lelia to help her expand the

INFLUENCES AND INSPIRATION

Madam C. J. Walker was a well-known philanthropist and supporter of black education. She was particularly impressed by Booker T. Washington. Much like Walker, Washington's life story was one of rags to riches. Born into abject poverty, Washington was endowed with a great intellect and a great will to succeed. He rose to become one of the most influential African American educators and thinkers of his time. Washington believed that African Americans needed to have vocational skills in order to survive financially. In 1888 he was appointed head of the Tuskegee Institute in Tuskegee, Alabama. The school's curriculum included such subjects as carpentry, printing, and farming for male students, and cooking, sewing, and domestic skills for female students. Tuskegee became an important black educational facility, attracting leading intellectuals such as Monroe Nathan Work and George Washington Carver to its faculty.

Walker asked Washington for an opportunity to speak at the college, and then requested that hairdressing become a course option. She became a generous supporter of Tuskegee and established a scholarship for female students. She also supported Mary McLeod Bethune's Daytona Normal and Industrial Institute for Negro Girls and set up a school for girls in West Africa. In her own businesses Walker sought to provide African American women with more vocational options and greater financial independence. She also encouraged her agents to support charitable courses, establishing social clubs for them to do this.

business into uncharted territories. As her income increased, Walker began contributing generously to a variety of charitable causes, including the YMCA and the National Association for the Advancement of Colored People (NAACP). She became a fierce critic of lynching, using her speaking engagements as opportunities to bring attention to the issue. Walker held national conventions, bringing her agents together to discuss new techniques and business experiences. She also set up Walker Clubs to promote philanthropy among her agents and encouraged them to give time and money to their communities.

By 1917 Walker's business empire was worth $500,000 and was the largest black-owned business in the United States. She moved her business center to New York and bought a 20-room mansion on the banks of the Hudson River in Irvington, although she spent little time there as she continued traveling the country, recruiting new agents.

On her travels Walker not only developed new business relationships but established many friendships with such prominent African American leaders as Booker T. Washington, Ida B. Wells-Barnett, and W. E. B. DuBois.

Legacy

Walker's hectic schedule took a toll on her health, however. In 1916 she was diagnosed with a kidney disease and hypertension. She became ill in St. Louis, and was transported back to New York, where she died of kidney failure on May 25, 1919. Walker left a personal fortune of more than $1 million: two-thirds of her estate was donated to charitable and educational institutions and the rest went to her daughter, who also became company president. Walker's role in empowering African American women through training and education was noted by many African American leaders, including DuBois, who published a dedication to Walker in the NAACP's journal *Crisis*.

KEY DATES

1867	Born in Delta, Louisiana, on December 23.
1905	Produces the Wonderful Hair Grower.
1906	Marries Charles Joseph Walker on January 4.
1917	The Madame C. J. Walker Manufacturing Company has revenues of more than $500,000, making it the largest black-owned business in the United States.
1919	Dies in New York on May 25.

See also: Bethune, Mary McCleod; Carver, George Washington; DuBois, W. E. B.; Malone, Annie T.; Washington, Booker T.; Wells-Barnett, Ida B.; Work, Monroe Nathan

Further reading: Bundles, A'Lelia. *On Her Own Ground: The Life and Times of Madam C.J. Walker.* New York, NY: Scribner. 2001.
http://www.princeton.edu/~mcbrown/display/walker.html (Biography).

WALKER, David
Abolitionist, Entrepreneur

David Walker was an abolitionist who wrote *David Walker's Appeal to the Colored Citizens of the World* (1829), a call to slaves to rise up against their white masters and arguably the most powerful militant document written by an African American until that time.

Early life
Born in Wilmington, North Carolina, in about 1796, Walker is believed to have been the son of a black slave and a freed black woman. Little is known of his early life in the South, however. In 1815 Walker moved to the city of Charleston, South Carolina, which had a large free black population. While living there Walker joined slave resistance movements and the newly formed American Methodist Episcopal (AME) Church, which was established in Charleston in 1817. Walker became a devoted follower of the AME Church; attempts by white people to close the church caused bitter resentment in the black community. Walker was certainly still living in Charleston when Denmark Vesey, who was a fellow member of the AME Church, planned his unsuccessful uprising against the city's white officials in 1822.

A businessman
In about 1825 Walker moved to Boston, Massachusetts, where he opened a used clothing shop. Walker married Eliza Butler and became part of Boston's black community. He joined the Prince Hall Masonry Lodge No. 459, the first black masonic lodge, and mixed with the city's black elite. He wrote regular contributions, and helped raised funds, for the nation's first African American newspaper, *Freedom's Journal*. In 1828 Walker helped create the Massachusetts General Colored Association in order to advocate better rights for all black Americans.

An appeal
Walker changed the national debate on slavery in 1829 when he published *David Walker's Appeal to the Colored Citizens of the World*. In this historic document Walker created an articulate and radical antislavery argument. He described slavery in the United States as the most oppressive form of slavery in world history. Referring to the U.S. Constitution and the Bible, he explored the inconsistencies of Christian Americans who fought for emancipation from Britain while allowing racial slavery

to persist. In addition, Walker also encouraged African Americans to stand up and violently oppose racial injustice. The book fired the spirit and cause of slaves and abolitionists, but it terrified white people, already worried by Vesey's failed revolt. They sought to prevent Walker's message from spreading and causing further dissent among black people. Several states enacted legislation to prevent the circulation of antislavery literature. At one point some states offered a $3,000 reward for Walker's head and $10,000 for bringing him to the South alive. He was also denounced by more moderate abolitionists such as William Lloyd Garrison for being too radical.

Conspiracy
A year after first publication, Walker's book was on its third edition, but Walker himself was found dead in mysterious circumstances in his home. There was much conjecture that he had been poisoned, but later scholarship suggests that he died of tuberculosis. In a short life Walker had overcome the obstacles of a racialized America to become not only a successful entrepreneur, but also a revolutionary messenger for the abolition of slavery in the country.

See also: Garnet, Henry Highland; Vesey, Denmark

Further reading: Hinks, Peter (ed.). *David Walker's Appeal to the Colored Citizens of the World.* University Park, PA: Penn State University Press, 2000.
http://www.nps.gov/boaf/davidwalker.htm (Biography).

WALKER, Herschel
Football Player

With his dominating combination of speed and power, Herschel Walker was one of the greatest running backs in college and pro-football history. Walker led the University of Georgia Bulldogs to the national title in 1980, and in 1982 won the Heisman Trophy, which is given to the nation's best college football player. As a professional, Walker achieved over 25,000 all-purpose yards (22,860m) in the upstart United States Football League (USFL) and National Football League (NFL). However, Walker played in two different leagues, and as a result his importance to football is often overlooked when compared to the careers of other running backs who played their entire careers in the more prestigious NFL. For NFL record purposes, Walker's USFL totals do not count. Nevertheless, Walker is remembered for his rambling rushing style on the field and as a model citizen off it—he once pulled an elderly woman from a burning car. Walker was so popular with fans and the media that he even had a thoroughbred race horse named after him.

Early life

Born in Augusta, Georgia, on March 3, 1962, Walker should have been born in his family's hometown of Wrightsville, Georgia. His mother had complications while giving birth to him and was sent to Augusta for treatment, where there were better medical facilities. The fifth of seven children, Walker did not seem destined to be a great football player as a young boy. He was happiest in his own company, reading books and writing poetry.

At age 12, Walker weighed only about 100 pounds (45.35kg) and stood 5 feet 3 inches (1.92m) tall. Over the next year, to increase his height and size (*see box*), Walker did more than 100,000 situps and 100,000 pushups and built up a muscular, athletic physique. By the time he entered Johnson County High School, Walker weighed nearly 200 pounds (90.71kg) and stood 5 feet 10 inches (1.55m) tall. Walker went on to lead his high school football and track teams to state championships. He scored a record-breaking 85 touchdowns during his high school football career. In his senior year alone he rushed for 3,167 yards (2,895.90m), averaging 211 yards (192.92m) per game.

Road to success

The valedictorian of his senior class, Walker was one of the most recruited athletes in the country. Ultimately, he chose to stay close to home and attend the University of Georgia in Athens. During his first year in 1980, Walker rushed for 1,616 yards (1,477.67m)—a National Collegiate Athletic Association (NCAA) freshman record—in leading the Bulldogs to the national title with a 17–10 win over Notre Dame in the Sugar Bowl. In the January 1981 game, Walker rushed for 150 yards (137m) and two touchdowns despite playing nearly the entire contest with a dislocated shoulder. The Bulldogs finished the season undefeated with a 12–0 record. Walker rushed for 1,891 yards (1,729m) as a sophomore, and as a junior won the Heisman Trophy after amassing a three-year total of 5,259 yards (4,808.82m) rushing. He was named an All-American in each of his three collegiate seasons. He also ran track, and was one of the world's best in the 60-meter dash.

▼ *In 1999 Herschel Walker came second in the top 100 greatest college football players ever.*

INFLUENCES AND INSPIRATION

When Herschel Walker was in the sixth grade he was a scrawny boy who wanted to know how to make himself bigger and stronger. He asked for help from Tom Jordan, the young track coach at Johnson County High, Georgia, who also coached physical education at the local grade school. Jordan told him: "Do pushups, situps, and run sprints." Subsequently Jordan became

Walker's mentor, and he helped him build a proper training regime. When Walker got to Johnson County High, Jordan made him run pulling car tires attached to his waist to build strength. Jordan, who was also an assistant coach for the football team, helped instill a strong work ethic in Walker. Combined with Walker's own sense of self-discipline, it led the young man

to dominate his high school competition. He went on to attain national fame as an athlete. While studying at the University of Georgia, Walker attributed his fame to Tom Jordan's strong influence. When Walker returned to Johnson County High in May 2003 for the renaming of the school's stadium in his honor, he requested Tom and his wife, Jani, be there to share in the glory.

After the 1982 football season there was speculation that Walker was about to turn professional early, but to the delight of Georgia fans he said he would return for his senior season. In February 1983, however, reports surfaced that Walker was about to join the New Jersey Generals in the NFL's rival league, the USFL. When the NCAA believed Walker had signed with a professional agent, they ruled him ineligible. NFL rules prevented underclassmen from joining the league—players had to have been beyond their high school graduation by four years. Walker finally decided to forego his senior season at Georgia and signed with the Generals. When he left Georgia he owned 15 Southeastern Conference records and 10 NCAA records.

A professional career

Walker's decision to leave college was prompted by the offer of a multimillion-dollar contract with the Generals, who were owned by real estate mogul Donald Trump. There was also an expectation that he would make a considerable amount of money in endorsements by signing with a team in the New York City metropolitan area. Nevertheless, after his first pro season Walker completed his degree in criminal justice at Georgia.

Walker played three seasons in the USFL, rushing for 5,562 yards (5,085m) and 54 touchdowns (he added seven touchdown receptions). His 2,411 yards (2204.61) in rushing in 1985 is a pro football single-season record. The USFL folded in 1986, however, after being awarded only $3.00 in damages from a monopoly antitrust suit that it brought against the NFL. The Dallas Cowboys, sensing the USFL would not last, had earned Walker's NFL rights by picking Walker in the fifth round of the 1985 draft.

Walker did not find as much success with Dallas as he had enjoyed at Georgia or with the USFL's Generals,

however. Early in the 1989 season he was traded to the Minnesota Vikings in exchange for five draft picks and the rights to several players. From 1989 to 1997 Walker played three seasons in Minnesota, three seasons in Philadelphia, a year with the New York Giants, and again with the Cowboys for his final two seasons. He finished his 12-year NFL career with 18,168 all-purpose yards (16,612.81m), rushing, receiving, and kickoff returns—which ranks eighth all-time. If Walker's USFL totals are added to his NFL totals, he would rank No. 1 on the list. Before his retirement Walker achieved more fame when he competed on the U.S. bobsled team in the 1992 Winter Olympics in Albertville, France. In 1999 Walker was inducted into the College Football Hall of Fame. He owns and runs the company, Renaissance Man Inc.

KEY DATES

1962   Born in Augusta, Georgia, on March 3.

1982   Wins the Heisman Trophy.

1983   Makes his professional debut with the N.J. Generals of the United States Football League.

1986   Joins the NFL with the Dallas Cowboys; later moves to the Minnesota Vikings, Philadelphia, and the New York Giants, before returning to the Cowboys.

1997   Retires from the NFL.

1999   Inducted into the College Football Hall of Fame.

Further reading: Cromartie, Bill. *There Goes Herschel.* New York, NY: Leisure Press, 1983.
http://collegefootball.org/famersearch.php?id=80026 (Biography).

WALKER, Maggie L.
Businesswoman, Social Activist

Maggie Lena Walker was a social activist and successful businesswoman. She became the first woman bank president in the United States after she founded the Saint Luke Penny Savings Bank in 1903.

Early life

Born in Richmond, Virginia, on July 15, 1867, Walker was the daughter of Elizabeth "Lizzie" Draper, a former slave, and Eccles Cuthbert, a white writer. Draper had worked for Elizabeth Van Lew, an abolitionist and Union spy. In 1869 Draper married William Mitchell, Van Lew's butler, and the family moved to downtown Richmond. In 1878, however, Mitchell was murdered, leaving his wife with two young children to support—Walker had a half brother—without the benefit of any insurance or income support. The experience was to influence Walker's later work.

The Order of Saint Luke

In 1881 Walker joined the Grand United Order of Saint Luke, which offered essential services to the aged and infirm, promoted services such as health care, and helped with burial expenses. Although she taught after leaving school, Walker retained a strong association with the organization and held several key positions. In 1886 she married building contractor Armstead Walker, Jr., with whom she had three sons, although one died as a baby.

In 1899 Walker was given the highest position in the order, the right worthy grand secretary. Under her leadership the organization, which was on the point of financial ruin, was revitalized. She renamed it the Independent Order of Saint Luke, founded a newspaper,

▲ *Maggie L. Walker dedicated her life to giving black people economic independence by setting up a bank, insurance company, and other businesses.*

the *Saint Luke Herald*, and in 1903 set up the Saint Luke Penny Savings Bank, which encouraged people to turn one-cent coins into dollars by saving. The bank promoted black home ownership and by 1920 had helped buy 600 homes. In 1905 Walker opened a department store, the Saint Luke Emporium; it closed by 1912 because of white opposition to its much lower prices.

Dedication to the community

In 1915 Walker's husband died but unlike her mother she was in a good financial position and could raise her children comfortably. Walker continued to support community enterprise and was also a suffragist, serving on the board of several women's groups. In 1921 Walker ran unsuccessfully for the position of state superintendent. Having given great service to the black community, she died in 1934. In 1978 Walker's Richmond home became a National Historic site.

Further reading: http://mdmd.essortment.com/
maggielenawalk_rglv.htm (Biography).

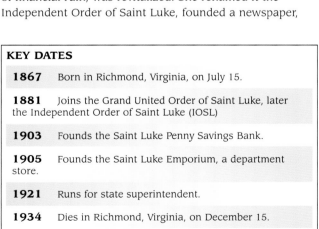

KEY DATES	
1867	Born in Richmond, Virginia, on July 15.
1881	Joins the Grand United Order of Saint Luke, later the Independent Order of Saint Luke (IOSL)
1903	Founds the Saint Luke Penny Savings Bank.
1905	Founds the Saint Luke Emporium, a department store.
1921	Runs for state superintendent.
1934	Dies in Richmond, Virginia, on December 15.

WALKER, Margaret
Writer

Believing it to be the "business of all writers to write about the human condition," teacher, novelist, essayist, and poet Margaret Walker dedicated her life to documenting the history of African Americans.

Early life

The daughter of a Methodist minister and a music teacher, Margaret Abigail Walker was born in Birmingham, Alabama, on July 7, 1915, moving to New Orleans with her family in 1925. Walker read widely as a child, enjoying the works of poet Langston Hughes and British dramatist William Shakespeare, reading the Bible, and listening to her maternal grandmother's stories of her great-grandmother, a slave who had experienced the Civil War (1861–1865) and Reconstruction. The tales inspired Walker's 30-year endeavor to research and write her epic novel, *Jubilee*.

The emergence of a writer

In 1932 Walker met Langston Hughes, who urged her to become a writer, and she subsequently transferred from New Orleans University to Northwestern University, Illinois, graduating with a BA in English in 1935. That year she began her fruitful association with the Federal Writers Project, Chicago, mixing with other promising writers. She forged a creative partnership with Richard Wright, aiding him with research for his novel *Native Son* (1940).

Achieving an MA in creative writing from the University of Iowa in 1940, Walker began her teaching career at Livingstone College, North Carolina. She published her first collection of poetry, *For My People* (1942), after which she embarked on the research for her doctorate. She finally completed her thesis in 1965, published as her

▲ *This group photograph of poets attending the Jackson State College festival in 1945 features in the front row (from left to right) Sterling Brown, Zora Neal Hurston, Margaret Walker, Langston Hughes; and in the back row, Arna Wendell Bontemps, Melvin B. Tolson, President Jacob L. Reddix, Owen Dodson, and Robert C. Hayden.*

novel *Jubilee*. Her next published work, *Prophets For A New Day* (1970), reflected on the civil rights movement and in 1972 she published *How I Wrote Jubilee,* which documented her research and writing process.

Walker taught at Jackson State College (later Jackson State University), Mississippi, from 1949. She established the Institute for the Study of History Life and Culture of Black People there. She retired from teaching in 1979, but continued to write, publishing among other works, *October Journey* (1973), *Richard Wright: Demonic Genius* (1987), and *This Is My Century* (1989). Walker was inducted into the African American Literary Hall of Fame in 1998, just before her death in November.

See also: Hughes, Langston; Wright, Richard

Further reading: Walker, Margaret. *How I Wrote Jubilee.* Chicago, IL: Third World Press, 1977.
http://www.ibiblio.org/ipa/walker/ (Biography).

KEY DATES	
1915	Born in Birmingham, Alabama, on July 7.
1942	Publishes her first volume of poetry, *For My People.*
1965	Publishes her debut novel, *Jubilee.*
1968	Founds the Institute for the Study of History Life and Culture of Black People.
1970	Publishes civil rights poetry, *Prophets For A New Day.*
1998	Dies in Chicago, Illinois, in November.

WALKER, Wyatt Tee
Civil Rights Activist, Religious Leader

Activist Wyatt Tee Walker was a close associate of Martin Luther King, Jr., and was executive director of the Southern Christian Leadership Conference (SCLC). An important strategist, Walker helped plan such successful nonviolent protests as the Birmingham Confrontation of 1963. Walker has been a prominent figure in fighting for international human rights and has lectured in many countries around the world.

Early life
Born in Brockton, Massachusetts, on August 16, 1929, Walker grew up in Merchantville, New Jersey. After high school, Walker earned a BA at Virginia Union University (1950). He remained at Virginia Union to study divinity, during which time he became friends with Martin Luther King, Jr. Walker graduated with a doctorate in 1953.

In 1953 Walker was appointed minister of the Gillfield Baptist Church in Petersburg, Virginia, where he stayed for

▼ *Wyatt Tee Walker was the third SCLC executive director after John L. Tilley and Ella Baker.*

seven years. Like many black ministers of his generation, he used his position to promote the cause of civil rights. He became well known for his fiery political orations as well as for his brilliant organizational ability.

In 1960 Walker was appointed executive director of the SCLC, an organization set up by King to coordinate nonviolent protests across the Southern states. Under Walker's leadership, the SCLC orchestrated a succession of high-profile actions, including sit-ins, walkouts, and marches, many of which captured international attention.

Minister and musicologist
Walker resigned from the SCLC in 1964. King appointed him chief minister of the Canaan Baptist Church of Christ in Harlem three years later. At Canaan Walker became a catalyst for social change, using money donated by his congregation to regenerate Harlem's rundown areas. His church attracted high-profile guest speakers such as South African black leader Nelson Mandela into its pulpit.

In 1975 Walker gained a doctorate in divinity and went on to establish himself as one of the United States's leading experts on black religious music; he published several influential studies. For Walker, church music plays a central role in black life and religion. Activist Jesse Jackson called Walker "Harlem's Renaissance man" because of his wide range of talents and diverse interests; he has published more than 20 books. In 2003 Walker suffered a stroke and in the following year retired from his ministry.

See also: Jackson, Jesse; King, Martin Luther, Jr.

Further reading: Walker, Wyatt Tee. *Somebody's Calling My Name.* Vally Forge, PA: Judson Press, 1979.
www.vuu.edu/alumni/WyattTeeWalker.htm (Biography).

WALLER, Fats
Composer, Musician

The composer of hit songs such as "Ain't Misbehavin'," Fats Waller was also an extremely talented pianist. Recordings such as "Handful of Keys" and "Smashing Thirds" showcased Waller's innovative techniques, such as gliding walking tenths with the left hand. Leading musicians such as Louis Armstrong and Fletcher Henderson recorded Waller's work.

Early life

Born in New York City on May 12, 1904, Thomas Wright Waller was one of the five children of Edward and Adeline Waller. In an open air church and on Harlem's streets, Edward, a Baptist lay preacher, delivered sermons while Adeline played the piano. As a young boy Waller sometimes accompanied his father while he preached, playing the harmonium. At age six, Waller began to perform with the high school orchestra, already showing some of the comedic style that would make him such a popular performer with audiences. He entertained his classmates by making funny faces and rolling his eyes dramatically while he played. By age 15 Waller was playing professionally as an organist for the Lincoln Theater.

In 1920 Waller's mother died and he moved into the home of pianist Russell Brooks, who encouraged his musical development. He studied with James P. Johnson, who greatly influenced Waller's rollicking stride piano style, and he studied classical piano and composition with pianist Leopold Godowsky and composer Carl Bohm.

The emergence of a star entertainer

By 1922 Waller was performing in New York theaters and clubs, accompanying vaudeville stars such as Alberta Hunter. He also recorded "Muscle Shoals Blues" and "Birmingham Blues." In 1923 he wrote and published "Wild Cat Blues" with the help of Clarence Williams.

▲ *Fats Waller's large physical presence and huge personality led him to be nicknamed "Fats."*

Through the 1920s Waller's reputation grew as a vibrant performer and as a gifted composer. Fletcher Henderson, one of the leading artists of the time, recorded and performed Waller's compositions, including "Crazy 'Bout My Baby." In the late 1920s Waller collaborated with his former teacher James P. Johnston on the show *Keep Shufflin'* (1928) and with lyricist Andy Razaf to write the all-black hit musical *Hot Chocolates* (1929)

In the early 1930s Waller had his own regular radio programs in New York and Cincinnati. He also toured extensively. In 1934 he signed an exclusive recording contract with Victor Records, mainly recording with his ensemble group, Fats Waller and His Rhythm. Waller died of pneumonia in 1943.

See also: Armstrong, Louis; Henderson, Fletcher; Hunter, Alberta

Further reading Shipton, Alyn. *Fats Waller: The Cheerful Little Earful.* New York, NY: Continuum International Publishing Group, 2002.
http://www.redhotjazz.com/fats.html (Biography).

KEY DATES	
1904	Born in New York City on May 12.
1929	The musical *Hot Chocolates* opens on Broadway, featuring the song "Aint Misbehavin."
1934	Forms Fats Waller and His Rhythm.
1943	Dies in Kansas City, Missouri, on December 15.

WARD, Samuel Ringgold
Abolitionist, Minister

The abolitionist and minister Samuel Ringgold Ward dedicated his life to the abolition of slavery. Famous for impassioned public speaking, Ward spoke out against slavery in all the Northern states.

Early life
Ward was born on October 17, 1817, on Maryland's eastern shore. Since his parents were slaves, he was also born a slave. His parents escaped to freedom when Ward was a young child, although they spent most of their lives fearing recapture, a fear that they passed on to their son. In 1826 the Wards moved to New York City, where Ward attended the Mulberry School for Negro Children, along with Henry Highland Garnet and Alexander Crummell.

Ward taught in black schools until 1839, when he was ordained as a pastor by the New York Congregational Association. He was also appointed as an agent for the American Anti-Slavery Society. While preaching Ward embarked on a career as a public speaker, earning a reputation as a formidable orator as he campaigned against slavery. Some commentators referred to him as the "black Daniel Webster" (the statesman and famous orator), although Ward later criticized Webster for his acceptance of the Fugitive Slave Act (1850). Ward joined the Liberty Party in 1843, and served as a vice president of the American Missionary Association, which concerned itself with the abolition of slavery

A fugitive himself
Following the passage of the Fugitive Slave Act, Ward helped slaves escape. He was involved in the rescue of the fugitive slave William "Jerry" Henry and as a result fled to Canada in 1851, worried that he might be captured himself. In Canada, where he stayed for two years, he lectured against slavery and worked for the Anti-Slavery Society of Canada while helping fugitive slaves who had fled north.

▲ *This photograph appeared in the English edition of Ward's autobiography (1855).*

Autobiography
Ward traveled to England in April 1853, seeking help for exiled and immigrant former slaves. He addressed the British and Foreign Anti-Slavery Society in 1853 and 1854. In 1855 he published *The Autobiography of a Fugitive Slave: His Anti-Slavery Labors in the United States, Canada, and England.* In that same year an English Quaker friend gave Ward some land in Jamaica, where he moved with his family. Ward worked as a Baptist minister in Kingston until 1860. He then moved to St. George Parish. Little is known of his final years, but it is thought that he died in Jamaica in 1866.

See also: Crummell, Alexander; Garnet, Henry Highland

Further reading: www.aaregistry.com/africa_american_history/1584 (Biography).

KEY DATES	
1817	Born in Maryland on October 17.
1839	Ordained as a minister.
1855	Publishes *The Autobiography of a Fugitive Slave.*
1866	Dies in Jamaica at about this time.

WARWICK, Dionne
Singer

Award-winning singer Dionne Warwick is probably best known for her long and successful association with the singer–songwriter Burt Bacharach. In 1968 Warwick became the first female black singer to win a Grammy ("Do You Know the Way to San Jose?"). Warwick also organized a 1986 charity recording of "That's What Friends Are For," featuring Gladys Knight, Elton John, and Stevie Wonder, which earned millions of dollars for AIDS research.

Early life
Born in East Orange, New Jersey, on December 12, 1940, Marie Dionne Warrick, whose name became "Warwick" following a spelling mistake on her first single in 1962, was the daughter of Mancel Warrick, a gospel record promoter for the Chicago-based label Chess Records. Her mother, Lee Drinkard, managed a gospel group named the Drinkard Singers. Warwick sang in the local church choir from an early age and as a teenager formed a singing group named the Gospelaires with her sister Dee Dee and aunt Cissy (later the mother of Whitney Houston).

▼ **Dionne Warwick singing at the Olympia, Paris, France, on December 31, 1965: The show helped establish her international reputation.**

Success
While studying music at the University of Hartford, Connecticut, Warwick began to do session work in New York. After singing backing vocals for the Drifters, she came to the attention of Burt Bacharach and his partner Hal David, who asked her to record some of their songs. Scepter record label president Florence Greenberg heard a demo and signed Warwick. In 1962 Warwick's first single, a Bacharach–David song entitled "Don't Make Me Over," reached No. 5 on the rhythm-and-blues (R&B) charts and the Top 20 of the pop charts. Over the next 10 years the trio had 30 hit singles, including the Grammy-winning "I'll Never Fall in Love Again" (1970).

In 1971 Warwick moved to Warner Brothers, taking Bacharach and David with her as part of the deal. In 1972, however, Bacharach and David split and Warwick was forced to sue them for breach of the contract with Warner. She did not work with Bacharach again until the 1980s. Warwick continued to have hit records such as the 1974 million-selling chart topper "Then Came You," and the albums *Dionne* (1976) and *Heartbreaker* (1982). She also collaborated with singers such as Stevie Wonder. Warwick set up a TV/film production company and in the 1990s hosted a TV show promoting the Psychic Friends Network.

See also: Houston, Whitney; Knight, Gladys; Wonder, Stevie

Further reading: www.thehistorymakers.com/biography/biography.asp?bioindex=645&category=musicMaker (Biography).

WASHINGTON, Augustus
Photographer

Augustus Washington was one of the earliest photographers. He ran a successful photographic studio before immigrating to Liberia, where he hoped African Americans would have a better future.

Early life

Washington was the son of a former slave and a woman of South Asian descent. He was born in Trenton, New Jersey, in either 1820 or 1821. It is thought that his mother died when Washington was very young, as he was brought up by a stepmother. As a teenager Washington decided that he wanted to become "a scholar, a teacher, a useful man," but he struggled to get a decent education because of his race.

Education

Washington managed to study at the Oneida Institute, Whitesboro, New York, and at Kimball Union University, New Hampshire, before entering Dartmouth College in 1843. During this time he took up photography to fund his studies, but he was forced to leave Dartmouth the following year as a result of his poor finances. He then moved to Hartford, Connecticut, where he taught in schools before opening a photographic studio in 1846. It specialized in the daguerre technique, which produced images on light-sensitive, silver-coated metallic plates and resulted in a very clear image.

A popular photographer

By the early 1850s Washington was established as one of Hartford's leading portrait photographers, charging between 50 cents and $10 per portrait. One of his best-known portraits was of abolitionist John Brown (1800–1859), taken between 1846 and 1847. Like Brown, Washington was an abolitionist.

Lack of equality

Despite his success as a photographer, Washington never really believed that African Americans would ever achieve true equality in the United States. He expressed his pessimism about the future of black Americans in a letter published in the July 3, 1851, edition of the *New York Tribune* newspaper. Washington entitled it "African Colonization—By a Man of Color," and wrote "He who would not rather live anywhere on earth in freedom than in this country in social and political degradation, has not attained half the dignity of his manhood." Washington began to look to Liberia, West Africa, as a suitable home.

Liberia

In November 1853 Washington and his wife and two young children sailed for Liberia, which had been established in 1816 by the American Colonization Society for the resettlement of free African Americans in Africa. Although Washington had earlier opposed the activities of the white-led Colonization Society, he eventually decided to leave America for what he hoped would prove to be a better life for his family.

In Liberia's capital, Monrovia, Washington resumed his work as a daguerreotypist. As he grew more successful he expanded his operation into neighboring Sierra Leone, Gambia, and Senegal, setting up studios in each country.

Diversification

After a few years in Liberia Washington diversified into farming, becoming one of the country's main sugarcane growers. Washington ceased working as a daguerreotypist in 1858. His success as a farmer resulted in his owning a large plot of land on the St. Paul River. Washington also became involved in Liberian politics, serving in the House of Representatives and the Senate. On his death in 1875, Washington was widely mourned in Liberia.

KEY DATES	
1820	Born in Trenton, New Jersey, at about this time.
1843	Attends Dartmouth College, New Hampshire, but leaves a year later.
1846	Opens one of earliest daguerreotype galleries.
1850s	Is established as one of the leading portrait photographers in Hartford, Connecticut.
1853	Sails for Liberia, West Africa.
1875	Dies in Monrovia, Liberia, on June 7.

Further reading: Schumard, Ann M. *A Durable Memento: Portraits by Augustus Washington.* Washington , D.C.: National Portrait Gallery, 1999.
www.npg.si.edu/exh/awash (Biography).

WASHINGTON, Booker T.
Intellectual, Educator

Born five years before the start of the Civil War (1861–1865) to a slave mother and a white father whom he never knew, Booker Taliaferro Washington became one of the most prominent and influential black Americans in the postwar South. Though often criticized by black critics for being an accommodationist, Washington was a complex figure who did much to help improve the lives of African Americans. He also influenced the development of the modern civil rights movement.

Early life
Born on a plantation near Hale's Ford in Franklin County, Virginia, on April 5, 1856, Washington was brought up in poverty as a slave of James Burroughs. After the Civil War, Washington moved with his mother, Jane, stepfather, and half brother and sister to Malden, West Virginia. He worked in various manual occupations, including salt packer, coal miner, and house servant. Washington was educated at Hampton Institute from 1872, where the school's principal, Samuel Chapman Armstrong, became a great influence and was Washington's mentor (*see box on p. 36*). Armstrong believed strongly in vocational education for freed black people.

Tuskegee
Armstrong recommended Washington for the position of principal and first teacher at Tuskegee Institute, a fledgling Negro Normal School created as part of a scheme to raise black votes for a white legislator seeking reelection in Macon County, Alabama. From a foundation of 30 adult

▲ *Washington's opinions upset W. E. B. DuBois, who wrote* **The Souls of Black Folk** *in response.*

students, a one-room shack, and a promise of $2,000 from the Alabama legislature, Washington built Tuskegee into the best-known black educational facility of his time. Along the way he became an informal adviser to presidents, a fund-raiser, and one of the most recognizable black leaders of his day. In his study of black education, Horace Mann Bond suggested Washington was so powerful that "almost no Negro institution could collect funds" without his approval.

Following Armstrong's example, Washington believed that practical skills would provide meaningful jobs for black Americans. Tuskegee students in Washington's day did not declare majors as much as they signed up for trades. The main courses on the campus were basketmaking, shoemaking, carpentry, farming, cabinet-making, tin-smithing, blacksmithing, and other industrial skills. The institution had grown to 2,000 students by the time of Washington's death in 1915.

At a time when black leaders such as W. E. B. DuBois were advocating a more confrontational approach to advancing black rights, Washington was conciliatory toward Southern whites, rarely threatening the status quo in his public pronouncements. In his 1901 autobiography,

KEY DATES

1856   Born near Hale's Ford, Franklin County, Virginia, on April 5.

1865   Moves with his mother to Malden, West Virginia, following the end of the Civil War.

1881   Becomes principal of Tuskegee School.

1895   Gives famous "Atlanta Compromise" speech.

1901   Publishes autobiography *Up From Slavery*.

1903   W. E. B. DuBois publishes *The Souls of Black Folk* in repudiation of Washington's accommodationist stance.

1915   Dies in Tuskegee on November 14.

INFLUENCES AND INSPIRATION

One of the most influential people in Booker T. Washington's life was Samuel Chapman Armstrong, principal of the Hampton Institute, where Washington studied.

Armstrong (1839–1893), who was born in Hawaii, had fought for the Union Army in the Civil War (1861–1865), rising to the rank of major general. After the war he worked for the Freedmen's Bureau in Virginia. Armstrong believed that it was essential to give freed black people a practical and industrial education, and with the help of the American Missionary Association in 1868 he founded Hampton Normal and Agricultural Institute (now the Hampton Institute). Washington, who studied there from 1872, learned such skills as carpentry. One of Armstrong's most devoted students, Washington continued after graduation to follow Armstrong's teachings; he believed they provided black people with key training and strength of character.

Up From Slavery, he wrote: "The agitation of questions of social equality is the extremist folly." Black Southerners, Washington assured white audiences, were much more concerned with education and economic advancement than political rights or integration. "I believe," he wrote, "it is the duty of the Negro—as the greater part of the race is already doing—to deport himself modestly in regard of political claims, depending upon the slow but sure influences that proceed from the possessions of property, intelligence, and high character for the full recognition of his political rights."

Public perception

Washington's ideas were popular with some black people reeling from the intense racial violence of the 1890s, but even more so with Southern whites. The Tuskegee leader's criticism of labor unions and radicalism further endeared him to conservative political and economic leaders. Northern whites and some from the South expressed their deep appreciation for Washington's gradualism by donating money to a man whose social philosophy seemed to mirror their own. White audiences greeted Washington's powerful but brief speeches enthusiastically.

Nowhere was Washington more applauded by white people than following his speech in Atlanta during the 1895 Cotton States and International Exposition. "In all things that are purely social," he declared, "we can be as separate as the fingers, yet one as the hand in all things essential to mutual progress." His critics argued that he had effectively told white Southerners that black people were willing to abandon hopes of holding political office and being equal partners in the social contract. DuBois later dubbed the speech the "Atlanta Compromise," an indication that some black people thought that trading integration and suffrage for property rights and industrial work was a poor bargain. Although some commentators suggested that Washington's rhetoric was designed more to raise money from white philanthropists in the North, other blacks called the Tuskegee leader an "Uncle Tom," arguing that he had turned a blind eye to violence and other forms of injustice. Washington himself never claimed to speak for the entire U.S. black population.

Though his critics raised valid points, few knew the extent of Washington's somewhat more militant work behind-the-scenes. He railed against segregated railroad cars and encouraged boycotts in order to win concessions. He secretly funded several organizations seeking to topple segregation and pass antilynching laws, and funded and provided legal support for court challenges to all-white juries in Alabama. After the release of D. W. Griffith's movie *The Birth of a Nation* (1915), Washington objected to its stereotypical portrayals of black people as untrustworthy.

Washington's stance alienated some of the leading black intellectuals of the day, including DuBois and William Monroe Trotter, who organized the Niagara movement to advocate full political and civil rights for all black people. This was the forerunner of the National Association for the Advancement of Colored People (NAACP). Although Washington's correspondence shows that he supported the NAACP, he never did so publicly. He died on November 14, 1915, in Tuskegee, where he was eulogized in front of 8,000 mourners.

See also: Bond, Horace Mann; DuBois, W. E. B.; Trotter, William Monroe

Further reading: Harlan, Louis R. *Booker T. Washington: The Wizard of Tuskegee, 1901–1915*. New York. NY: Oxford University Press, 1983.
http://www.nps.gov/bowa/home.htl (National monument site).
http://library.thinkquest.org/10320/Washngtn.htm (Biography).

WASHINGTON, Buck
Musician, Entertainer

During the early 20th century Ford Lee Washington, better known as "Buck" Washington, became known as part of the popular vaudeville act Buck and Bubbles. Playing with John Bubbles (John Sublett) in fast-paced, humorous song-and-dance routines, Washington most often provided the piano accompaniments as Bubbles performed improvised tap routines. Washington also often danced and clowned in the act.

Early life

Washington was born in Louisville, Kentucky, on October 6, 1903. By about 1913, when he met near-lifelong stage partner John Sublett, he was already an accomplished musician. Washington and Sublett began to perform as Buck and Bubbles in about 1917; Washington played jazz piano while Bubbles danced. They began their performance careers in local black theater, but their routine was so successful and popular with audiences that within two

▼ *Buck Washington (right) and John Bubbles (left) were known for their witty, fast-paced routine.*

KEY DATES

1903   Born in Louisville, Kentucky, on October 6.

1917   Begins to perform with John Sublett as "Buck and Bubbles" in about this year.

1930   Records with jazz trumpeter and singer Louis Armstrong.

1953   Buck and Bubbles split up.

1955   Dies in New York City on January 31.

years they were already headlining the nation's top vaudeville venues, including New York's Palace Theater. From this point on the two men performed largely for white audiences.

Musician

As a pianist Washington took his main inspiration from the strident, almost brassy playing style developed in the 1920s by Earl Hines. During the 1930s Washington was able to record alongside some of the greatest black jazz musicians of the era, including Louis Armstrong—notably on "Dear Old Southland" (1930)—Billie Holiday, and Coleman Hawkins. For many critics, however, his playing never really rose above the merely competent.

During the 1930s and 1940s Buck and Bubbles often made appearances in Hollywood musicals, including *Cabin in the Sky* (1943), whose all-back cast also featured Lena Horne, Ethel Waters, and Duke Ellington, and *A Song Is Born* (1948), starring Danny Kaye. Such movies brought them to the attention of an international audience. They performed together to much acclaim until 1953, when they both decided to concentrate on separate careers. Washington died two years later.

See also: Armstrong, Louis; Bubbles, John; Ellington, Duke; Hawkins, Coleman; Hines, Earl; Holiday, Billie; Horne, Lena; Waters, Ethel

Further reading: Feather, Leonard, and Ira Gitler: *The Biographical Encyclopedia of Jazz.* New York, NY: Oxford University Press, 1999.
www.aaregistry.com/african_american_history/ 1711/Buck_Washington_dancer_extraordinaire (Biography).

WASHINGTON, Denzel
Actor, Director

Denzel Washington is one of the most intelligent and charismatic actors of his generation. His portrayals of morally complex characters infused with wry wit, intelligence, and a hint of underlying anger have garnered him numerous awards, including two Oscars. Washington describes himself as a rarity in Hollywood, "a minority among minorities—a working black actor." Although Washington takes pride in his African American heritage, and has portrayed several important black figures such as South African activist Steve Biko and the civil rights leader Malcolm X, he insists that he wants to be thought of as an "actor" and not a "black actor."

Early life

Born on December 28, 1954, in Mt. Vernon, New York, Denzel Washington was named after his father, a Pentacostal minister. His mother, Lennis, was a beautician and gospel singer. Washington and his two siblings grew up in a racially diverse, middle-class neighborhood at the edge of the Bronx, where his childhood friends were of West Indian, Irish, African American, and Italian origin. His parents discouraged their children from watching television or going to the movies. Washington remarked, "It's a wonder I ever went into acting [because my] father was down on the movies, and his idea of something worthwhile would be *The King of Kings, The Ten Commandments,* and *101 Dalmations.*"

After his parent's divorce the 14-year-old Washington won a scholarship to attend Oakland Academy, an exclusive boarding school in upstate New York. After graduating he went to Fordham University in the Bronx, enrolling as a premed student. While working as a counselor at a YMCA-sponsored camp one summer during his college years, Washington organized a talent show. Someone at the camp told him that he looked natural on stage and asked if he had ever considered acting. The suggestion sparked Washington's interest in acting and, when he returned to Fordham in the fall, he auditioned for and won the lead part in the university's production of Eugene O'Neill's *The Emperor Jones.* He also switched courses to study journalism and major in drama.

Washington starred in several other plays in college, including *Othello.* Robinson Stone, his drama teacher,

▼ **Denzel Washington is well respected by fellow actors. Ethan Hawke, his costar in Training Day, hailed Washington as "...A great movie star. Each generation there's two or three—and he's it."**

Denzel Washington is often compared to Sidney Poitier and is called his successor. In 2002 both Poitier and Washington were honored with Academy Awards—Poitier's was for Lifetime Achievement and Washington's was for Best Actor.

One of the most respected figures in American cinema during the 20th century, Poitier was the first black man to be nominated for the Best Actor Academy Award for his performance in *The Defiant Ones* (1958); five years later he won the Oscar for his role in *Lilies of the Field*. Poitier acted on both stage and screen and participated in the civil rights movement. His roles in the 1967 films *Guess Who's Coming to Dinner* and *To Sir, With Love* were landmarks that helped highlight social problems between blacks and whites and also to break down barriers that prevented black actors from getting mainstream lead film roles.

In his 2002 Oscar acceptance speech, Washington paid tribute to Poitier when he said, "Forty years I've been chasing Sidney, they finally give [an Oscar] to me, what do they do? They give it to him the same night.... I'll always be chasing you Sidney, I'll always be following in your footsteps."

KEY DATES

1954   Born in Mt. Vernon, New York, on December 28.

1977   Lands his first television role in *Wilma*.

1982   Begins a five-year stint as Dr. Philip Chandler on *St. Elsewhere*.

1990   Wins the Oscar for Best Supporting Actor for his performance in *Glory*.

1992   Stars as Malcolm X in Spike Lee's film biographical movie of the same name.

2002   Awarded Oscar for Best Actor for *Training Day*; directs his first film, *Antwone Fisher*.

thought that Washington was the best Othello that he had seen and arranged for agents to see Washington's performance. Before he graduated in 1977 Washington was offered a small part in a television drama, *Wilma*.

The making of a star

Early in his career Washington starred with George Segal in *Carbon Copy* (1981) and accepted a role in a television mini-series called *Flesh and Blood*. These parts brought Washington to public attention and he was soon cast as Dr. Phillip Chandler in the popular TV drama *St. Elsewhere*. The role, which Washington played for five seasons, led to his being cast as Private Peterson in the Off-Broadway stage show *A Soldier's Play* (1982). He won an Obie Award and went on to play the role in the film version, *A Soldier's Story* (1984), leading *Chicago Tribune* correspondent Bob Thomas to call him "one of the most versatile of the new acting generation."

Hollywood soon recognized Washington's star potential: He was handsome, intelligent, articulate, talented, and had a compelling screen presence and great dignity. When Washington started acting there were very few lead roles for black actors. This changed when Washington was cast as Steve Biko in *Cry Freedom*, a role for which he earned his first Academy Award nomination in 1989. He went on to play the part of Trip, a runaway slave who fights with the first black regiment in the Civil War film *Glory*. In 1990 Washington won the Best Supporting Actor Oscar for this role. It was only the fifth Oscar ever won by a black actor.

From the 1990s onward Washington appeared in leading roles in such movies as Spike Lee's *Mo' Better Blues* and *Malcolm X,* Jonathan Demme's *Philadelphia,* and *Devil in a Blue Dress,* based on Walter Mosely's book of the same name. He became known for his charismatic, often sensitive performances. In 2002 Washington received the Best Actor Academy Award (*see box*) for his role as Alonzo Harris, a crooked Machiavellian police detective in the acclaimed movie *Training Day*. In that same year Washington turned his talents to directing when he made *Antwone Fisher*. One of the highest paid black actors in Hollywood, Washington is also a generous supporter of his church and of charitable causes.

See also: Lee, Spike; Malcolm X; Mosely, Walter; Poitier, Sidney

Further reading: Brode, Douglas. *Denzel Washington: His Films and Career.* Seacaucus, NJ: Carol Publishing Group, 1997.
http://www.imdb.com/name/nm0000243 (Filmography).

WASHINGTON, Dinah
Singer

Singer Dinah Washington has influenced generations of blues and jazz singers. In her relatively short career Washington, who was called "Queen of the Blues," was famous for her remarkable voice, clear enunciation, great sense of timing and delivery, and emotive quality, which enabled her to sing anything from rhythm and blues and gospel to jazz. The musician and producer Quincy Jones, who arranged songs for Washington early in his career, said that she "could take the melody in her hand, hold it like an egg, crack it open, fry it, let it sizzle, reconstruct it, put the egg back in the box, and back in the refrigerator, and you would've still understood every single syllable."

Early life
Born in Tuscaloosa, Alabama, on August 29, 1924, Ruth Lee Jones moved with her family to Chicago, Illinois, when she was very young. Washington grew up singing at St. Luke's Baptist Church. Influenced by singer Billie Holiday, Washington began singing in small clubs; she also performed with Sallie Martin's gospel group. She won first prize in an amateur singing competition at the Regal Theater and played at the Garrick Bar, where she came to the attention of band leader Lionel Hampton. In about 1943 she changed her name to Dinah Washington; some sources claim that Hampton chose the name.

The making of a star
From 1943 to 1946 Washington sang with Hampton's band, eventually rising to become its major attraction. Jazz critic and composer Leonard Feather saw Washington while she was playing with Hampton and persuaded Keynote Records to sponsor her debut recording session.

Signed to Mercury Records, in 1946 Washington left Hampton's band. In the 1940s Washington worked with

▲ *Dinah Washington, photographed in about 1940, when she was still performing under her original name of Ruth Jones.*

some of the leading musicians of the time, including Clifford Brown, Max Roach, and Cannonball Adderley. In 1959 "What a Difference a Day Makes" propelled Washington into the popular marketplace, earning her a Grammy. She built on the success with such songs as "Unforgettable" and "Baby, You Got What It Takes" (both 1959) with Brook Benton. However, as Washington's career became more established, her personal life suffered. Married seven times, with substance addictions, Washington died from an accidental overdose of diet pills and alcohol in December 1963, at age 39.

See also: Adderley, Cannonball; Brown, Clifford; Holliday, Billie; Jones, Quincy; Roach, Max

Further reading: Cohodas, Nadine. *Queen: The Life and Music of Dinah Washington.* New York, NY: Pantheon Books, 2004.
http://www.aaregistry.com/african_american_history/333/Dinah_Washington_a_passionate_blues_singer (Biography).

KEY DATES	
1924	Born in Tuscaloosa, Alabama, on August 29.
1943	Changes her name to Dinah Washington at about this time; tours with Lionel Hampton and his band for three years.
1959	Records "What a Difference a Day Makes," which wins her a Grammy; records "Unforgettable."
1963	Dies in Detroit, Michigan, on December 14.

WASHINGTON, Harold
Politician, Activist

As mayor of Chicago (1983–1987), Harold Washington was responsible for reforming the city's system of political patronage. He introduced the Shakman Decree (1983), which outlawed patronage and the political firing of municipal employees. He also appointed women and people from ethnic minorities to his administration and hired the city's first black police chief.

Early life
Born on the South Side of Chicago, Illinois, on April 15, 1922, Washington was the son of domestic worker Bertha Jones and Roy Lee Washington, a stockyard worker who retrained as an attorney and became a precinct captain for the Democratic Party. Until the age of six, Washington boarded at a Benedictine school in Milwaukee, Wisconsin, after which he attended public schools in Chicago. He left school to work in a factory, but with his father's help began working at the Chicago office of the U.S. Treasury Department. He married Dorothy Finch in 1941, but they divorced nine years later.

Moving on
After being drafted into the Army during World War II (1939–1945) and serving in the South Pacific, Washington started to study, taking correspondence courses to get his high school diploma. He studied at Roosevelt College, Chicago, after the war ended, graduating in 1949 with a political science degree. Washington went on to Northwestern University Law School, where he gained his degree in 1952. Following his father's death, he was hired to replace him as captain of his precinct.

▲ *Just before his death in 1987, Harold Washington was elected mayor of Chicago for a second term.*

Politics
Washington proved to be an asset to the Democratic Party. He was assistant corporation counsel (1954–1958) and arbiter for the Illinois Industrial Commission (1960–1964), before being elected state representative for the Third Ward in 1964. He gained a reputation as a civil rights advocate, supporting fair employment bills and helping form the Black Caucus in 1969. In 1977 he was elected to the state senate, and campaigned unsuccessfully to become mayor a year later. From 1981 to 1983 he served as a Democratic representative in the 97th and 98th Congresses. In 1983 Washington was elected mayor of the city with 52 percent of the vote; he effectively ended the system of patronage. Reelected mayor in February 1987 with 53 percent of the vote, Washington died nine months later.

Further reading: Rivlin, Gary. *Fire on the Prairie: Chicago's Harold Washington and the Politics of Race.* New York, NY: H. Holt, 1992.
http://bioguide.congress.gov/scripts/
biodisplay.pl?index=W000180 (Brief biography).

KEY DATES	
1922	Born in Chicago, Illinois, on April 15.
1952	Receives law degree from Northwestern University Law School.
1964	Elected state representative for the Third Ward of Chicago.
1977	Elected into the state senate.
1983	Elected Mayor of Chicago; introduces the Shakman Decree.
1987	Elected for a second term; dies on November 25.

WASHINGTON, Isaiah
Actor

Referred to by some Hollywood insiders as "the next Denzel Washington," Isaiah Washington, who is no relation to Denzel, is a talented young actor. Washington has gained prominence in recent years for his outstanding roles in a number of acclaimed films and TV shows, working with directors such as Spike Lee.

Early life
Born in Houston, Texas, on August 3, 1963, Washington did not consider becoming an actor until he was an adult. He graduated from Willowridge High School and thought about pursuing a football career before deciding to study aerospace engineering at Holloman Air Force Base in New Mexico. After a number of unfulfilling work experiences—time spent in the Air Force and working a traditional nine to five job—Washington turned to acting in 1986 after seeing Spike Lee's *She's Gotta Have It*. "I hadn't seen

▼ **Isaiah Washington says his personal philosophy is: "You don't have the time 'to make the time' to do something. You have to do it now!"**

that many African Americans on screen before," he commented. "I thought, 'Let me see if I can get in to see this guy named Spike Lee.'"

Acting career
Washington's path began when a coworker dared him to audition for a part in a local play. He got the part and became intrigued by the process of creating a role. "I had always enjoyed watching performers, my favorites being Clint Eastwood and Charles Bronson, so I decided I would pursue the career full time.... I was seeking a way to be gainfully employed while also doing something that I enjoyed."

This decision led Washington to the drama program at Howard University, Washington, D.C., where he studied with Vera Katz and Harry Poe and appeared in Ntozake Shange's play *Spell No. 7*. After graduating from Howard, Washington moved to New York City and became one of the original members of the City Kids Repertory Group. As he performed at inner-city schools with the group, he developed and honed his craft.

Washington soon began take on film and television work in addition to the theater. An acclaimed performance on NBC's *Homicide* in 1994 caught the attention of Spike Lee, who cast him in *Crooklyn*. Since then, he has appeared in several other films directed by Lee, including *Clockers* (1995), *Girl 6*, and *Get on the Bus* (both 1996). In the years following his work with Lee, Washington appeared in the acclaimed films *Bullworth*, *Out of Sight*, and *Romeo Must Die*. His TV work included *Ally McBeal*, *Law and Order*, and *NYPD Blue*. In 2005 he was cast as Dr. Preston Burke in the hit TV show *Grey's Anatomy*.

See also: Lee, Spike; Shange, Ntozake

Further reading: http://www.imdb.com/name/nm0913460/ (Biography and filmography).

WASHINGTON, Ora
Tennis Player

Ora Washington was a pioneering athlete. However, despite dominating the all-black American Tennis Association (ATA) for many years during segregation, and spending 18 years as a center, coach, and scorer for the Philadelphia Tribune basketball team, she died in relative obscurity.

Early life
Born in Philadelphia on January 23, 1898, Ora Mae Washington came of age during a period of great change for American women. During World War I (1914–1918) the position of both black and white women was transformed as they moved out of the home and into jobs previously done by men. Women started to work in factories and won the vote in 1920. Female athletes began to make a mark on what was previously a male-dominated area, which allowed women such as Washington to excel in sports. She became one of the most successful African American athletes of her generation.

A sports phenomenon
Washington played in the ATA from the 1920s. She was noted for her individualistic tennis style, particularly her fast footwork and unusual racket grip; she held it half way up the handle and seldom took a full swing. Between 1929 and 1937 Washington won eight ATA titles, remaining undefeated, until Lulu Ballard stopped her winning streak. She also won all the women's doubles championships between 1925 and 1936, as well as the mixed doubles in 1939, 1946, and 1947.

Washington's speedy footwork helped her in her other career as a basketball player. She began playing the sport in 1930 with the Germantown Hornets, black America's first star female sports team. Her 22–1 record earned her the national female title. In 1932 she started playing for the Philadelphia Tribune

▲ **Between 1924 and 1936 Ora Washington remained the undefeated champion of the ATA.**

Girls, the other top African American women's team, sponsored by the prominent black newspaper the *Philadelphia Tribune*.

Giving back to the community
When Washington finally retired in the mid-1940s she had won more than 200 trophies. Afterward she worked with African American children, offering them free training sessions and coaching. She was inducted into the Black Athletes Hall of Fame in 1976, five years after her death. Washington had lived in such seclusion that the organization had not realized until then that she had died. Despite her tremendous sporting ability, Washington's stature as one of the first great African American sports stars has rarely been recognized.

Further reading: Ashe, Arthur. *A Hard Road to Glory: A History of the African-American Athlete 1919-1945.* New York, NY: Ballantine Books, 1994.
www.aaregistry.com/african_american_history/633 (Biography).

KEY DATES	
1898	Born in Philadelphia, Pennsylvania, on January 23.
1929	Wins first of her eight ATA singles titles.
1971	Dies in Philadelphia.
1976	Inducted into the Black Athletes Hall of Fame.

WATERS, Ethel
Singer, Actor

Blues and jazz singer Ethel Waters was one of the first successful African American female singers. Waters's first big break came after she recorded "Down Home Blues" and "Oh Daddy" with Harry Herbert Pace's African American label Black Swan in the 1920s. Waters sang with most of the leading musicians of her time, including Fletcher Henderson and Duke Ellington before establishing a successful acting career.

The road to success

Waters was born in Chester, Pennsylvania, on October 13, 1896 (some sources give the date as 1900). Her teenage mother had been raped by her white father, John Wesley Waters. Raised in extreme poverty by her grandmother in Chester and Philadelphia, Waters grew up around prostitutes and thieves. Although she completed sixth grade, she could neither read nor write well, but she could sing and her voice earned her the name "Baby Star."

Aged 12 or 13 Waters married Merritt Pernsley, but the marriage was unhappy because Pernsley beat her. They separated when Waters was 14. Waters went on to work in Philadelphia hotels and other establishments as a maid, dishwasher, and waitress. Determined to be a singer, she first performed in a nightclub in Baltimore, Maryland, and was well received. Influenced by white vaudeville-style singers such as Fannie Brice, the 17-year-old Waters became a professional singer in Baltimore, performing as Sweet Mama Stringbean, a name that reflected her tall, lean build.

Spotted in the 1920s by Fletcher Henderson, musical director of the Black Swan label, Waters went on to record with the label. She also performed with Henderson and his orchestra at clubs such as Harlem's Plantation Club, later performing with other jazz greats such as Duke Ellington.

▲ **Ethel Waters rose from poverty to become an internationally acclaimed singer and actor.**

Following her appearance in the all-black revue *Africana* in 1927, Waters also appeared in Lew Leslie's *Blackbirds*, replacing Florence Mills, who had died. In 1928 she married Clyde Matthews, but the following year was declared bankrupt.

From the 1930s onward Waters began to appear increasingly in musicals and on film. She performed in Irving Berlin's Broadway revue *As Thousands Cheer* (1933) and DuBose Heyward's *Mamba's Daughter* (1939). She also starred in such movies as *Cabin in the Sky* (1943), *Pinky* (1949), for which she received an Academy Award Best Supporting Actress nomination, and Carson McCullers's *A Member of the Wedding* (1952). From the late 1950s Waters became a regular singer in Billy Graham's Crusades. She died of a heart attack in September 1977.

See also: Ellington, Duke; Henderson, Fletcher; Mills, Florence; Pace, Harry Herbert

Further reading: Samuels, Charles (ed.). *Ethel Walters. His Eyes on the Sparrow.* New York, NY: Doubleday, 1951.
http://www.redhotjazz.com/waters.html (Biography).

KEY DATES	
1896	Born in Chester, Pennsylvania, at about this time.
1920s	Records with Black Swan and Columbia Records.
1949	Nominated for an Academy Award for *Pinky*.
1957	Joins Billy Graham's Crusades and tours with him until 1976.
1977	Dies in Chatsworth, California on September 1.

WATERS, Muddy
Musician

Muddy Waters, born McKinley Morganfield, was one of the most popular and influential blues singers and guitarists of his time. He had a string of hits during the 1950s, and his combination of Delta Blues and electric music influenced many later rock-'n'-roll bands.

Early life
Born in Rolling Forks, Mississippi, on April 4, 1915, Waters was the son of sharecroppers Ollie Morganfield and Bertha Jones. His grandmother Della Jones nicknamed him Muddy Waters because he liked to play in the swamps near his home. After his mother died when Waters was three, his grandmother brought him up at her home at Stovall's Plantation near Clarksdale. While picking cotton the young man also learned to play the harmonica; he later switched to guitar, influenced by Eddie "Son" House, who specialized in the bottleneck style of slide guitar.

Blues star
Waters performed in juke-joints in a country–blues style and was sufficiently well known to be recorded by John Work of Fisk University, Nashville, and Alan Lomax for the Library of Congress during 1941–1942. He subsequently moved to Chicago, where he played with John Lee "Sonny Boy" Williamson and harmonicist and guitarist Jimmy Rogers; he also changed to electric guitar.

After recording an unreleased session for Columbia Records in 1947 Waters signed to Aristocrat Records. In 1948 Waters released "I Can't Be Satisfied" backed with "I Feel Like Going Home," which sold 3,000 copies within 48 hours. It was followed by further successes, including "Rollin' Stone."

Waters's own electric slide guitar was backed by a band that included Jimmy Rogers, harmonicist Little Walter Jacobs, and drummer Baby Face Leroy. The group had a series of major hits, including "Louisiana Blues"

▲ *Muddy Waters plays at the Capital Radio Jazz Festival, Alexander Park, London, England, in 1979.*

(1950), "I'm Your Hoochie Coochie Man" (1953), and "I'm Ready" (1954). Waters toured Britain in 1958, where his tough electric style was a revelation to British rhythm-and-blues groups—the Rolling Stones named themselves after his early hit. His performance at the Newport Jazz Festival in 1960 brought him to the attention of mainstream audiences. In the late 1960s Waters's work went out of fashion, but he made an artistic comeback on his last four albums with the guitarist Johnny Winter, which restored his reputation. Waters continued to play and tour until his death in 1983.

See also: Williamson, John Lee

Further reading: Gordon, Robert. *Can't Be Satisfied: The Life and Times of Muddy Waters.* London, England: Jonathan Cape, 2002.
http://www.muddywaters.com (Official site).

KEY DATES	
1915	Born in Rolling Fork, Mississippi, on April 4.
1947	Signed to Aristocrat Records
1950	Has first major hit, "Louisiana Blues."
1983	Dies in Chicago, Illinois, on April 30.

WATSON, Bobby
Musician, Composer

Bobby Watson is an alto saxophonist and composer, who has worked with some of the leading names in jazz. Influenced by the work of such greats as Art Blakey and Miles Davis, Watson has made many successful recordings as a solo artist and with his bands the 29th Street Saxophone and Horizon.

Early life
Born in Lawrence, Kansas, on August 23, 1953, Watson grew up around music: His father tuned pianos and sang in the church choir. Watson started playing the clarinet, switching to the saxophone at age 13. Although he played a lot of church music, Watson remarked: "I ended up gravitating toward jazz because I liked to change things. Jazz gives a musician total freedom. The more you learn about the craft and science of notes the more it frees you.… Once you start to understand that relationship it gives you the freedom to express yourself."

Making a career
Watson went on to study music at the University of Miami, graduating in 1975, after which he moved to New York City. His first performance was at Harveys on 50th Street and Broadway. Watson joined Art Blakey's Jazz Messengers (also known as the University of Blakey) in 1977, staying with the group for four years and becoming its musical director. While with the Messengers, Watson also collaborated with other musicians, including drummers Max Roach and Louis Hayes.

From the 1980s Watson worked with Curtis Lundy, and formed the 29th Street Saxophone Quartet with alto saxophonist Ed Jackson, tenor saxophonist Rich Rothenberg, and baritone saxophonist Jim Hartog. He cofounded the hard bop quintet Horizon with drummer Victor Lewis, and led the High Court of

▲ *Bobby Watson on stage in 2000, the year he released the album* **Live & Learn.**

Swing, formed as a tribute to the late alto saxophonist Johnny Hodges.

Watson's albums include *Love Remains* (1998) and *Live & Learn* (2000). He also composed the music for Robert DeNiro's directorial debut film, *A Bronx Tale*. In 2001 Watson became the first William and Mary Grant/Missouri Professor of Jazz. He is director of jazz studies at the University of Missouri–Kansas City Conservatory of Music.

See also: Blakey, Art; Davis, Miles; Hodges, Johnny; Roach, Max

Further reading: http://bobbywatson.com (Official site for Watson, including biography, discography, and links).

KEY DATES

1953   Born in Lawrence, Kansas, on August 23.

1975   Graduates from the University of Miami with a music degree.

1977   Joins Art Blakey's Jazz Messengers.

2001   Becomes the first William and Mary Grant/Missouri Professor of Jazz.

WATTLETON, Faye
Public Health Advocate

During the 1980s Faye Wattleton rose to prominence as one of the United States's leading advocates of women's reproductive rights in the controversial subject of abortion. As president of the Planned Parenthood Federation of America (PPFA), the largest and oldest of the nation's family-planning organizations, Wattleton fought passionately for women's right to choose and to preserve access to safe and publicly funded abortions. Wattleton's celebrated public-speaking skill, glamorous television-friendly image, and powerful sense of mission have made her not only a formidable figurehead in the prochoice movement but also a role model for many young African American women.

Early life

Alyce Faye Wattleton was born in St. Louis, Missouri, on July 8, 1943, the only child of George and Ozie Wattleton. Her father was a factory worker, and her mother worked as a seamstress and as a minister in the fundamentalist Church of God (*see box on p. 48*). As a popular preacher, her mother was often away from home and Wattleton, as a young girl, often spent long periods in the care of relatives and family friends. Her upbringing was extremely strict and repressive, and she received little in the way of sex education.

In 1958 Wattleton enrolled to study nursing at Ohio State University, from which she graduated with a BA degree in 1964. After a two-year stint teaching at Miami Valley Hospital School of Nursing in Dayton, Ohio, she won a scholarship to follow graduate studies at Columbia University in New York City. She also completed an

▲ Faye Wattleton has claimed "my satisfaction comes from my commitment to advancing a better world."

internship in Harlem Hospital, where she witnessed at first hand the injuries and deaths caused by self-administered and illegal back-alley abortions. Abortion was illegal in the majority of U.S. states at the time: In 1965 alone, illegal terminations caused almost 200 deaths.

Reproduction rights

In 1967 Wattleton earned her master's degree in maternity and infant care, after which she returned to Dayton, where she took up the position of assistant public health director for Montgomery County. She also began voluntary work for the Dayton chapter of the PPFA, and from 1969 to 1978 served as its executive director. Finally, in January 1978 she was appointed the youngest president of the PPFA, based in its New York headquarters. Wattleton was the first woman and first African American to head the organization since its founding in 1942. Under her forthright leadership the PPFA became the United

KEY DATES

1943 Born in St. Louis, Missouri, on July 8.

1964 Earns a BA degree in nursing from Ohio State University.

1978 Becomes the first black president of the Planned Parenthood Federation of America (PPFA).

1992 Resigns as president of PPFA.

1995 Cofounds the Center for Gender Equality in New York City.

1996 Publishes autobiography, *Life on the Line*.

INFLUENCES AND INSPIRATION

Faye Wattleton has often paid tribute to the powerful influence that Ozie Wattleton has had over her life and career, even though mother and daughter have taken opposing positions on the issue of abortion. As a woman minister in a male-dominated church, Ozie Wattleton had to show courage, determination, and independence. Although poor she believed passionately that she had a duty to help those less fortunate than herself. Ozie Wattleton passed on these qualities and values to her daughter, along with a gift for public speaking. On the other hand, Faye Wattleton's passionate commitment to women's reproductive rights and to sexual health is in many ways a reaction to the poor sex and health education she herself received as a teenager. Apart from giving her some advice after she began menstruation, her mother told her very little about sexual relationships or birth control. Wattleton has written that partly to compensate for this she has always spoken openly about sexual matters to her own daughter. Throughout her career Wattleton has argued that education plays a primary role in preventing unwanted pregnancy and therefore influences abortion rates.

States's seventh-largest charitable organization, providing medical services and birth-control counseling to four million Americans every year.

Family planning in the United States

Since World War II (1939–1945) the PPFA had played a key role in raising public consciousness about family planning and had helped bring about the U.S.-wide legalization of abortion following the historic *Roe v. Wade* Supreme Court decision in 1973. Nevertheless, during the 1970s the PPFA maintained a moderate, conservative public image and had tried to maintain a low profile in the increasingly strident abortion debate that was polarizing the country.

During the 1980s the Republican administration of President Ronald Reagan made several moves to restrict funding for and access to abortion services. While Wattleton has always downplayed the question of race, in the United States, nonwhite women are almost twice as likely than whites to resort to abortion, in large part because they are more poorly educated about and have less access to methods of contraception. In response Wattleton spearheaded a national campaign to protect a woman's right to choose and also to preserve federal funding for family-planning services. She made numerous appearances on television and radio, and traveled the country to speak at rallies and conferences.

For Wattleton, government attempts to restrict access to abortion were an assault on women's liberty. In one speech in 1989 she argued that "the power of the government to control women's reproduction is more frightening than any other tyranny, more binding than any other prison." She insisted that abortion was a question of private rather than public morality.

An ongoing struggle

Wattleton's high media profile led her to become a target for antiabortion extremists, who sent her death threats and taunted her in the street. In 1989 Wattleton and the pro-choice movement received a significant setback when the Supreme Court ruled that it was up to individual state legislatures to decide on the issue of abortion. Meanwhile, Wattleton was also facing opposition from within the PPFA, where some people considered that her vehement pro-choice line was compromising the wider goals of the organization. In 1992 Wattleton resigned as president.

Life after the PPFA

Since 1992 Wattleton has continued to campaign for women's reproductive rights, as well as on wider issues of equality. In 1995 she helped found the nonpartisan, nonprofit research and development Center for Gender Equality, later renamed the Center for the Advancement of Women, of which she is president.

Wattleton's courage and determination have won her many honors, including 12 honorary doctoral degrees from such institutions as Northeastern University Law School, the University of Pennsylvania (both 1990), and Wesleyan University (1991). She was a 1993 inductee into the National Women's Hall of Fame. Wattleton's memoir, *Life on the Line*, was published in 1996.

Further reading: Wattleton, Faye. *Life on the Line.* New York, NY: Ballantine, 1996.
www.healthnewsdigest.com/site/wattleton.html (Biography).
http://www.plannedparenthood.org/pp2/portal/ (PPFA site).

WATTS, André
Pianist

André Watts was a concert pianist who achieved fame while still a child and went on to develop a distinguished recording and performing career. He is best known for his interpretations of the classical European Romantic repertoire, combining technical mastery and passionate musicality.

Early life
Born on an army base in Nuremberg, Germany, on June 20, 1946, Watts was the son of Herman Watts, an African American soldier, and Maria Alexander Gusmits, a Hungarian. He began to study violin at age four and piano at age six with his mother. Watts's musical talent was obvious and in 1954 the family moved to Philadelphia, Pennsylvania, where he attended the Philadelphia Academy of Music. At age nine he won first prize in a competition to play in a Children's Concert with the Philadelphia Symphony Orchestra; he played Haydn's Piano Concerto

▼ *André Watts was a child prodigy, winning piano competitions from an early age.*

KEY DATES

1946   Born in Nuremberg, Germany, on June 20.

1963   Makes his first public appearance with the New York Philharmonic Orchestra.

1966   Makes first international appearance in London, England.

1976   Appears in first solo recital on national television.

in D. At age 10 he played a Mendelssohn piano concerto, and in 1962 he played Cesar Franck's Symphonic Variations with the orchestra.

Critical acclaim
Watts came to public attention when he played Liszt's Piano Concerto No. 1 with the New York Philharmonic Orchestra in a Young Person's Concert in 1963, televised by CBS. He performed it again at the request of the orchestra's director, Leonard Bernstein, when the scheduled performer, the Canadian pianist Glen Gould, became too ill to play.

While developing his performing career Watts continued his musical studies at the Peabody Institute in Baltimore, Maryland, graduating in 1972. In 1966 he made his European debut with the London Symphony Orchestra in England. In 1967 he went on a world tour with the Los Angeles Philharmonic, and in 1973 took part in a tour of the Soviet Union with the San Francisco Symphony Orchestra, both with the support of the State Department.

Watts made his debut televised solo recital from Lincoln Center, New York, in November 1976, the first of many such performances. His concert with the New York Philharmonic Orchestra in 1988, the 25th anniversary of his first concert with them, was also televised.

Watts continues to tour, principally in the United States. The recipient of many awards, he received honorary doctorates from Yale University in 1973 and Albright College in 1975, and the Avery Fisher Prize in 1988. He holds a chair at the Indiana University School of Music.

Further reading: http://www.will.uiuc.edu/fm/programs/classicallyblack/cbwatts.htm (Biography).

WATTS, J. C.
Football Player, Politician

One of the first African Americans integrated into his local elementary school, J. C. Watts has broken down barriers in education, sports, and politics.

Early life
Born in Eufaula, Oklahoma, on November 18, 1957, Julius Caesar Watts was the fifth of six children born to Buddy and Helena Watts. From his early years as an elementary school student, Watts found ways to break through the subordinate roles expected of black Americans in the southern United States.

Sporting excellence
After graduating from high school in 1976, Watts studied at the University of Oklahoma, becoming the first black man to play quarterback for the college. He led the Oklahoma Sooners to two consecutive Big Eight Championships and to Orange Bowl victories in 1980 and 1981. After being voted Most Valuable Player of both the 1980 and 1981 Orange Bowls, Watts graduated in 1981 and signed a contract with the Canadian Football League (CFL).

Watts enjoyed a successful career as a CFL quarterback, starting for Ottawa and Toronto from 1981 through 1986. In his rookie season Watts gained increased visibility when he was voted the Most Valuable Player in the CFL championship game.

After five years in Canadian football Watts returned to Oklahoma. Serving as youth minister at Sunnylane Baptist

▲ *J. C. Watts speaks at a rally for the reelection of George W. Bush and Dick Cheney in 2004.*

Church in Del City, Oklahoma, he made a name for himself as a community activist. Watts trained to become an associate pastor, and in 1990 he was elected to the Oklahoma State Corporation Commission, a state regulatory agency. He became the chairman of the commission before setting his sights on Congress.

Politics
Less than 10 years after he retired from professional football, the fourth Congressional district of Oklahoma elected Watts to the U.S. Congress in 1994. Watts won four consecutive elections, increasing his margin of victory each time. In his final campaign in 2000 Watts was reelected with 65 percent of the vote. In 1998, and again in 2000, his House colleagues elected him as chair of the House Republican Conference, making Watts the fourth most powerful Republican in the House of Representatives.

After four successful terms Watts retired from the House to serve as chairman of the J. C. Watts Companies. Since 2003 he has been chairman of GOPAC, a training organization for Republican political candidates. He and his wife founded the J. C. and Frankie Watts Foundation to promote service, leadership, and self sufficiency in young people.

Further reading: Watts, J. C. *What Color is a Conservative? My Life and My Politics.* New York, NY: HarperCollins, 2002. http://www.jcwatts.com (Official site).

KEY DATES

1957   Born in Eufaula, Oklahoma, on November 18.

1981   Graduates from University of Oklahoma with a BA in journalism.

1994   Elected to Congress from the fourth district of Oklahoma.

1997   Delivers the Republican response to President Clinton's 1997 State of the Union address.

1998   Elected chair of the Republican Conference; elected again in 2000.

2003   Becomes chairman of GOPAC, a training organization for Republican political candidates.

WAYANS Family
Writers, Directors, Actors, Comedians

A huge entertainment dynasty, the Wayans family has had a massive effect on the movie, TV, and comedy scene. The award-winning family has successfully turned their hands to writing, directing, and acting. The series *In Living Color* and the *Wayans Brothers,* and films such as *Scary Movie*, which made fun of Hollywood blockbuster horror films such as *Scream*, helped establish the Wayans as one of Hollywood's premiere entertainment families. The family uses comedy to challenge stereotypes and preconceived ideas.

The Wayans
The Wayans have their roots in New York City. Their parents Howell and Elvira Wayans had 10 children and six established successful careers in entertainment: Dwayne (1957–), Keenan (1958–), Damon (1960–), Kim (1961–), Shawn (1971–), and Marlon (1972–).

Keenan started to study at Tuskegee University, but he dropped out in his senior year to pursue a career in comedy, following in the footsteps of his hero, Richard Pryor. Keenan went on to have a successful career in TV

▼ *Keenan Ivory, Marlon, and Damon Wayans at the BET Comedy Awards in Pasadena, California, in 2004.*

KEY DATES

1990   In *Living Color* airs for the first time.

2000   *Scary Movie* grosses over a $150 million at the domestic box office.

2004   The family wins the BET Comedy Icon Award for its contributions to the field of comedy.

and film, establishing the way for his family. After the movie *I'm Gonna Git You Sucka* (1988), he hit the big time in the early 1990s with his creation of the popular Emmy award-winning TV series *In Living Color*, in which his sister Kim and brother Shawn also starred.

Shawn went on to coproduce, cowrite, and costar with younger brother Marlon in *Don't Be a Menace to South Central While Drinking Your Juice in the Hood* (1996), a spoof of several black movies.

Marlon graduated from the School of Performing Arts in New York and from Howard University, Washington, D.C., going on to act in the films *Requiem for a Dream* and *Scary Movie* (both 2000). Created by yet another family member, cousin Craig Wayans, and directed by brother Keenan, *Scary Movie* was a surprise smash at the box office, out-grossing the films they set out to parody and producing two sequels.

Damon found success in the mid-1980s in *Saturday Night Live*. He is also the star of the show *My Wife and Kids* (2001), on which his sister Kim has worked as a story editor. Kim has collaborated with her brothers on several projects and also does stand-up comedy. Damon has appeared in several films, including Spike Lee's *Bamboozled* (2000).

In 2004 Keenan wrote, produced, and directed the comedy film *White Chicks*, which starred Shawn and Marlon. In that same year the Wayans family was awarded the BET Comedy Icon Award. In a 2005 interview, Oprah Winfrey called the Wayans America's funniest family.

See also: Lee, Spike; Pryor, Richard; Winfrey, Oprah

Further reading: Wayans, Shawn. *150 Ways to Tell If You're Ghetto*. New York, NY: Dell, 1997.
http://www.afroamericansyndicate.com/OprahWayans.html (Oprah Winfrey's interview with the Wayans family).

WEATHERS, Carl
Football Player, Actor

A famous and professionally successful football player, Carl Weathers also achieved his ultimate ambition to become a successful actor and movie star.

Early life

Weathers was born in New Orleans, Louisiana, on January 14, 1948. He attended San Diego State University in California, where he excelled at sports and quickly became a football star. He went on to play professionally with the Oakland Raiders, acting in local stage productions during the off-season. He joined British Columbia Lions in the Canadian Football League (1971–1973), before retiring from football to pursue his dream of becoming a professional actor in 1974, at age 26.

A rocky road to fame

Weathers first starred in two low-budget blaxploitation films, *Bucktown* and *Friday Foster* (both in 1975). He also made guest appearances in several popular TV shows such as *Starsky and Hutch, Kung Fu*, and the *Six-Million Dollar Man*. However, it was for his appearance as Apollo Creed in Sylvester Stallone's smash hit boxing movie, *Rocky* (1976), that he was best remembered. The film was such a success that he reprised it three times in sequels in 1979, 1982, and 1985.

Weathers cemented his image as an action star, starring in such films as *Force 10 From Navarone* (1978) and *Predator* (1987). In 1988 he had his first leading role in *Action Jackson*, but the film performed poorly at the box office and was panned by critics. However, during the 1990s, he substituted for Howard E. Rollins in four *In the Heat of the Night* TV specials that were popular with critics and viewers alike. Weathers returned to the action genre in two TV-movies with Hulk Hogan: *Assault on Devil's Island* (1997) and *Shadow Warriors II: Hunt for the Death Merchant* (1999). He also proved himself a versatile actor in a series of comedies alongside Adam Sandler in *Happy Gilmore* (1996), *Little Nicky* (2000), and *Eight*

▲ **Carl Weathers (above) played Apollo Creed in the hit movie Rocky with Sylvester Stallone in 1976.**

Crazy Nights (2002). Weathers also played himself in three episodes of the Fox Television comedy series *Arrested Development*.

Weathers continued his interest in sports and is a member of the U.S. Olympic Committee, which handles the career of athletes in various sports. He is also a supporter of charitable causes, including the Big Brothers Association, which mentors children in need.

See also: Rollins, Howard E.

Further reading: http://www.hollywoodcultmovies.com/html/carl_weathers.html (Short biography of Weathers and capsule review of his cult movies).

KEY DATES	
1948	Born in New Orleans, Louisiana, on January 14.
1974	Retires from football to embark on an acting career.
1976	Plays Apollo Creed for the first time in the film *Rocky*.

WEAVER, Robert Clifton
Public Servant

Robert Clifton Weaver, the great-grandson of a slave, was the first African American appointed to a cabinet position. An outstanding economist, Weaver worked in government for many years before embarking on an academic career.

Early life

Born in Washington, D.C., on December 29, 1907, Weaver was the son of a university graduate mother and a father who worked as a postal clerk. Weaver and his older brother, Mortimer, Jr., were raised in a largely white Washington neighborhood. Both boys were outstanding students at school, following their mother's advice that the best way to fight racial prejudice was to do well.

After school both brothers went to Harvard University. When Weaver was refused a room in a dorm because of his color, he and his brother lived together off-campus. In 1929 Weaver graduated cum laude but in that same year Mortimer died of a mystery illness. Weaver stayed on at Harvard to complete an MA in 1931; he received a doctorate in economics in 1934.

Political career

By the time he earned his doctorate, Weaver was employed by the government. In 1933 Harold L. Ickes, the secretary of interior, hired him to be a race relations adviser in the Housing Department. While there Weaver became an active member of the so-called Black Cabinet, an influential group of African Americans, such as Mary McLeod Bethune, in the administration of Franklin D. Roosevelt.

During World War II (1939–1945) Weaver held different positions in the government concerned with mobilizing black labor. In 1944 he left the government to direct the Mayor's Committee on Race Relations in Chicago. He then directed the fellowship program of the John Hay Whitney Foundation, publishing two studies about discrimination.

▲ **Robert Clifton Weaver takes his oath as Secretary of Housing and Urban Development in 1966.**

In 1955 Weaver was appointed as rent commissioner for New York State and became the first African American to hold a state cabinet position. Following the election of John F. Kennedy as president in 1960, Weaver was appointed director of the U.S. Housing and Home Finance Agency, the highest federal position ever held by an African American. Kennedy wanted to give him a position on his cabinet, but was opposed by senators on the grounds of Weaver's race. When Lyndon B. Johnson won the presidential election in 1966, he appointed Weaver as head of the newly established Department of Housing and Urban Development (HUD), making him the first black person to serve in the federal cabinet.

In 1969 Weaver left politics to start an academic career. Between 1970 and 1978 he was professor of urban studies at CUNY's Hunter College. Weaver won many awards, including the Equal Opportunity Day Award of the National Urban League in 1987. He died on July 17, 1997.

See also: Bethune, Mary McLeod; Political Representation

Further reading: www.pbs.org/wnet/aaworld.reference/articles/robert_clifton_weaver.html (Biography).

KEY DATES	
1907	Born in Washington, D.C., on December 29.
1934	Receives PhD from Harvard.
1966	First African American appointed to the cabinet.
1997	Dies in New York City on July 17.

WELLS, Junior
Musician

Junior Wells was a pioneer of the blues harmonica. Influenced by such musicians as John Lee "Sonny Boy" Williamson and Little Walter Jacobs, Wells helped define the Chicago blues sound.

Early life

Born Amos Blakemore in Memphis, Tennessee, on December 9, 1934, Wells was raised on farms in West Memphis and Arkansas. Growing up around the music of the blues culture of Memphis, Wells was taught to play the harmonica by musician Little Junior Parker. Following his parents' separation, Wells moved with his mother to Chicago, Illinois, where he skipped school to play his harmonica.

In 1950 Wells joined guitarists Louis and David Myers to form the band the Deuce. They changed their name to the Aces after drummer Fred Below joined them.

▼ *Junior Wells and his band perform on the NBC TV program* **The Sounds and Sights of Chicago** *in the 1950s.*

KEY DATES

1934	Born in Memphis, Tennessee, on December 9.
1946	Moves to Chicago, Illinois, with his mother.
1952	Begins playing with Muddy Waters.
1959	"Little by Little" reaches No. 23 on the rhythm-and-blues charts.
1965	Releases the album *Hoodoo Man Blues*.
1997	Awarded the W. C. Handy Blues Award for the album *Come on in This House*.
1998	Dies in Chicago, Illinois, on January 15.

Wells's big break came when he persuaded his sister and her boyfriend to take him to see Muddy Waters play. Wells said: "I went up to Muddy and told him I played harp.... Muddy said he'd let me try. Little Walter [Jacobs] said, 'That little shrimp.' They stood me on a Coke box to reach the mike and I made $45 in tips."

Music

In 1952 Little Walter Jacobs left Waters's band and Wells replaced him. In 1953 Wells was drafted into the Army, serving two years. When he returned to Chicago he met Mel London, who produced some of Wells's best-known songs, including "Little by Little" (1957) and "Messin' With the Kid" (1960).

In the 1960s Wells began a long collaboration with guitarist Buddy Guy, who played on Wells's first acclaimed album, *Hoodoo Man Blues* (1965). The two men toured with the Rolling Stones in 1970, beginning an association that was to last for the rest of Wells's life. Bassist Bill Wyman backed Wells at the Montreaux Jazz Festival (1974) and Wells produced a track for the Rolling Stone's tribute album *Paint It Blue: Songs of the Rolling Stones* (1997). Wells's 1997 album *Come on in This House* was nominated for a Grammy and won the W. C. Handy Blues Award for a traditional blues album. Wells died in Chicago in 1998.

See also: Waters, Muddy; Williamson, John Lee

Further reading: http://www.bluesharp.ca/legends/jwells.html (Biography).

WELLS, Ruth
Social Activist

Ruth Wells led a long and ultimately successful campaign against realtors who were exploiting African American homebuyers in Chicago, Illinois.

Early life
Born in West Point, Mississippi, on August 1, 1934, Ruth Darnell was educated at public schools in Calendonia, Mississippi. At age 13 Wells and her family moved to Gary, Indiana, where she attended Roosevelt High until 11th grade, after which she left to work for the Standard Oil Company in Whiting.

Housing scam
In 1959 Wells joined the 3M Company and relocated to Chicago, Illinois. When she and her husband bought a house in Lawndale on the city's West Side, they fell victim to a scam. As increasing numbers of blacks moved into the district, many prejudiced whites took fright and sold their homes cheaply in order to make a quick escape. The properties were bought up by realtors who resold them to African Americans and provided finance enabling them to buy the properties. At the time few financial institutions would lend money to black people, so the buyers were forced to accept the sellers' extortionate terms. The house remained the property of the realtor until the whole purchase price plus the interest had been paid in full, late payment would result in immediate repossession, and early repayment was not allowed. Meanwhile the occupant was responsible for paying for all repairs and maintenance.

Fighting injustice
Wells was horrified by the injustice of the scheme. She decided to fight the realtors but initially found it difficult to get enough support from other black Americans who had suffered in the same way because they were afraid of reprisals and eviction. However, with the help of Father Jack McNamara, a local Jesuit priest, Wells founded the Contract Buyers League (CBL). Inviting all the local residents to meetings held on Wednesday evenings in a local school, McNamara and Wells got people to admit that they had been exploited. The CBL also protested outside contractors' offices and homes, carrying signs that said "Your Neighbor is a Slum Landlord." The organization enlisted the assistance of Robert Ming, a black civil rights attorney, and lawyers from the firm of Jenner and

▲ **Ruth Wells and the CBL fought discriminatory and exploitative practices on behalf of black homeowners.**

Block, who agreed to handle a case *pro bono*, meaning without a fee. Legal action began in 1968, and in 1972 a federal court found that the realtors had acted unlawfully and ruled that all the existing arrangements be replaced by regular mortgages. Later the same year Wells was recruited by Citizens Alert, a criminal justice watch organization, for which she worked until her retirement in 1990.

KEY DATES	
1934	Born in West Point, Mississippi, on August 1.
1950	Joins Standard Oil.
1959	Moves to Chicago, Illinois.
1972	Wins legal action against corrupt realtors; joins Citizens Alert.
1990	Retires from Citizen's Alert.

Further reading: McPherson, James Allen. "In My Fathers House There are Many Mansions—And I'm Going to Get Me Some of Them Too: The Story of the Contract Buyers League." *Atlantic Monthly*, April 1972.

WELLS-BARNETT, Ida B.

Civil Rights Activist, Writer

A fearless civil rights activist, Ida B. Wells-Barnett fought hard against racial and gender injustice in the United States. Wells-Barnett, who added the name of her husband, journalist and lawyer Ferdinand L. Barnett, to her maiden name, was a vocal opponent of lynching. She meticulously researched and wrote a pamphlet on the issue. She was also a great defender of women's rights.

Early life

Born in Holly Springs, Mississippi, on July 16, 1862, Ida Bell Wells was the eldest child of an enslaved cook, Elizabeth, and carpenter, James. Although the Wellses stayed on with their former owners after Emancipation, they were forced to move by retaliation

▼ **Ida B. Wells-Barnett was one of the founding 40 members of the NAACP.**

against James Wells for voting in the election of 1867. White Southerners resented the African Americans entitlement to vote during Reconstruction.

Wells-Barnett's parents died within a day of one another in the yellow fever epidemic of 1878. One infant brother also perished, and Wells-Barnett insisted on returning home to care for her remaining five siblings, in spite of the threat of contracting the disease herself. Relatives and well-meaning friends wanted to separate the children to enable several families to care for them, but Wells-Barnett refused. With the help of her grandmother, she planned to take care of her brothers and sisters; she passed the local teaching examination and worked as a teacher to help support the family. She lived at the schoolhouse during the week, and traveled home to care for a house full of children and grade her students' work on the weekends. After about two years Wells-Barnett and two of her sisters went to live with an aunt in Memphis, while the other children were cared for by another aunt. In Memphis Wells-Barnett continued to teach and also took summer classes at Fisk University and LeMoyne Institute.

Challenging the status quo

In 1884 Wells-Barnett was on her usual train to school when she was asked to move to the colored section of the car. She refused and the conductor, along with two other railroad employees, proceeded to physically eject her from the car. Wells-Barnett sued the Chesapeake and Ohio Railroad for discrimination and won a $500 judgment. Wells-Barnett never saw the money, however. In 1887 the Tennessee Supreme Court overturned the verdict on appeal and Wells-Barnett was ordered to pay the railroad $200 in costs.

Shortly after her initial winning verdict Wells-Barnett, who was still teaching, began to write for two church publications, the *Evening Star* and the *Living Way*. Writing under the name Iola, she was invited to contribute on various issues by black papers around the country. She was soon referred to as the "Princess of the Press."

In 1887 Wells-Barnett was offered the position of regular reporter for a black Memphis newspaper named *Free Speech and Headlight*. In 1891 she wrote several articles criticicizing the Memphis school board for giving black children separate but unequal educational

INFLUENCES AND INSPIRATION

In 1892, when three friends of Ida B. Wells-Barnett's were lynched by a white mob because they were taking away business from white competitors, Wells-Barnett put her investigative and writing skills to exposing the truth about lynching. A long accepted practice, particularly in the rural South and West of America, many white supporters argued that lynching stopped marauding black men from raping decent white women. Wells found that less than a third of victims had even been accused of rape, let alone were guilty of it and argued that it was in fact black women who were more often subjected to interracial sexual violence. Wells-Barnett presented her findings to a group of black women activists in Chicago in 1892. Wells-Barnett wrote that this was the beginning of the women's club movement in the United States, which evolved four years later into the National Association of Colored Women, the first national black women's organization.

opportunities. Her teaching contract was not renewed, and she invested her savings in a part-interest in the paper, shortening its name to the *Memphis Free Speech*.

Lynching

On May 21, 1892, Wells-Barnett published an editorial discussing one of the most frequent scenarios for lynching black men (*see box*). She intimated that the liaisons between black men and white women were relationships between consenting adults, and that by lynching black men, white men were really trying to hide from this fact. Enraged whites vowed to kill her and destroyed the office of the *Free Speech*. Wells-Barnett, who was traveling when the article was published, did not return to Memphis. She moved to New York City and then on to Chicago.

Wells-Barnett published a pamphlet on lynching, and began to speak around the country and overseas on the subject. In 1895 she published *The Red Record: Tabulated Statistics and Alleged Causes of Lynching in the United States,* a compilation of all her investigation into lynching up until that date. She also married Ferdinand L. Barnett, a Chicago-based newsman and attorney in that year, taking his name.

Activism

Wells-Barnett was a great believer in asserting her rights both as a woman and as a person of color. She was a suffragist and promoted women's rights around the country. She attended the 1905 Niagara movement conferences organized by W. E. B. DuBois, and was critical of Booker T. Washington, whom she accused of accommodating white views at the expense of African Americans. She was also one of the founding members of the National Association for the Advancement of Colored People (NAACP) in 1909, but eventually accused it of being a conformist group geared toward the needs of the black American elite. Threatened by the government when she protested the hanging of 12 black soldiers executed for their part in a Texas riot, Wells-Barnett was refused a passport to attend the Versailles Peace Conference in 1919. She continued to tackle difficult issues for the rest of her life, writing about the 1919 Arkansas riot in which more than 200 black Americans died, for example. She stood unsuccessfully for the Illinois state legislature at age 68. Wells-Barnett died in 1931.

See also: DuBois, W. E. B.; Washington, Booker T.

Further reading: McMurray, Linda O. *To Keep the Waters Troubled: The Life of Ida B. Wells-Barnett.* New York, NY: Oxford University Press, 1998.
http://www.duke.edu/~ldbaker/classes/AAIH/caaih/ibwells/ibwbkgrd.html (Article about Wells-Barnett and her passion for justice).

KEY DATES

1862	Born in Holly Springs, Mississippi, on July 16.
1878	Parents die during a yellow fever epidemic.
1884	Successfully sues the Chesapeake and Ohio Railroad for discrimination on public transportation.
1892	Publishes antilynching pamphlet; addresses black women activists in Philadelphia.
1931	Dies in Chicago, Illinois, on March 25.
1970	Autobiography, *Crusade for Justice,* is published.
1990	U.S. Postal Service issues a stamp in her honor as part of its Black Heritage series.
2005	The United States Senate apologizes for not enacting antilynching legislation on June 13.

WELSH, Kariamu
Choreographer, Academic

A leading African American dance scholar and choreographer, Kariamu Welsh is best known for her influential dance technique Umfundalai, an athletic blend of traditional African movement, song, and ritual, and African American modern dance. Since the 1970s Welsh has been an important figure in Afrocentricity, the scholarly movement that has sought to review world history and culture from an African perspective. Welsh was married to Afrocentric scholar Molefi Kete Asante.

Early life

Born in 1948, Welsh initially studied dance at the State University of New York, Buffalo, where she received her BA in 1972 and went on to take an MA in choreography (the process of creating and arranging dances) in 1975. Inspired by the black arts movement, Welsh focused her studies on the rich traditions of African dance and sought to forge a modern dance that was a full expression of African American culture and heritage. A crucial influence was African American dance pioneer Katherine Dunham.

Making a mark

In 1981 Welsh went to Zimbabwe in southern Africa, where she helped set up the country's National Dance Company, of which she became the first artistic director. Two years later she returned to the United States, where she became the director of the Institute for African Dance Research and Performance at Philadelphia's Temple University. During the following decade Welsh and Asante turned Temple University, Philadelphia, into the United States's most important center for Afrocentric scholarship. They collaborated on such groundbreaking works as the edited collection *African Culture: The Rhythms of Unity* (1985).

Academic

In 1987 Welsh became a professor at Temple University. She went on to gain her doctorate in dance history and choreography from New York University, New York City. Welsh teaches in both the African American studies and women's studies departments at Temple. Her ongoing researches have led to extended field trips to Ghana, Cote-d'Ivoire (Ivory Coast), Benin, and Zaire. In addition, Welsh has contributed articles to several publications, including the *International Journal of African Dance*. She edited a special issue on black women and dance for *SAGE: A Scholarly Journal on Black Women*. Welsh also wrote *Zimbabwean Dance: Rhythmic Forces, Ancestral Voices, and An Aesthetic Analysis* (1997) and the *Umfundalai Technique: An African Dance Technique* (2001).

Choreographer

As a choreographer Welsh has created an innovative and exhilarating body of work, which includes *Nubian Caravan* (1993), *Bolokalafini* (1994), and *Raaaahmona*. Her work is usually performed by her dance troupe, Kariamu and Company Traditions, which uses Welsh's contemporary dance technique of Umfundalai. Welsh's work often deals with political themes such as racism and covers contemporary events. Her work has influenced many younger African American dancers and choreographers, and has been recognized with honors and awards, including three senior Fulbright Scholarships and a Guggenheim Fellowship. Welsh has served on several national and regional arts councils, including the National Endowment of the Arts, the Pennsylvania Council on the Arts, and the New York State Council on the Arts.

See also: Asante, Molefi Kete; Dunham, Katherine

Further reading: Welsh-Asante, Kariamu (ed.). *African Dance: An Artistic, Historical, and Philosphical Inquiry.* Lawrenceville, NJ: Africa World Press, 1996.
umfundalai.com (Site devoted to Umfundalai, Welsh's dance technique).

KEY DATES

1948	Born in this year.
1970	First develops Umfundalai dance technique in about this year.
1981	Becomes artistic director of the National Dance Company of Zimbabwe.
1983	Becomes director of the Institute for African Dance Research and Performance at Temple University, Philadelphia, Pennsylvania.
1994	Boklolafini performs at the Merriam Theater in Philadelphia.

WESLEY, Charles Harris
Historian, Educator, Writer

Charles Harris Wesley was a highly regarded teacher, historian, and author. The fourth African American to receive a doctorate from Harvard University, Wesley was a fierce advocate of education. He led several educational organizations throughout his distinguished career. He was also an ordained minister in the African Methodist Episcopal (AME) Church, to which he provided more than 40 years of service.

Early life
Born in Louisville, Kentucky, on December 2, 1891, Wesley attended local public schools and then entered the Preparatory School at Fisk University, from which he received a BA in 1911. An exceptional student, Wesley excelled in a range of subjects. He was a talented musician with an excellent baritone voice; he performed in several operas and sang with Roland Hayes and the Fisk Jubilee Singers.

Wesley went on to study at Yale University. While there he became a member of the Zeta Chapter of the Alpha Phi Alpha fraternity. Wesley published the first and definitive history of the fraternity, *The History of Alpha Phi Alpha: A Development in Negro College Life* in 1929. He later served as the national general president of the fraternity from 1931 to 1940. After receiving his MA from Yale in 1913, Wesley began working for the AME Church, serving as a minister and later as an elder until the 1930s.

A career in academia
Wesley received a doctorate from Harvard in 1925 after which he joined the faculty of Howard University in Washington, D.C. He taught there 17 years before being appointed president of Wilberforce University in Ohio, a school affiliated with the AME Church. In the five years that Wesley was in the post he made several improvements, hiring talented members of staff, integrating the student body, and introducing new programs, including African studies. In 1947 Wesley took up an appointment as the first president of Central State College, Ohio, where he remained until 1965.

Black studies
Throughout his career Wesley promoted black studies. Since his mid-20s Wesley had been involved with black intellectual Carter G. Woodson's Association for the Study of Negro Life and History. In 1950 he was appointed president of the organization and served as the executive director from 1965 until 1972, after which he became executive director emeritus. In 1976 Wesley was appointed director of the Afro-American Historical & Cultural Museum in Philadelphia (now the African American Museum).

The author of several books on black history such as *Negro Labor in the United States, 1850–1925* (1927) and *Collapse of the Confederacy* (1937), Wesley was general editor of the 10-volume *International Library of Negro Life and History* (1968). Wesley's wife, Dorothy Porter Wesley, was also a noted author and a librarian, and collector of materials relating to the African American diaspora. Her book *Modern Negro Art* (1943) is a classic treatment of black American artists and art.

Wesley received numerous awards and honors for his outstanding work, including a Guggenheim Fellowship in 1930–1931, the Scottish Rite Gold Medal Award in 1957, and the Armistad Award in 1972. He died in Washington, D.C., on August 16, 1987. He was buried at Lincoln Memorial Cemetery, in Maryland.

KEY DATES	
1891	Born in Louisville, Kentucky, on December 2.
1911	Receives BA from Fisk University.
1913	Receives MA in economics from Yale University.
1925	Receives PhD in history from Harvard University.
1965	Becomes executive director of the Association for the Study of Negro Life and History (until 1972); later becomes executive director emeritus.
1976	Becomes director of the Afro-American Historical and Cultural Museum in Philadelphia, Pennsylvania.
1987	Dies in Washington, D.C., on August 16.

See also: Woodson, Carter G.

Further reading: Conyers, James L. (ed.). *Charles H. Wesley: The Intellectual Tradition of a Black Historian*. New York, NY: Garland, 1997.
http://dpw-archives.org/chw.html (Timeline).

WEST, Cornel
Intellectual, Scholar

Cornel West is an influential scholar who is known for his opinions on a range of subjects, including race relations, politics, and cultural diversity. West has collaborated with leading scholars such as Henry Louis Gates, Jr., and bell hooks. A sometimes controversial figure, West had a well-publicized dispute with Harvard University president Lawrence Summers in 2002, which led him to leave the institution to join Princeton University as the Class of 1943 University Professor of Religion and African American Studies.

Early life
Born in Tulsa, Oklahoma, on June 2, 1953, West was the son of Irene Bias, a schoolteacher, and Clifton L. West, an Air Force administrator. Brought up in a Baptist family—his

▼ *Cornel West has lectured all over the world on on such issues as homophobia, racism, and poverty.*

grandfather was Reverend Clifton L. West, Sr., pastor of the Tulsa Metropolitan Baptist Church—West grew up a devout Christian. The church and his family helped instill in him a sense of racial pride. He took part in civil rights marches in the 1960s and in his own words grew up with ideals and images of "dignity, integrity, majesty, and humility."

A voracious reader, West excelled at school. He became influenced by Malcolm X and the Black Panther movement, and became acquainted with the principles of Marxism and the writings of such people as the Ghanaian philosopher and independence leader Kwame Nkrumah.

Toward academia
In 1970 West went to Harvard University, graduating three years later with a BA cum laude. While there he was mentored by the first black American professor of political science, Martin Kilson, who said that West was the most "intellectually aggressive and highly cerebral student" that

INFLUENCES AND INSPIRATION

One of the people who most influenced Cornel West was Richard Rorty, professor of philosophy at Princeton University. West called Rorty's attention to history as "music to my ears." Rorty's teachings influenced West in writing his book *The American Evasion of Philosophy: A Genealogy of Pragmatism* (1989).

Rorty was born in New York on October 4, 1931. After studying philosophy at the University of Chicago with philosophers Rudolph Carnap, Charles Hartshorne, and Richard McKeon, he was awarded a BA in in 1949, after which he received his MA in 1952. Four years later Rorty was awarded a doctorate from Yale for his dissertation "The Concept of Potentiality." In 1958 Rorty began teaching at Wellesley College, after which he moved to Princeton University in 1961. In 1982 he moved to the University of Virginia as Kenan Professor of the Humanities. He stayed there until 1998, when he moved to the department of comparative literature at Stanford University. A respected scholar, Rorty has received numerous academic awards and honors, including Guggenheim and MacArthur fellowships.

he had taught at the university. West was also part of the Black Student Union and took part in anti-Vietnam War and antiracism protests.

West went on to do his postgraduate work at Princeton, New Jersey, where he was influenced by Richard Rorty (*see box*). He earned his MA in 1975 and his doctorate in 1980; his thesis was later published as *The Ethical Dimensions of Marxist Thought* (1991). While at Princeton, West taught at New York federal prisons and joined the Union Theological Seminary, where he taught the philosophy of religion. He began to practice as a lay preacher.

In 1984 West joined Yale Divinity School, Connecticut, a post that eventually became a joint appointment with the American studies department. He also taught at the University of Paris, France, in 1987, a year before he was appointed director of Afro-American studies and professor of religious studies at Princeton. He moved to Harvard six years later, becoming the Alphonse Fletcher, Jr., University Professor in 1998. During this time he published several books, including *Prophetic Fragments* (1988) and *Breaking Bread: Insurgent Black Intellectual Life*, with bell hooks (1991). West was a vocal rights activist, taking part in such protests as Louis Farrakhan's Million Man March (1995) to raise the profile of African American men. He was also a senior adviser to Democratic presidential contender Bill Bradley in 2000, and publicly endorsed Ralph Nader, an activist lawyer who ran as presidential candidate for the Green Party in 2000.

Controversy

In 2002 West returned to Princeton after a controversial altercation with Harvard's president, Lawrence Summers, who accused West of dedicating too much time to nonacademic pursuits, such as his political activities and recording a rap CD, *Sketches of My Culture*, to the detriment of his teaching. Summers also accused West of inflating grades and missing classes.

In 2003 West starred in the *Matrix Reloaded* and *Matrix Revolutions*. In 2004 he was adviser to Al Sharpton's presidential campaign. In 2005 West criticized the government for its lack of action in helping New Orleans's black community following Hurricane Katrina.

KEY DATES

1953	Born in Tulsa, Oklahoma, on June 2.
1973	Receives BA from Harvard.
1975	Earns MA from Princeton; completes his doctorate five years later.
1988	Appointed director of Afro-American studies and professor of religious studies at Princeton.
1994	Moves to Harvard; becomes the Alphonse Fletcher, Jr., University Professor four years later.
2002	Returns to Princeton as the Class of 1943 University Professor of Religion and African American Studies.
2004	Acts as adviser on Al Sharpton's presidential campaign.

See also: Farrakhan, Louis; Gates, Henry Louis, Jr.; hooks, bell; Malcolm X; Sharpton, Al

Further reading: Cowan, Rosemary. *Cornel West: The Politics of Redemption.* Cambridge, England: Polity Press, 2003. http://archives.cnn.com/2002/fyi/teachers.ednews/01/10 /west.harvard.ap/ (Article about West).

WEST, Dorothy
Writer

Writer Dorothy West was involved in the Harlem Renaissance, the 1920s black arts movement that was centered in Harlem, New York City. One of the youngest writers in the movement, West was known as "the Kid" by her contemporaries Langston Hughes and Zora Neale Hurston. In the 1930s West founded the short-lived *Challenge* to publish young black writers.

Early life
Born in Boston, Massachusetts, on June 2, 1907, West was the only child of a former slave who became a prosperous Boston fruit trader and his much younger wife. She enjoyed a comfortable childhood, spending summers at Martha's Vineyard. An intelligent child, West started school at age five. She attended the prestigious Girls' Latin School in Boston, graduating in 1923, after which she studied at Boston University and later at the Columbia University School of Journalism.

A lifelong writing career
West wrote fiction all her life. She wrote her first story at age seven; at age 14 West won several competitions sponsored by the *Boston Post* newspaper. She moved to New York City in the 1920s, where she associated with members of the Harlem Renaissance. In 1926 she tied for second place with Zora Neale Hurston in a competition run by *Opportunity* magazine with a short story titled "The Typewriter." West also became a member of the Saturday Evening Quill Club, an African American writers' group.

In 1932 West visited the Soviet Union with a group of African American writers and artists that included Langston Hughes to work on a film, *Black and White,* which was never completed. She returned to the United States the next year, following her father's death.

▲ *Dorothy West dedicated the 1995 novel* **The Wedding** *to the memory of the former first lady Jacqueline Kennedy Onassis, who encouraged her to write the book but died before its publication.*

West published very little but concentrated instead on her own literary magazine, *Challenge*. Started in 1934 as a forum for black American writers, it ran for three years until financial problems closed it down. A successor magazine, *New Challenge*, was also forced to close because of money problems.

During the 1940s West worked for a short time with the Federal Writers Program. She published her first novel, *The Living is Easy*, in 1948. The largely autobiographical book was well received but West then faded from public view. In the 1960s she started to write a weekly column, "Oak Bluffs," for the *Vineyard Gazette*, about goings-on in her largely black neighborhood. She continued writing the column well into the 1990s.

West found fame and success very late in her life with the publication of her second novel, *The Wedding*, written with the encouragement of her editor, Jacqueline Kennedy Onassis. Oprah Winfrey made the book into a two-part TV miniseries. West died on August 16, 1998.

See also: Harlem Renaissance; Hughes, Langston: Hurston, Zora Neale; Winfrey, Oprah

Further reading: West, Dorothy. *The Wedding*. New York, NY: Anchor, 1996.
www.pw.org/mag/west.htm (Biography).

KEY DATES	
1907	Born in Boston, Massachusetts, on June 2.
1934	Starts *Challenge* magazine.
1948	Publishes first novel, *The Living Is Easy*.
1995	Publishes second novel, *The Wedding*.
1998	Dies in Martha's Vineyard on August 16.

WEST, Kanye
Musician, Activist

Award-winning musician Kanye West is an established producer and acclaimed musician. Working with such stars as Jay-Z and Alicia Keys, West had a successful career as a producer and mixer before he released his critically acclaimed albums *The College Dropout* (2004) and *Late Registration* (2005). Known for forthright lyrics that highlight political and social issues, West received a lot of media attention when he accused President George W. Bush of "not caring about black people" in the aftermath of Hurricane Katrina in 2005.

Early life
Born in Atlanta, Georgia, on June 8, 1977, Kanye Omari West was the son of Donda West, a professor of English, and Ray West, a former Black Panther turned photographer and pastoral counselor. His parents divorced when he was three. He lived in China for a year when he was 10, while his mother taught English there. An intelligent and confident young man, West attended Columbia College, Chicago, for a semester, and Chicago State University for a year before dropping out to pursue a career in music in 1996.

Learning a craft
West worked as a producer and mixer in the rap scene. He admitted that he initially found it difficult mixing with rappers. He said, "Other people came from hustling and all that. Sometimes it was hard to relate."

Working with artists such as Alicia Keys and Ludacris, West began to build up a reputation as a leading producer, often using vintage samples and live instrumentals. In 2001 he was invited by the rapper Jay-Z to work on the album *The Blueprint* (2001). Signed to Roc-a-Fella Records, West believed that his rapping was not good enough to be

▲ *Kanye West collects several awards at the 2004 BMI Urban Awards, held in Miami Beach, Florida.*

a performer and spent the next few years perfecting it. He said: "There's nothing I really wanted to do in life that I wasn't able to get good at. That's my skill. I'm not specifically talented at anything except for the ability to learn. That's what I do."

Celebrity
Following a bad car accident in 2002, West had his jaw wired. He wrote about the experience in the song "Through the Wire" for his debut solo album *The College Dropout*, which went on to be a huge success, selling three million copies. The album picked up three Grammys, including Best Album and Best Rap Song for "Jesus Walks." West was often in the news, once for walking out of the 2004 American Music Awards, when he lost the best new artist award to country singer Gretchen Wilson. West appeared at the Philadelphia Live8 show in 2005, hosted by Will Smith, at which he performed "Diamonds from Sierra Leone," from his hit album *Late Registration* (2005).

See also: Jay-Z; Keys, Alicia; Smith, Will

Further reading: http://www.rocafella.com/Artist. aspx?v=bio&key=40 (Biography). http://www.kanyewest.com/ (Official site).

KEY DATES	
1977	Born in Atlanta, Georgia, on June 8.
2001	Produces songs for Jay-Z's album, *The Blueprint*.
2004	Releases debut solo rap album, *The College Dropout*; wins three Grammys.
2005	Releases the album *Late Registration* to critical acclaim; denounces the government for lack of action after Hurricane Katrina in September.

WHARTON, Clifton R., Jr.
Politician, Educator

Like his father Clifton R. Wharton the politician and educator Clifton R. Wharton, Jr., has held so many positions in his lifetime that a summary cannot do justice to his accomplishments. Wharton, who has taught at many prestigious universities, has been awarded honorary doctorates from more than 25 international universities, and has authored four books and more than 50 articles.

Early life
Born in Boston, Massachusetts, on September 13, 1926, Wharton spent six years living in the Spanish Canary Islands, where his diplomat father was posted as a consul. An extremely bright youngster, Wharton was admitted to Harvard University at age 16, graduating with a BA in history in 1947. He immediately pursued an MA in international affairs at Johns Hopkins School of Advanced International Studies, concentrating on Latin America affairs; he graduated in 1948. From 1948 to 1953 he worked as an economist with the American International Association for Economic and Social Development. Wharton then enrolled at the University of Chicago, where he earned another an MA and PhD in economics in 1958.

▼ *Bill Clinton named the former MSU president deputy secretary of state in 1993.*

From 1958 to 1970 Wharton was chairman of the Rockefeller Family Philanthropic Foundation, first in Latin America (Brazil, Costa Rica, and Venezuela) from 1948 to 1957 and then in Southeast Asia (Malaysia, Vietnam, Cambodia, and Thailand) from 1958 to1970.

Academic
During his 22 years of experience at home and abroad, Wharton built such an impressive record that he was hired as president of Michigan State University in 1970. Serving in a decade full of turmoil, Wharton focused on specific goals such as improving the quality of the curriculum at Michigan State in the face of budget cuts, providing educational opportunities for underprivileged students, and merging the School of Osteopathic Medicine with the other medical schools at the university. Wharton created a Presidential Commission on Admissions and Student Body Composition to draw up policies on enrollment, and a Presidential Fellows Program designed to train students and junior faculty for university administration positions. He also built the Clifton and Delores Wharton Center for the Performing Arts, which opened in 1982.

In December 1977 Wharton resigned from Michigan State University to become chancellor of the State University of New York (SUNY). The largest university system in the country, comprising 64 colleges and universities, SUNY had about 380,000 students. Wharton held the position until 1987.

Politics and international affairs
Wharton served as chairman of Congress's Food Advisory Committee on World Hunger in the Carter administration. In 1987 he became chairman and chief executive officer of Teachers Insurance and Annuity Association and the College Retirement Equities Fund (TIAA–CREF), the world's largest private pension provider with assets of some $112 billion. He also served on the Overseas Development Council and was a trustee of the Council on foreign Relations.

In January 1993 President Bill Clinton appointed Wharton deputy secretary of state, a position from which he resigned on November 9, apparently because of a barrage of negative reports from the media about his performance in foreign affairs.

INFLUENCES AND INSPIRATION

There is no doubt that the person who influenced the young Wharton most was his father, Clifton Reginald Wharton. (1899–1990), a distinguished career diplomat, who served in Africa and Europe. Wharton, Jr., has credited much of his success to his father, with whom he traveled across the oceans when he was young. The influence of this time abroad seeing and experiencing other cultures, political systems, and economies can be seen in the educational choices he made: He studied history, international affairs, and economics.

Clifton R. Wharton was born in Baltimore, Maryland. After studying law he became the first black person to take the Foreign Service examination. He was one of 20 candidates who passed. He was posted to Liberia. In 1930 he became the consul to Las Palmas in the Canary Islands. After a series of minor appointments, Wharton became first secretary and consul in Lisbon, Portugal, rising to be consul general (1950), after which he served in Marseilles, France (1953–1957).

In 1958 Dwight D. Eisenhower gave him the posting of minister to Romania; he became the first black career Foreign Service officer to serve as chief of a mission. Under John F. Kennedy he was appointed Ambassador to Norway, the first black ambassador to serve in Europe. A true pioneer, Wharton set his son a fantastic example.

Wharton has summed up his achievements in terms of the firsts he achieved: "I was the first black to attend and graduate from the Johns Hopkins School of Advanced International Studies; the first black to earn a PhD in economics from the University of Chicago; the first black to head a major predominantly white university; the first black to head the largest university system in the U.S.; the first black elected chairman and CEO of a Fortune 500 company; the first black to chair a major U.S. foundation, the Rockefeller Foundation; and the first black person to occupy the No. 2 position in the U.S. Department of State."

Honors

Wharton has received over 20 honorary degrees, as well as the Alumni Medal from the University of Chicago; the Distinguished Service Award for Lifetime Achievement from the Council on Education, the Black History Makers Award, and the President's Award for World Hunger.

KEY DATES	
1926	Born in Boston, Massachusetts, on September 13.
1958	Earns MA and PhD in economics.
1970	Becomes president of Michigan State University.
1978	Appointed chancellor of the State University of New York.
1987	Becomes chairman of the TIAA–CREF.
1993	Appointed deputy secretary of state; resigns from post; retires from TUIAA–CREF.

Wharton has served on nine private boards and commissions, including the Ford Motor Company, Time-Warner, Equitable Life, Tenneco, and Harcourt General, and on such federal boards as the Federal Reserve Bank of New York, the New York Stock Exchange, the Public Broadcasting Service, the Presidential Advisory Commission on Trade Policy and Negotiations, and the Board for International Food and Agriculture Development, of which he was the chairman.

Wharton has authored or edited four books and monographs and more than 50 professional journal articles. Drawing on his training and his experience in economic development in developing countries, Wharton edited the important *Subsistence Agriculture and Economic Development* (1969).

Between his 1958 graduation from the University of Chicago and his retirement from the State Department in 1993 he served under Presidents Lyndon B. Johnson, Gerald Ford, Jimmy Carter, Ronald Reagan, George Bush, and Bill Clinton.

Wharton married Delores Duncan Wharton (1927–), who was the first black executive director for the Kellogg Foundation and Philips Petroleum.

Further reading: Clarke, Caroline V. *Take a Lesson: Black Achievers on How They Made It and What They Learned Along the Way.* New York, NY: John Wiley & Co., 2002. http://www.news.cornell.edu/Chronicle/96/4.25.96/Wharton-bio.html (Biography).

WHEATLEY, Phillis
Writer

Phillis Wheatley was an African-born slave who achieved great fame during her life for her poetry. By age 19, Wheatley was already a well-known writer, even though she was not able to publish her poems in the United States. *Poems on Various Subjects, Religious and Moral* was published in London, England, in 1773.

Early life

Thought to have been born in 1753 in Senegal, Sierra Leone, or Gambia on the western coast of Africa, Wheatley was captured by the master of the slave ship *Phillis* in 1761. She was brought to Boston, Massachusetts, where she was judged to be about seven or eight years old, on account of her size and her missing front teeth. On July 11, 1761, the young child was bought by John and Susanna Wheatley, a white couple in search of a personal servant; they named her Phillis, after the ship that brought her to America.

Kind benefactors

Susanna Wheatley and her eldest daughter, Mary, taught the young Phillis to read (*see box*). The family soon noted that she seemed to have an aptitude for language. Susanna encouraged Phillis partly to test whether Africans could be

▲ *Phillis Wheatley in about 1773, the date in which her book was published in London, England.*

educated. At that time most whites believed in the intellectual, emotional, and cultural inferiority of the black race. Black people were not considered human beings and therefore were seen as having no past, no civilization, and no future. Such a denial of the humanity of Africans was one way in which whites justified their enslavement and brutalization.

When Wheatley was able to learn to write as well as read, she was given a pen, ink, and paper. As a young girl she read many of the Greek and Latin classics. She was a gifted student and by 1765 had composed a letter to Reverend Samson Occom, a Native American minister of the Mohegan group. In 1767 she penned her first published poem, "On Messrs. Hussey and Coffin." The poem, which described the near-destruction in a storm of the boat of Hussey and Coffin en route from Nantucket to Boston, was published in the *Newport Mercury* newspaper. Hussey and Coffin had been dinner guests of the Wheatleys, where they had recounted their harrowing tale; Phillis, tending table at the time, overheard the story.

KEY DATES

1753   Born in either Senegal, Gambia, or Sierra Leone at about this time.

1761   The *Phillis* docks in Boston, Massachusetts; John Wheatley buys the young girl for "a trifle"; his wife Susanna decides to call her Phillis, after the boat.

1767   Publishes her first poem, "On Messrs. Hussey and Coffin" in the *Newport Mercury.*

1773   Publishes *Poems on Various Subjects, Religious and Moral.*

1778   Marries John Peters.

1784   Dies in Boston in March.

1786   First American printing of Wheatley's book in Philadelphia, Pennsylvania.

1998   "Ocean," a 1773 ode to the sea that was not included in her published book of poetry, is sold for $68,500 at a Christie's auction.

INFLUENCES AND INSPIRATION

Phillis Wheatley owes her writing career to a group of women who provided her with an education and with support.

Taught to read by Susanna Wheatley, Phillis was also taught Latin and the Bible by Susanna's daughter Mary. Wheatley was able to read Latin well enough to familiarize herself with Ovid's *Metamorphoses.* Susanna Wheatley also encouraged Phillis to send her poems out for publication and promoted them in the local press. Susanna tried to get Wheatley's volume of poetry published, but many people did not believe that a black woman could have written such work and she was not able to interest a Boston publisher. Instead, Susanna's English friend Selina, the Countess of Huntington, arranged for *Poems on Various Subjects, Religious and Moral* to be published in London, England, in 1773.

Wheatley's closest friend was Obour Tanner, an African slave who is believed to have made the Middle Passage with Wheatley. Thought to have been older than Wheatley, Tanner provided emotional support to the author. Their letters show a very close, nurturing relationship. Without the support of these women Wheatley's work might not have been published.

Wheatley in turn influenced the slave Jupiter Hammon, who was the first published black writer in America. In 1778 he published an "Address to Miss Phillis Wheatly [sic], Ethiopian Poetess, in Boston, who came from Africa at eight years of age, and soon became acquainted with the gospel of Jesus Christ." Hammon acknowledged Wheatley as a sister, in race and in spirit, and encouraged her to continue to improve her writing and to remain grounded in her faith.

Writing

Wheatley's work falls into several poetic forms of which the most prominent is the elegy. An elegy is a poem written in sorrow or mourning for a dead person. Wheatley's most famous elegy, "On the Death of the Rev. Mr. George Whitefield," greatly increased her exposure to the public. Whitefield was a popular Methodist minister in the colonies as well as in England, where he was the personal chaplain to the Countess of Huntington. The countess, who often corresponded with the Wheatleys, later financed the publication of Wheatley's landmark book, *Poems on Various Subjects, Religious and Moral,* when American publishers rejected the work.

In anticipation of the hostile public response to the premise that an enslaved black woman could write a book of poetry, in 1722 John Wheatley assembled what he called a "group of the most respectable characters in Boston" to establish the authenticity of the verse as Wheatley's own. The 18 men were sufficiently satisfied with Wheatley's performance and signed a declaration to that effect. The statement accompanied Wheatley on her voyage to England, and was added as a preface to her poems by her London publisher. At about this time Wheatley was also given her freedom.

In London Wheatley was introduced to society. Although she was due to be presented at court, she had to return home following the news that Susanna Wheatley was ill. Susanna died in 1774.

Although *Poems on Various Subjects, Religious and Moral* contained more than 30 poems, Wheatley had written many more. In addition to the many elegies she wrote, she also penned the occasional narrative and epic poem of which "Goliath of Gath" is an excellent example. The best example of her historical narratives is "Affray in King Street, on the evening of the 5th of March," her account of the Boston Massacre.

Last years

In 1778 Wheatley married a free black man named John Peters, with whom she had three children. The marriage was not a happy one and Peters abandoned Wheatley after her fortunes began to fail.

Wheatley tried to publish two more books of poetry, *Proposals* and *Poems and Letters on Various Subjects,* but she was not successful. She died, along with her newborn child, in March 1784, in a shack in Boston, probably from an infection relating to childbirth.

See also: Hammon, Jupiter

Further reading: Shields, John C. (ed.). *The Collected Works of Phillis Wheatley.* New York, NY: Oxford University Press, Inc., 1988.
http://www.forerunner.com/forerunner/X0214_Phillis_Wheatley.html (Biography).

WHITAKER, Forest
Actor, Director

Forest Whitaker is a versatile and talented actor, equally at home playing jazz superstar Charlie Parker (*Bird*, 1988), an assassin (*Ghost Dog: The Way of the Samurai*, 1999), or Ugandan dictator Idi Amin (*The Last King of Scotland*, 2006). Whitaker has also established himself as a director with such films as *Waiting to Exhale* (1995), based on Terry McMillan's novel of the same name, *Hope Floats* (1998), starring Sandra Bullock, and *First Daughter* (2004).

Early life
Born in Longview, Texas, on July 15, 1961, Forest Steven Whitaker was one of three sons of insurance salesman Forest Whitaker and special needs teacher Laura Whitaker. When Whitaker was a baby his family moved to California, where he grew up. In school Whitaker excelled at sports, and he received a sports scholarship to attend Pomona College. In his first year he appeared in college stage productions and was signed up by an agent. His tenor voice led to a classical music scholarship at the University of Southern California. While there he decided to go into film, and after two years at USC he won a scholarship to the Drama Studio London, at Berkeley.

A versatile career
In 1982 Whitaker made his screen debut as a football player in *Fast Times at Ridgemont High*. He went on to work with many fine directors, cast in such movies as Oliver Stones's *Platoon*, Martin Scorsese's *Color of Money* (both 1986), and Barry Levinson's *Good Morning Vietnam* (1987). In 1988 Clint Eastwood cast Whitaker in *Bird*. In his first lead role Whitaker played jazz musician

▲ *Although Forest Whitaker is an established actor, he is also a respected director, specializing in films that deal with relationships and family.*

Charlie "Bird" Parker to critical acclaim, and was given the Best Actor Award at the Cannes Film Festival in France. The movie increased Whitaker's public profile and he went on to perform in many successful movies, including Neil Jordan's *Crying Game* (1992), Robert Altman's *Pret-a-Porter* (1995), and Wayne Wang's *Smoke* (1995). In addition Whitaker started to direct. His first big-budget feature was the HBO drama *Strapped* (1993), but his big-screen directorial debut came in 1995 with *Waiting to Exhale*, starring Angela Bassett. His later movies include *A Little Trip to Heaven* (2005) and *The Last King of Scotland* (2006).

See also: Bassett, Angela, McMillan, Terry; Parker, Charlie

Further reading: http://www.starpulse.com/Actors/ Whitaker,_Forest (Biography).

KEY DATES	
1961	Born in Longview, Texas, on July 15.
1982	Makes screen debut in *Fast Times at Ridgemont High.*
1988	Plays Charlie Parker in Clint Eastwood's *Bird;* wins the Best Actor Award at Cannes Film Festival.
1995	Directs *Waiting to Exhale.*
1999	Stars in Jim Jarmusch's *Ghost Dog: The Way of the Samurai.*
2005	Joins the hit TV show *The Shield.*

WHITAKER, Mark
Journalist, Editor

An influential U.S. journalist, Mark Whitaker was appointed as editor of the weekly news magazine *Newsweek* in 1998, making him the first African American to head a major U.S. news weekly. Since his appointment the magazine has won two prestigious National Magazine Awards for General Excellence—one for its coverage of the events of the terrorist attacks on Washington and New York on September 11, 2001, and the other for its coverage of the 2003 U.S.-led invasion of Iraq.

Early life
Born in Lower Merion, Pennsylvania, on September 9, 1957, Whitaker was the son of a white French professor, Jeanne Theis Whitaker, and Cleophus Sylvester "Syl" Whitaker. The relationship caused a stir as Syl was Jeanne's student; although the couple married, they divorced when Whitaker was eight.

Whitaker won a scholarship to Harvard, graduating in 1979. While still an undergraduate he worked as an intern in *Newsweek*'s San Francisco and Washington, D.C., bureaus. He joined the magazine staff full time in 1981, initially working in the international section. In 1987 he became business editor, overseeing the reporting of such events as the "Black Monday" crash on Wall Street.

During the 1990s Whitaker was rapidly promoted, serving as assistant managing editor (1991–1996) and managing editor from 1996. In 1998, after the death of *Newsweek* editor Maynard Parker, Whitaker took his place. Black Americans are poorly represented in journalism, and it was hoped that Whitaker's high-profile editorship would encourage young black people to enter the profession. However, Whitaker said that his aim was to be "the very best editor of *Newsweek*, not just the best black editor."

▲ *Mark Whitaker at the 2005 National Magazine Awards held in New York City.*

Achievements and controversy
At the time of Whitaker's appointment *Newsweek*, like other weekly news magazines, faced falling circulation figures, as people increasingly turned to the 24/7 news coverage available on television. Whitaker, however, believes that there is a market for quality, in-depth reporting. This was confirmed, when in the three weeks following 9/11, *Newsweek* put out five editions and its circulation temporarily increased as much as tenfold. In 2005, however, Whitaker attracted widespread criticism when *Newsweek* published, and later retracted, an uncorroborated story about the desecration of a copy of the Koran by U.S. soldiers serving at the Guantanamo Bay prison in Cuba.

Further reading: www.msnbc.com/modules/newsweek/info/nwinfo_whitaker.asp (Biography).

KEY DATES

1957 Born in Lower Merion, Pennsylvania, on September 9.

1977 Begins working for *Newsweek* as a reporting intern.

1979 Graduates from Harvard.

1998 Appointed editor of *Newsweek*.

2005 Publishes an unsubstantiated report about the desecration of the Koran by U.S. soldiers in Cuba.

WHITAKER, Pernell
Boxer

Pernell Whitaker quickly rose through the boxing ranks, winning the U.S. lightweight Golden Gloves title in 1982 and the Olympic gold medal in the same division in 1984. Nicknamed "Sweet Pea," after a journalist misheard a crowd calling him "Sweet Pete," he was the champion of the world for a decade in the welterweight and lightweight divisions (1987–1997).

Early life

Born in Norfolk, Virginia, in 1964, Whitaker grew up in the city's Young Park projects. He became a boxer at age nine, when he got into a fight with another boy in front of a neighborhood recreation center. The center's boxing coach spotted the boys fighting and told them to come inside and put gloves on. Afterward the coach made them get their parents' permission to continue boxing. Whitaker lost his first three fights and quit, but he returned to the sport at age 11. After winning his first 25 amateur fights, he never looked back. At age 18 he won the Golden Gloves title and at age 20 became an Olympic gold medalist.

A professional boxer

Three months after his Olympic triumph Whitaker made his professional debut, knocking out Ferrain Comeaux in the second round. Whitaker went on to win his next 14 fights to earn a shot at the World Boxing Council (WBC) lightweight crown against Jose Luis Ramirez, but Ramirez won a controversial decision on March 12, 1988. One judge told Whitaker afterward: "There is no doubt in my

▲ *In his prime Whitaker often outclassed his opponents with his close-range counterpunching.*

mind you won." Whitaker bounced back a year later, defeating Greg Haugen for the International Boxing Federation (IBF) lightweight title and adding the WBC crown in a rematch with Ramirez.

In 1992 Whitaker won the IBF light welterweight title from Rafael Pineda. In 1993 he won the WBC welterweight title from James McGirt. Later that year he retained the title in a match with Julio Cesar Chavez that most observers thought Whitaker had won but which resulted in a draw.

After several successful defenses of the welterweight title Whitaker lost it on April 12, 1997 to Oscar De La Hoya. Several more losses and a no decision (for testing positive for cocaine) followed. In 2001 he lost to the unheralded Carlos Bojorquez, who broke Whitaker's collarbone in the fourth round, forcing him to retire. Whitaker had won 40 of his 45 professional fights. Many fight pundits regard him as "pound for pound" the best fighter in the world during his era.

Further reading: http://www.boxrec.com/boxer_display.php? boxer_id=00555 (Detailed list of Whitaker's boxing record).

KEY DATES	
1964	Born in Norfolk, Virginia, on January 2.
1982	Wins the U.S. Golden Gloves lightweight title.
1984	Wins Olympic lightweight gold medal in Los Angeles; has his first pro fight on November 15.
1989	Wins IBF title; wins the WBC lightweight title in a rematch with Jose Luis Ramirez in his hometown of Norfolk.
1993	Wins the WBC welterweight title from James McGirt.
1997	Loses a decision and the WBC welterweight title to Oscar De La Hoya on April 12.
2001	Loses to Carlos Bojorquez in Stateline, Nevada, which ends his career.

WHITE, Barry
Musician

Known as the "Walrus of Love" and "Sultan of Soul," Barry White was the king of romance. With his larger-than-life physique and deep, sexy, velvet baritone voice, White had massive hits with such songs as "You're the First, My Last, My Everything," which also became his theme tune. Despite being unable to read or write music, White built up a successful and lucrative career, selling more than 100 million records. In the 1990s he became known to new audiences through his guest appearances on the TV show *Ally McBeal*.

The making of a star

Born in Galveston, Texas, on September 12, 1944, White was raised in South Central Los Angeles. He began singing in the local Baptist Church choir at a young age. Brought up by a single mother in a tough neighborhood, by age 16 White, already the father of two, was sent to jail for theft. He later said that music saved him. He heard Elvis Presley's "It's Now or Never" and decided that he wanted a career in music. Following his release he worked with several small record companies. He sang with the Upfronts, worked on the arrangement of Bob and Earl's 1963 song

▼ *Barry White in his recording studio at his home in Sherman Oaks, California, in 2003.*

KEY DATES	
1944	Born in Galveston, Texas, on September 12.
1970s	Forms Love Unlimited and the Love Unlimited Orchestra.
1973	Has first hit "I'm Going to Love You Just A Little Bit More, Baby."
1990s	Songs appear in the hit show *Ally McBeal*.
2003	Dies in Los Angeles, California, on July 4.

"The Harlem Shuffle," and released a song as Lee Barry in 1965. Deciding to write and produce rather than sing, White worked with singer Felice Taylor, who had a No. 11 hit on the British charts with "I Feel Love Comin'."

In 1969 White met Diane Taylor and sisters Linda and Glodean James (Glodean later became his wife). White groomed the trio as the group Love Unlimited and produced their million-selling single "Walkin' In The Rain With The One I Love" (1972). White's own recording career began again with the album *I've Got So Much to Give*, which spawned the single "I'm Going to Love You Just a Little Bit More, Baby," which went to No. 3 on the rhythm-and-blues charts.

In 1973 White formed the 40-piece Love Unlimited Orchestra, releasing the instrumental piece "Love's Theme," which some music critics claim launched disco. Between 1974 and 1979 White had numerous hits including the *Billboard* chart toppers "Can't Get Enough of Your Love, Babe" (No. 1) and "You're the First, My Last, My Everything" (No. 2), which helped the album *Can't Get Enough* reach the top of the charts. He released eight Barry White Albums, four Love Unlimited records, four Love Unlimited Orchestra albums, toured, and scored a movie soundtrack (*The Together Brothers*, 1974), before taking a break. In the 1990s White released a series of hit albums, including *The Icon is Love* (1994) and *Staying Power* (1999), which won two Grammys. He wrote an autobiography, *Love Unlimited*, before his death in 2003.

Further reading: White, Barry, with Marc Eliot. *Love Unlimited.* Louisville, KY: Broadway Books, 1999.
ttp://www.findarticles.com/p/articles/mi_m1355/is_4_104/ai_105619330 (Obituary).

WHITE, Bill
Baseball Player, Commentator

An outstanding first baseman, Bill White prided himself on not fitting into any mold. Through hard work and determination White made himself into a great hitter. After his professional baseball playing career ended, White became the first black major league broadcaster. In 1989 he became the highest ranking black executive in sports when he was named president of Major League Baseball's National League. Throughout his career White was also an outspoken advocate for black players in the major leagues.

In 13 major league seasons White batted .300 or greater four times, had seven seasons with 20 or more home runs, drove in 100 runs in a season four times, and won the World Series with the 1964 St. Louis Cardinals. In that same year White told *Sport* magazine: "I wasn't a great athlete, but I worked harder than anyone else."

Early life
Born in Lakeland, Florida, on January 28, 1934, William DeKova White was the son of a steelworker. His family instilled a strong work ethic in him at an early age. The Whites moved to Warren, Ohio, where White attended Harding High School, graduating second in his class with hopes of becoming a doctor.

White received an academic scholarship to attend Hiram College and enrolled as a premed major, but he began to play baseball as a diversion to his studies. A scout for the New York Giants spotted White playing and signed him for a $2,500 bonus. White later said he quit Hiram's premed program because he needed the money, but his success in baseball more than justified his decision.

A career in baseball
At age 19 White was sent to play for the Giants' minor league team in Danville, Virginia, becoming the Carolina League's only black player. At the time segregation laws in Southern states forced black players to stay in separate hotels and eat in separate restaurants. Despite having to deal with the racial abuse hurled at him from the stands, White put up impressive statistics in Danville, hitting .298 with 20 home runs and 80 runs batted in. From Danville White moved to the minor league team in Sioux City, Iowa, in the Western League. White soon impressed the Giants, and he was called up to the major leagues, where he immediately made an impact. In his major league debut

▲ *As a baseball player, commentator, and president of the National League, Bill White was not shy about speaking his mind: Hall of Famer Bob Gibson said that White was never one to let problems "slide by."*

with the Giants, White hit a home run in his first at-bat on May 7, 1956. He compiled an impressive rookie season, smashing 22 home runs and batting .256. His career was interrupted by a two-year stint in the Army, however. He returned to the Giants for the final few weeks of the 1958 season in San Francisco, where the franchise had moved earlier that year.

Cardinals
In 1959 White was traded to the St. Louis Cardinals. It was during his first stint with the team that White's career really skyrocketed. After taking the advice of Cardinals hitting coach Harry Walker (*see box*) to hit for average and try knocking the ball up the middle instead of out of the ballpark, White flourished. He hit for the cycle (single, double, triple, and a home run) in one game in 1960, and in 1961 he totaled 14 hits in two days while playing back-to-back doubleheaders; the feat tied with a record set by Ty Cobb in 1912. Fellow African American pitcher Bob Gibson nicknamed White "Robot" because of his careful, plodding style. White worked so hard that he had to scrawl on his glove, "RELAX."

INFLUENCES AND INSPIRATION

One of the most influential people in Bill White's career was Cardinals's hitting coach Harry Walker, a white Southerner whose brother Dixie had expressed doubts about being Jackie Robinson's teammate in the Brooklyn Dodgers in 1947. Although it seemed unlikely that White, a black northerner from Ohio, would have much time for a white Southerner who often called black people shiftless and lazy, White needed Walker's hitting instruction to improve and such stereotypical comments made White work even harder.

Walker advised White to hit for average with grounders into the holes in the infield, instead of trying to slug home runs. Following Walker's advice, White helped the Cardinals overcome a six-and-a-half game deficit with two weeks to play to beat the Phillies for the NL East division title in 1964. The Cardinals went on to win the World Series over the Yankees. White came to respect Walker's fairness, and the two later became fishing companions.

KEY DATES

1934   Born in Lakeland, Florida, on January 28.

1953   Signs for the New York Giants as an amateur free agent.

1956   Makes his major league debut on May 7.

1959   Signs for the Cardinals.

1964   Helps Cardinals win the World Series.

1989   Is named president of baseball's National League, the first black American to head a major sports league.

1994   Resigns as National League president.

In the early 1960s White gained a reputation for speaking out on racial issues. He was among a vocal minority of black players who protested the inequalities between black and white players at spring training sites in Florida and in minor league cities in the South.

White had his best season in 1964, hitting .303 with 21 home runs, and helping lead the Cardinals to the World Series title in seven games over the N.Y. Yankees. White was traded to the Philadelphia Phillies following the 1965 season. He drove in 103 runs in 1966, but injured his Achilles tendon playing handball the next offseason and missed a third of the 1967 season. In 1969 White returned to the Cardinals, appearing in just 49 games before retiring. He finished his playing career with a .286 batting average, 202 homers, 870 RBIs (runs batted in), and was a six-time All-Star and seven-time Gold Glove winner.

More than just a player

White became a baseball broadcaster following his retirement. He served as a Yankees broadcaster with booth partner Phil Rizzuto for 18 years from 1971 to 1989. When he first started in the broadcast booth, White continued to speak out against racial inequality. He highlighted such issues as the lack of black managers and executives in the game. He turned down an offer from Yankees' owner George Steinbrenner to become the team's general manager in 1975 as he thought the job would not last.

On February 3, 1989, the owner of the 12 teams named White the 13th president of the National League. It was the first time an African American had been appointed to head a major professional sports league. Although White had no prior administrative or business experience, he was very personable: As former teammate Jim Brosnana said, "Bill White was able to get along with anybody." White had the support of many of his peers in baseball. At the press conference to announce his appointment, White tried to downplay the racial significance of his new post. After being asked about it on several occasions, he commented that he would have been "foolish" to take on any job for "whatever historical significance there might have been" if he had not been able to do what the job required.

As NL president White fought against such things as the shift of the Chicago Cubs to the NL West and vehemently defended black rights. He came to feel that he lacked real influence, however, and resigned from the position in 1994. He retired to Bucks County, Pennsylvania, where most of his time is dedicated to fishing.

See also: Gibson, Bob; Robinson, Jackie

Further reading: Halberstam, David. *October 1964.* New York, NY: Villard, 1994.
http://www.baseballhalloffame.org/library/columns/rw_041117.htm (Baseball Hall of Fame essay)

WHITE, Charles Wilbert
Artist

Charles Wilbert White was an important 20th-century black artist. A painter, lithographer, and teacher, White often produced work influenced by his race. Fascinated by intellectual Alain Locke's 1925 book *The New Negro*, White tried to represent the dignity and pride of the New Negro in the United States. During his career he moved from producing monumental abstract compositions representing important historical events in African American life to intense studies of individuals.

Early life
Born in Chicago, Illinois, on April 2, 1918, White came from a poor family. His mother saw education as a way out of poverty and encouraged White's artistic pursuits. He was a talented violinist but from an early age had an obvious gift for drawing and painting.

A brilliant career
White began studying at the Arts and Crafts Guild for Negro Artists in 1932. He was turned down by two art schools on racial grounds but won a scholarship to the Art Institute of Chicago in 1936. There he was introduced to the work of

▼ *White dedicated the first part of his career to representing the African American experience.*

KEY DATES

1918	Born in Chicago, Illinois, on April 2.
1939	Creates first mural, *Five Great American Negro Heroes.*
1956	Moves back to California from Mexico.
1979	Dies in Los Angeles, California, on October 3.

Harlem Renaissance artists such as Charles Alston, Aaron Douglas, and Hale Woodruff, and to the Mexican muralists Diego Rivera, David Siqueiros, and José Clemente Orozco.

On graduating in 1938 White joined the Federal Art Project, part of the Works Progress Administration. A Julius Rosenwald Fellowship in 1942 allowed him to travel in the South and to study at the Art Students League, New York, where he met and married artist Elizabeth Catlett. During these few years he produced his most important large-scale murals, *Five Great American Negro Heroes* (1939), *History of the Negro Press* (1940) and *Contribution of the American Negro to American Democracy* (1943). White was drafted into the Army in 1944 but continued to draw and paint. While undertaking flood relief work in the Mississippi Valley he contracted severe tuberculosis, which led to him being hospitalized for two years.

In 1946 White accompanied Catlett to Mexico City, where he studied lithography at the Taller de Gráfica Popular. The couple separated and White moved to California with his new wife, the white political activist Frances Barrett, in 1956. His worsening health meant that he was physically unable to continue making large-scale works and in the 1950s he started to produce highly expressive figurative drawings. Elected a member of the National Academy of Design in 1975, White was professor and chairman of Otis Art Institute, Los Angeles, and a professor at Howard University. He died in 1979.

See also: Catlett, Elizabeth; Douglas, Aaron; Harlem Renaissance; Locke, Alain

Further reading: Barnwell, Andrea D. *Charles White*. San Francisco, CA: Pomegranate, 2002.
http://www.artlex.com/ArtLex/a/african_american_6.html (Biography).

WHITE, George Henry
Politician

George Henry White was a lawyer, politician, and activist. A member of the Republican Party, White was elected to Congress in 1896.

Early life
Born in Rosindale, North Carolina, on December 18, 1852, White was the son of Mary and Wiley F. White, and was of mixed black, Irish, and Native American heritage. He was not able to get much of an education when he was a child as he worked on the farms and in the forests near his home. From age 17 White set about educating himself, attending high school while working hard to save money to finance himself at college. He graduated from Howard University, Washington, D.C., in 1877 and returned to North Carolina, where he settled in New Bern. White taught school and studied law with Judge William J. Clark.

A political career
A member of the Republican Party, White decided to pursue public office. He was elected to the North Carolina House of Representatives in 1880, campaigning on issues such as the financing of black education. In 1885 White was elected to the state Senate; a year later he was named solicitor and prosecuting attorney for the second judicial district of North Carolina, a post he held for eight years.

In 1896 White was elected to the U.S. Congress despite a campaign by white supremacists to stop him from being elected. By 1898 he was the only African American in the House of Representatives. He fought fiercely against racial discrimination and introduced the first federal antilynching bill, although it was stalled by his political opponents. Like activist and journalist Ida B. Wells-Barnett,

▲ *George Henry White campaigned throughout his life for better civil rights for black people.*

White argued that the rape of white women was not the main reason for lynchings. In 1901, however, White left North Carolina after an amendment was introduced that disenfranchised most black voters. Realizing that he would not be elected to a third term, White delivered a famous speech called "Defense of the Negro Race," in which he refuted charges of African American inferiority. He said, "This is perhaps the Negroes' temporary farewell to the American Congress.... Phoenix-like he [the Negro] will rise up some day and come again." Oscar DePriest was the next black American to be elected to Congress, in 1928.

White went on to practice law in the District of Columbia and Philadelphia. He helped establish Whitesboro, a black community in New Jersey, and worked with Booker T. Washington and the NAACP. He died in 1918.

See also: DePriest, Oscar; Political Representation; Washington, Booker T.; Wells-Barnett, Ida B.

Further reading: http://www.infoplease.com/biography/us/congress/white-george-henry.html (Biography and bibliography).

KEY DATES	
1852	Born in Rosindale, North Carolina, on December 18.
1880	Wins a seat on the state House of Representatives.
1885	Elected to the state Senate.
1896	Elected to U.S. House of Representatives.
1900	Leaves North Carolina after passage of the state constitutional amendment disenfranchising most black voters.
1918	Dies in Philadelphia, Pennsylvania, on December 28.

WHITE, Reggie
Football Player, Preacher

Reggie White is one of the most-honored athletes ever to play defensive end in the National Football League. He was nicknamed the "Minister of Defense," a reference to both his football prowess and his evangelical Christian ordination.

Early life

Born to unmarried parents in Chattanooga, Tennessee, on December 19, 1961, White grew up in the projects. He had a very close relationship with his grandmother, who instilled in him a strong sense of religious faith, regularly taking him to the Alton Park Bible Church. When he was 12, White told his mother and grandmother that he was going to become a preacher. At age 17 he became an ordained minister, displaying an expert ability to hold an audience's attention.

The minister of defense

White was also an extremely talented athlete. He played football at the University of Tennessee, where he set school records for most sacks in a career, season, and game. After college he signed on with the Memphis Showboats of the United States Football League (USFL), where he played for two seasons, gaining 23.5 sacks, 192 tackles, and seven forced fumbles in 34 starts.

When the USFL folded, the NFL Philadelphia Eagles drafted White. He played with them for eight seasons, becoming their all-time sack leader. He also set a then-record season-best with 21 sacks in 1987.

In 1993 White went to the Green Bay Packers, where he played for six more seasons, helping them to two Super Bowls, including a victory in 1997. He was named the NFL Defensive Player of the Year in 1998. Later that year White announced his retirement following a bout of ill health. However, he made a short-lived comeback with the Carolina Panthers for the 2000 season. At the time of his retirement White was the NFL's all-time sacks leader with 198.

Preacher

Many commentators argue that White's influence went beyond sports. He was an outspoken critic of issues such the perceived lack of government action over the suspicious burning of 36 black churches in the South in 1995. He continued to preach during his retirement, setting

▲ *Reggie White, No. 92, in action playing for the Green Bay Packers against the Philadelphia Eagles on September 12, 1993.*

up charities and working with prisoners and drug addicts. In 2004 White died suddenly, at age 43. Both the Green Bay Packers and the Philadelphia Eagles retired White's No. 92 in 2005.

KEY DATES
1961　Born in Chattanooga, Tennessee, on December 19.
1996　Helps Green Bay Packers reach the Super Bowl; they won the following year.
1998　Is named the NFL's Defensive Player of the Year; announces his retirement.
2004　Dies in Huntersville, North Carolina, on December 26.

Further reading: White, Reggie. *Reggie White in the Trenches: The Autobiography.* Nashville, TN: Thomas Nelson Inc, 1996. http://espn.go.com/classic/obit/s/2004/1226/1953400.html (White's obituary and profile).

WHITE, Sol
Baseball Player, Team Manager, Writer

A remarkable figure in baseball's early history, Sol White was a black pioneer who captained and managed several top black teams during the era of segregated baseball in the late 1800s and early 1900s. While White was known as a hard-hitter, an outstanding all-around player, and a smart captain, some commentators consider his greatest contribution to the sport to be his book, *Sol White's History of Colored Base Ball,* the first recorded history of black baseball.

From integration to segregation

After the Civil War (1861–1865), under the protection of several constitutional amendments and the Civil Rights Act of 1866, newly freed blacks were given the opportunity to compete as equals in amateur baseball games and sometimes played with white players on the same teams. While several outstanding black baseball players did gain prominence during the integrated period of the 1870s and 1880s, White's athletic talent was not recognized until 1887, by which time Jim Crow laws were on the verge of reversing many of the gains African Americans had secured for themselves during Reconstruction.

Born in Bellaire, Ohio, on June 12, 1868, White excelled at sports. While attending Wilberforce University as a 19-year-old, White joined the Pittsburgh Keystones as a second baseman and started his career with a batting average of .308. The Keystones was one of eight teams that became charter (original) members of the League of Colored Baseball Clubs in 1887, but folded shortly after their incorporation. White then played for the Wheeling, West Virginia, Green Stockings, an integrated team, and batted .371 as a rookie third baseman, which helped to pull a team struggling to stay out of last place into fourth. At the end of the season color lines were drawn and White, despite his ability, was cut from the team.

From 1888 to 1895 White either played in organized white leagues as an alternate player or as a member of a black team representing a host city in an otherwise all-white league. He also played with two all-black teams, the Cuban Giants and the New York Gorhams. The Gorhams played in the Middle States League in 1889, and the Cuban Giants represented York, Pennsylvania, in the Eastern Interstate League in 1890, and Ansonia in the Connecticut State League in 1891. There was not a Cuban among the Cuban Giants, who took their name based on the racial realities of the day and the belief that white crowds would sooner pay to see Latinos play ball than they would blacks. During his first three seasons with the Cuban Giants and the New York Gorhams, White posted batting averages of .324, .356, and .375 respectively. In 1895 White played for Fort Wayne in the Western Tri-State League and hit .385.

▼ *Sol White fought hard against the color bar in sports, paving the way for men like Jackie Robinson.*

KEY DATES

1868	Born in Bellaire, Ohio, on June 12.
1887	Begins his career with the Pittsburgh Keystones.
1895	Plays for the last time on an integrated team from Fort Wayne, Indiana; later that year, bats .404 for the Page Fence Giants.
1902	Organizes and manages the Philadelphia Giants.
1904	Wins the Eastern Championship with the Philadelphia Giants.
1907	Publishes *Sol White's History of Colored Base Ball.*
1947	Jackie Robinson breaks color bar in baseball.
1955	Dies in New York in August.

<table>
<tr><td colspan="3" align="center">INFLUENCES AND INSPIRATION</td></tr>
</table>

Sol White briefly experienced the post-Reconstruction freedom to play integrated baseball, but his talent matured just as the color line was being drawn. Undaunted by the profound inequalities of segregation, White went on to captain top teams and dutifully recorded the achievements of black players in the hope that they would be assessed on the basis of their ability and not by the color of their skin. Two key black players who preceded White and were known to have inspired him were John A. Jackson, who played under the name Bud Fowler from 1872, and Moses Fleetwood Walker in 1884. Although Fowler and Walker were considered some of the best players of their time—Walker especially as he played in the major leagues—they were only grudgingly accepted by their teams. Both experienced racism, discrimination, and physical abuse, and were continually dropped by their teams. Despite these adversities, Fowler and Walker, and later White along with many other outstanding black American baseball players, paved the way for Jackie Robinson and the integration of baseball.

This would be the last time he would play baseball as a member of an integrated team. With the *Plessy v. Ferguson* (1896) Supreme Court decision, the era of segregation and of segregated baseball officially began.

Star player and team leader

During the 1890s and early 1900s White made significant contributions to black baseball, playing with many of the championship-winning teams of the era. In addition to playing for the Cuban Giants and the New York Gorhams, White played with the Big Gorhams, the Cuban X-Giants, the Columbia Giants, and the Philadelphia Giants. He also played with the Page Fence Giants, for whom he batted .404 in 1895.

Of all of these teams White was most closely identified with the Philadelphia Giants, the team he organized in 1902 with Walter Schlichter, a white sportscaster. White played shortstop for the Giants and also managed the team. In 1903 the team made the playoffs against the Cuban X-Giants for the eastern championship, but lost the Series, 5 games to 2, owing to the enormous talent of the Cubans' pitching star, Rube Foster. During the very next season White persuaded Foster to join the Giants and the subsequent playoff results were reversed as the Giants beat the Cubans to win their first championship. Under White's lead, the Giants won three more titles, thereby winning four consecutive eastern championships. Although White is said to have been a focused and intense player while on the field, he was a calm, forward-thinking manager who led his team to numerous victories.

In 1909 White left the Philadelphia Giants and signed with the Brooklyn Royal Giants. When the New York Lincoln Giants were organized in 1911, White became their manager for one season before retiring from baseball in 1912. White pursued other interests for the next several years, but returned to black baseball as the secretary of the Columbus Buckeyes when the Negro National League was established in 1920. After leaving the Buckeyes, White managed the Cleveland Browns in 1924. He then coached the Newark Stars in the Eastern Colored League in 1926 before retiring from baseball altogether. During his career White had been an active participant in the first three black leagues, beginning in 1887 with the League of Colored Baseball Clubs. After his retirement White wrote a column for the *Amsterdam News*.

Historic chronicler of black baseball

In 1907 White wrote *Sol White's History of Colored Base Ball*. The purpose of the book, of which it is said that only four original copies exist, was to record and celebrate the achievements of black baseball players so that their accomplishments would not disappear during the era of segregated baseball. The book covers key subjects such as the art of pitching, remarkable feats performed by black players, and the challenges of managing a team. Because black players had been prohibited from organized baseball and had to organize their own black leagues, White's documentation provides important historical data and social commentary that underscore the unfairness of segregation. He argued that no other sport had been hit as badly by segregation as baseball.

See also: Color Bar and Professional Sports; Foster, Andrew "Rube"; Robinson, Jackie

Further reading: White, Sol. *Sol White's History of Colored Base Ball, with Other Documents on the Early Black Game, 1886–1936.* Lincoln, NE: University of Nebraska, 1996.

WHITE, Walter F.
Civil Rights Activist

At the helm of the National Association for the Advancement of Colored People (NAACP) from the early 1930s to the mid-1950s, Walter Francis White steered the organization's staunch policy toward integration and its legalistic approach to civil rights. Although White was very light skinned and could easily have passed for white, he instead chose to dedicate his life to seeking to improve the lot of his fellow African Americans.

Early life
Born in Atlanta, Georgia, on July 1, 1893, White was the son of a postman and a former teacher. His mother stayed home to raise White and his six siblings. Both his parents were very light-skinned, but raised their children as part of Atlanta's black American community. White grew up recognizing the strong ties in the community, especially after the violence directed at black people during the 1906 Atlanta race riot. White attended a segregated public school, and then completed both his high school and college degree at Atlanta University.

NAACP and civil rights
While working at his first job, selling insurance for a black-owned company, White joined the NAACP and organized the first chapter in Atlanta in 1916. Two years later he became assistant secretary to James Weldon Johnson in the national NAACP. From 1918 to 1930 White made his name by undertaking dangerous undercover investigations of lynching, frequently traveling in the South and passing as a white man in order to learn details of racial crimes. He published two novels in 1924 and 1926: *The Fire in the Flint* and *Flight* gained him a Guggenheim Fellowship, which enabled him to write *Rope and Faggot: A Biography of Judge Lynch*, a book that

▲ **Walter F. White's blond, blue-eyed looks often made people doubt that he was African American.**

analyzed the role of lynching in the South as a means to control the black labor force.

In 1931 White became the executive secretary of the NAACP. Under his leadership the NAACP began court challenges of school segregation, restrictive voting, and housing laws. White also spent years pressuring Congress to pass a federal antilynching bill. Believing that white ignorance was a major obstacle to black advancement, White promoted black artists and writers whose work he hoped would change the white attitude toward African Americans. He lobbied Hollywood to present black people in more realistic roles, criticizing such actors as Hattie McDaniel for playing such roles as Mammy in *Gone with the Wind* (1939).

White was a delegate at the United Nations alongside Mary McLeod Bethune in 1945. Before his death from a heart attack in 1955 he worked with lawyer Charles Hamilton Houston on the *Brown v. Board of Education* case, which ended school segregation.

See also: Bethune, Mary McLeod; Houston, Charles Hamilton; Johnson, James Weldon; McDaniels, Hattie

Further reading: Janken, Kenneth Robert. *White: The Biography of Walter White, Mr. NAACP.* New York, NY: The New Press, 2003.
http://www.gwu.edu/~erpapers/abouteleanor/q-and-a/glossary/white-walter.htm (Biography).

KEY DATES	
1893	Born in Atlanta, Georgia, on July 1.
1924	Publishes the novel, *The Fire in the Flint*.
1931	Named executive secretary of the NAACP.
1948	Influences Harry S. Truman to appoint a presidential commission on civil rights.
1955	Dies in New York City on March 21.

WIDEMAN, John Edgar
Writer

The novelist John Edgar Wideman's early literary successes have been followed by difficult family circumstances that have deeply influenced his subsequent writing and career: Both his brother and son have been convicted of murder, for example. Wideman remarked in an interview with *Salon* magazine: "If something terrible happens, you've got to do something about it. Your choice is either to be crushed by it or to carry on. That's a choice all the time. At this point today, and in my work so far, I have tried to suggest that it is worth carrying on."

Early life
Born in Washington, D.C., on June 14, 1941, Wideman was brought up in a well-to-do but working-class family. He spent his first 10 years in the predominantly white neighborhood of Homewood in Pittsburgh, Pennsylvania, before moving to a largely African American area. From an early age he became used to moving between two very different worlds. Wideman attended Peabody High, where he excelled both academically and at sports.

After winning the Benjamin Franklin Scholarship, Wideman attended the University of Pennsylvania. He won a creative writing award and graduated Phi Beta Kappa from the college in 1963. As well as being a good student, Wideman was an extremely talented basketball player and became an All-Ivy League forward on the university's basketball team. Only the second African American to be awarded a Rhodes Scholarship, Wideman then spent the next three years studying at Oxford University in England.

Novelist
On his return to the United States in 1966, Wideman attended the creative writing workshop at the University of Iowa, publishing his first novel the following year. *A Glance Away* was critically acclaimed and two more novels, *Hurry Home* (1969) and *The Lynchers* (1973), followed. As well as writing, Wideman served as assistant basketball coach at the University of Pennsylvania between 1968 and 1972. In 1971 he became director of the African American studies program, a position he held until 1973.

Following Wideman's move to Wyoming in 1975, a six-year literary silence ensued. At the start of the 1980s he reemerged, publishing a trilogy that sealed his literary reputation. He won the 1984 PEN/Faulkner Award for the last part of the trilogy, *Sent For You Yesterday*.

▲ *John Edgar Wideman, photographed in September 1998, has drawn on personal tragedy in his writing.*

In 1976 Wideman's life changed abruptly when his brother was convicted of murder and sentenced to life imprisonment. He published a memoir, *Brothers and Keepers*, in 1984. In 1986 Wideman's son Jake was tried and convicted of the murder of a classmate. After his son's conviction Wideman moved back to the East Coast to teach at the University of Massachusetts at Amherst. Since then he has published a number of novels, short stories, and works of nonfiction. His 1990 novel *Philadelphia Fire* won the PEN/Faulkner Award, making Wideman the only novelist to win the award twice. Wideman has published a number of works since, including *God's Gym* (2005).

KEY DATES	
1941	Born in Washington, D.C., on June 14.
1963	Receives Rhodes Scholarship to study in England.
1967	Publishes his first novel, *A Glance Away*.
1984	Wins PEN/Faulkner Award.
1990	Wins the PEN/Faulkner Award for second time.

Further reading: Wideman, John Edgar. *Hoop Roots*. New York, NY: Houghton Mifflin, 2003.
http://aalbc.com/authors/johne.htm (Biography).

WIGINGTON, Clarence W.
Architect

During the early 20th century Clarence W. Wigington, or "Cap" Wigington as he was also known, became the first African American architect to be employed by a city authority. As municipal architect in the Minnesota capital, St. Paul, Wigington left a rich legacy of some 60 public buildings, from schools and fire stations to water towers and air terminals.

Early life
Clarence Wesley Wigington was born in Lawrence, Kansas, on April 21, 1883. When Wigington was a child his parents moved frequently and his education was often interrupted. However, he eventually graduated from a high school in Omaha, Nebraska, and went on to study briefly at the city's art school.

A love of architecture
In about 1902 Wigington became a junior draftsman at one of the city's most prestigious architectural practices and undertook six years of training. In 1908 he settled in Sheridan, Wyoming, where he had received his first

▼ *During the 1930s and 1940s Wigington built enormous ice castles for the St. Paul Winter Carnival.*

commission for building a potato-chip factory. Although he had won several competitions, Wigington at first found little success. Black architects were still rare and most found it hard to get commissions from anyone except black patrons. However, Wigington's luck changed when he moved to St. Paul in 1913. Two years after his arrival he was first in a civil-service entrance exam and was employed by the Office of the City Architect.

The functional and the fantastic
Over the following decades Wigington created some of the city's most notable landmarks, including the Highland Park Water Tower (1928) and the Harriet Island Pavilion (1941). However, perhaps his most original, although also his most transient, works were the exuberant "ice palaces" that he designed for the city's annual Winter Carnival. These massive and wonderful structures survive only in photographs and Wigington's architectural drawings.

Throughout his life Wigington played an active part in Minnesota's civic life. In 1919 he cofounded the Sterling Club, a social club for African American men that still flourishes today. During World War II (1939–1945) he was captain of a black battalion of the Minnesota Home Guard and gained the nickname "Cap." After he retired in 1949, Wigington and his buildings were largely forgotten, but toward the end of the 20th century his importance as one of the most successful early 20th-century black architects was reevaluated. In 1998 the Harriet Island Pavilion was renamed the Clarence W. Wigington Pavilion in his honor.

Further reading: Taylor, David Vassar, with Paul Clifford Larson. *Cap Wigington: An Architectural Legacy in Ice and Stone.* St. Paul, MN: Minnesota Historical Society Press, 2002. www.startribune.com/stories/389/52602.html (Newspaper article on Wigington's legacy).

WILDER, L. Douglas
Politician

The first elected black governor in the United States, L. Douglas Wilder served one term as governor of the state of Virginia (1990–1994). Wilder became the mayor of Richmond, Virginia, in 2004.

Born in Richmond on January 17, 1931, Lawrence Douglas Wilder was named for the poet Paul Laurence Dunbar and abolitionist Frederick Douglass. The penultimate child of Robert J. Wilder, Jr., and Beulah Richards, Wilder and his siblings were brought up in a poor but loving family in which discipline was important. He attended racially segregated schools, and earned money shining shoes and delivering newspapers.

After graduating from Virginia Union University with a chemistry degree, Wilder was drafted into the Army to serve in the Korean War (1950–1953). He won a Bronze Star for heroism during combat. When Wilder returned to Virginia after the war, he worked as a chemist in the state medical examiner's office. In 1959 he earned a law degree from Howard University, Washington, D.C. Soon afterward he established his own firm, Wilder, Gregory, and Associates, and became a successful trial lawyer in Richmond.

A career in politics

Wilder's life in public office began in 1969 after he won a special election for the Virginia state senate. He was the first black state senator in Virginia since Reconstruction and campaigned for fair housing, rights for government workers, and greater hiring of minorities in the private sector. Sixteen years later Wilder was elected to the post of Virginia lieutenant governor on a Democratic ticket. In 1990 Wilder narrowly defeated Republican Marshall Coleman by less than half a percent in the gubernatorial

▲ *In 2004 Wilder became the first directly elected mayor of Richmond in 60 years—the city council previously chose the mayor from its nine members.*

election. The close result prompted a recount but Wilder was sworn in as the first black governor on January 13, 1990.

During his time in office Wilder ushered in some of the steepest cuts in funds for higher education, but he also balanced the state budget. In 1991 he withdrew from the Democratic presidential candidate race after public arguments with other Democrats and members of the Black Caucus; he also withdrew from an independent run for the U.S. Senate in 1994. After his term as governor finished, Wilder taught and had a radio call-in show before being elected mayor of Richmond in 2004.

See also: Douglass, Frederick; Dunbar, Paul Laurence; Political Representation

Further reading: http://www.ci.richmond.va.us/citizen/city_gov/mayor/ (City of Richmond mayoral site).

KEY DATES

1931   Born in Richmond, Virginia, on January 17.

1959   Receives his law degree from Howard University, Washington D.C.

1969   Wins a special election for the Virginia state senate.

1990   Sworn in as Virginia's 66th governor on January 13.

2004   Becomes the first elected mayor of Richmond in 60 years on November 2.

WILKENS, Lenny
Basketball Player, Coach

Basketball legend Lenny Wilkens is one of only a few superstars to be inducted into the Naismith Memorial Basketball Hall of Fame as both a coach and player. On and off the court, Wilkens's calm and unselfish demeanor helped him win more games than any other coach in National Basketball Association (NBA) history.

Early life

Leonard Randolph Wilkens was born in Brooklyn, New York City, on October 28, 1937, to an African American father and an Irish mother. As a child the cards were stacked against him: He grew up in what was one of Brooklyn's toughest neighborhoods, and his father died when Wilkens was five years old. Wilkens made the best of things: He was an excellent student, and he worked tirelessly after school, earning money to help support his deeply religious mother.

Basketball

After graduating from Brooklyn's Boys High School, Wilkens attended Providence College on a basketball scholarship. In his first year his team went undefeated, a telling sign of what lay ahead for Wilkens's basketball career. At Providence he earned All-American team honors as a senior. After graduating with a degree in economics in 1960, Wilkens was drafted into the NBA by the St. Louis Hawks.

Over the next 15 years Wilkens played for the Hawks (1960–1968), Seattle SuperSonics (1968–1972), Cleveland Cavaliers (1972–1974), and the Portland Trail Blazers (1974–1975). A nine-time NBA All-Star, Wilkens was one of

▲ *Wilkens led his teams to nine 50-plus win seasons, two divisional championships, and two NBA world championships.*

the greatest point guards in the history of the league, with a career average of 16.5 points and 6.7 assists per game.

In 1969 Wilkens coached the SuperSonics in his first season as both player and head coach. In his first four seasons as a head coach, Wilkens was player-coach for the Sonics and then the Portland Trail Blazers. Wilkens coached six teams for 32 NBA seasons: Seattle (1969–1972, 1977–1985), Portland (1974–1976), Cleveland (1986–1993), Atlanta (1993–2000), Toronto (2000–2003), and New York (2003–2005). Over the course of his career, Wilkens coached 2,448 regular season games as head coach, more than any coach in history.

Some of the crowning moments of Wilkens's NBA career include winning two Olympic gold medals coaching the U.S. team (1992, 1996). In 1996 the NBA honored Wilkens as a unique sports legend, naming him one of the 50 greatest players and one of the 10 greatest coaches.

KEY DATES

1937 Born in Brooklyn, New York, on October 28.

1960 Graduates from Providence College; is drafted into the NBA by the St. Louis Hawks.

1969 Has first game as a player–coach on October 14, the opening game of the World Championship season.

1977 Becomes head coach in 1977–1978 season; Seattle wins NBA Championship the following year.

1996 Honored by the NBA as one of the 50 greatest players and one of the 10 greatest coaches in its history.

Further reading: Wilkens, Lenny, and Terry Pluto. *Unguarded : My Forty Years Surviving in the NBA.* New York, NY: Simon & Schuster, 2001.
http://www.nba.com/history/players/wilkens_summary.html (Biography).

WILKINS, Dominique
Basketball Player

Dominique Wilkins was one of the most prolific scorers in National Basketball Association (NBA) history. Named on seven All-NBA teams and nine consecutive All-Star squads, Wilkins is a two-time winner of the NBA Slam-Dunk Championship. His remarkable athleticism earned him the nickname "the Human Highlight Film." He is the older brother of NBA player Gerald Wilkins.

Jacques Dominique Wilkins was born in Paris, France, on January 12, 1960, where his father was stationed while serving with the Air Force. Wilkins moved to the United States, where he attended high school in Washington, North Carolina. He went to college in Georgia, where he excelled at basketball.

A career of highlights

In 1982, at age 22, Wilkins was drafted by the Utah Jazz; he was traded to the Atlanta Hawks later that year, beginning what was to be a 12-year stint with the team. Wilkins was instrumental in turning the Hawks from hardened losers into a winning team in the mid-1980s. His flamboyant, slam-dunk playing style made him an instant hit with crowds, and he quickly challenged Michael Jordan's status as the NBA's greatest scorer. However, the team still seemed to fail during the play-offs, which prompted some critics to accuse Wilkins of aiming for individual accomplishments at the expense of team goals. This and a career-threatening injury were blamed for keeping him off the "Dream Team" at the 1992 Olympics.

During the 1992–1993 season Wilkins made an impressive comeback, once again proving to be one of the league's premier defensive players. During the season he

▲ **Wilkins (No. 21, left) in action with Celtics' Xavier McDaniel (No. 31, right) on December 20, 1993.**

became the 17th player in NBA history to rack up 20,000 career points. Despite still being at the top of his game, he was traded by the Hawks to the Los Angeles Clippers during the 1993–1994 campaign. The following season he signed to the Boston Celtics, and the next to Panathinaikos Athens of the Greek League. For the 1996–1997 season he returned to the NBA with the San Antonio Spurs, before again going overseas to Italy. During the 1998–1999 campaign he returned to play his last season in the NBA alongside his brother Gerald with the Orlando Magic. In 2001 Wilkins had his NBA jersey retired. He was named vice president of the Hawks franchise in 2004.

Further reading: Bjarkman, Peter C. *Sports Great Dominique Wilkins.* Berkeley Heights, NJ: Sports Great Books, 1996. http://www.nba.com/history/players/wilkins_summary.html (Biography).

KEY DATES	
1960	Born in Paris, France, on January 12.
1982	Drafted by Utah Jazz; traded to the Atlanta Hawks.
1992	Stages a remarkable comeback after a career-threatening injury.
1994	Traded to L.A. Clippers; signs with Boston Celtics.
1996	Signs with San Antonio Spurs.
1999	Signs to Orlando Magic.
2001	Has his NBA jersey retired.

WILKINS, J. Ernest
Mathematician, Physicist, Engineer, Educator

One of the United States's most brilliant scientists and mathematicians, J. Ernest Wilkins, Jr., helped pioneer developments in the field of nuclear technology during and following World War II (1939–1945). In later decades Wilkins concentrated on his work as a teacher at the university level. In 1990 he became Distinguished Professor of Applied Mathematics and Mathematical Physics at Clark Atlanta University, Atlanta, Georgia.

Early life
Jesse Ernest Wilkins was born in Chicago, Illinois, on November 27, 1923. His father, J. Ernest Wilkins, (*see box on p. 86*), was a successful Chicago attorney, while his mother, Lucile Beatrice Robinson, was a public school teacher. Wilkins showed a gift for mathematics from an early age: He could do basic math at age three, and by age seven was solving complex mathematical puzzles set for him by his father. An intelligent child, Wilkins was able to advance rapidly through school, helped by his parents and his teachers.

A fantastic intellect
In 1936, at age 13, Wilkins graduated from Parker High School and enrolled to study mathematics at the University of Chicago, the youngest student ever to be admitted there. He was awarded his BA degree at age 16, his MA at 17, and a doctoral degree just a few days after his 19th birthday in 1942. Wilkins's precocious achievements were celebrated in the national press and won him a scholarship to the prestigious Institute for Advanced Study at Princeton University, New Jersey, where the celebrated physicist Albert Einstein (1879–1955) was a member of the faculty.

Making history
In 1943 Wilkins embarked on a career in teaching at the historically black Tuskegee Institute, Alabama, set up by Booker T. Washington. He left in 1944 after just one year to work as an associate physicist on the Manhattan Project at the University of Chicago.

As part of its military efforts during World War II (1939–1945) the U.S. government had set up the secret Manhattan Project to research and develop the world's first atomic weapons. There were laboratories working on the project across the country, but the University of Chicago laboratory focused on the production of plutonium 239, which was used in the weapons. Although some of the scientists who worked on the project later denounced it, in August 1945 the U.S. military dropped an atomic bomb on Hiroshima, Japan.

During his time on the project Wilkins worked under Eugene Wigner, who directed the Theoretical Physics Group, providing the design of the Hanford, Washington, nuclear reactor. Wilkins made several significant contributions to the development of nuclear-reactor physics.

Between industry and academia
In 1946, rather than returning to academia, Wilkins began to work in private industry, initially as a staff mathematician at the American Optical Company in Buffalo, New York. In 1950 he returned to the field of nuclear physics, working for the United Nuclear Corporation in White Plains, New York. After the war many small companies began to research peacetime uses for nuclear technology, including the development of nuclear power plants and nuclear-propelled boats and submarines.

The United Nuclear Corporation was one of the most successful of the new companies, and Wilkins remained with the company until 1960, eventually becoming its manager of research and development. Wilkins realized

KEY DATES	
1923	Born in Chicago, Illinois, on November 27.
1940	Receives BA degree in mathematics.
1942	Receives a PhD in mathematics.
1944	Works for two years on the secret Manhattan Project to produce the first atomic bomb.
1960	Awarded master's degree in mechanical engineering.
1977	Joins the Idaho National Engineering Laboratory to develop low-cost nuclear-power plants.
1990	Appointed Distinguished Professor of Applied Mathematics and Mathematical Physics at Clark Atlanta University.
2003	Retires from Clark Atlanta.

that in order to develop new technologies for his company, he needed to gain practical knowledge of engineering. In the mid-1950s he enrolled at New York University, graduating with a BS degree in mechanical engineering in 1957. He went on to complete a master's degree in the subject in 1960.

Later that year Wilkins left the United Nuclear Corporation to work for one of its rivals, the General Atomic Company in San Diego, California. Over the next 10 years he served in various senior positions, rising from assistant chair of the theoretical physics department and assistant director of defense sciences and engineering to director of computational research.

Wilkins returned to academia in 1970. As distinguished professor of applied mathematical physics at Howard University in Washington, D.C., he set up the United States's first doctoral program in mathematics in a historically black university. Wilkins's growing international reputation also led him to be selected as national president of the American Nuclear Association (1974–1975).

Wilkins took a year's sabbatical to work at the Argonne National Laboratory in Argonne, Illinois, where he provided mathematical consultation for reactor physics and engineering. Before he could return to Howard, he was offered another lucrative post in industry.

Returning to business

In 1977 Wilkins once again returned to industry, working at E. G. & G. Idaho, Inc., the prime operating contractor of the Idaho National Engineering Laboratory in Idaho Falls, Idaho. As deputy general manager for science and engineering and vice president, he drew on his experience as both an engineer and nuclear scientist. He was able to help develop and design nuclear power plants for the Department of Energy. In 1984 he retired from Idaho and married Maxine G. Malone. He returned to work at the Argonne National Laboratory as a distinguished Argonne Fellow, but retired in 1985. He acted as a consultant to various organizations and businesses, and conducted his own research. In 1990, however, he returned to teaching, when he was appointed Distinguished Professor of Mathematics and Mathematical Physics at Clark Atlanta University. Part of his decision was formed by his wish to work with the celebrated mathematician Albert Turner Bharucha-Reid, but he died before Wilkins arrived.

Awards and honors

Wilkins's contributions to science, mathematics, and technology have been widely honored. In 1976 he was elected to the National Academy of Engineering—only the second African American to achieve the honor—and in 1980 he received an Outstanding Civilian Service Medal from the Army. He is a fellow of the American Nuclear Society and an honorary life member of the National Association of Mathematicians.

Further reading: Kessler, James, et al. *Distinguished African American Scientists of the 20th Century*. Phoenix, AZ: Oryx Press, 1996.
www.math.buffalo.edu/mad/PEEPS/wilkns_jearnest.html (Biography.)
http://www.maa.org/summa/archive/WilkinsJ.htm (Mathematical Association of America biography).

WILKINS, Roy
Civil Rights Activist

Roy Wilkins maintained a close association with the National Association for the Advancement of Colored People (NAACP) for more than 40 years, serving for 22 of those years as the association's executive director. He led the NAACP through some of the most important and volatile struggles facing blacks in the country's history and helped organize key events in the civil rights movement.

Early life
Born in St. Louis, Missouri, on August 30, 1901, Roy Ottoway Wilkins was raised by his aunt and uncle in St. Paul, Minnesota, in a low-income, integrated community. He worked his way through college at the University of Minnesota, taking a variety of jobs ranging from stockyard worker to editor. He also joined the local chapter of the NAACP. After graduating with a degree in sociology in 1923, Wilkins took a job with the *Kansas City Call*, a major black weekly newspaper, first as a reporter and columnist then as managing editor. He worked there until 1931, when he was named assistant executive secretary of the national

▼ *Roy Wilkins is often referred to as the "senior statesman" of the civil rights movement.*

NAACP under director Walter F. White. He remained in that role until 1934, when he replaced W. E. B. DuBois as the editor of the NAACP's official magazine, *Crisis,* on DuBois's retirement. He remained editor until 1949.

A man of the people
During World War II (1939–1945) Wilkins served as consultant to the War Department on matters relating to black employment. He also joined DuBois and White in 1945 as consultant to the American delegation at the founding conference of the United Nations.

In 1955 Wilkins was named the NAACP's executive secretary, a title that changed to "executive director" in 1965. Staunchly antimilitant, Wilkins promoted a nonviolent role for the NAACP as he led the organization through the crucial civil rights years. Wilkins was one of the organizers of the historic 1963 March on Washington, and he participated in the 1965 Selma to Montgomery march. Wilkins and the NAACP were instrumental supporters of the Civil Rights Acts of 1957, 1960, 1964, and 1965. His commitment to peaceful protest and strict opposition to separatism brought him into conflict with many black militant activist groups, however.

Wilkins received the Presidential Medal of Freedom in 1967. In 1977, at age 76, he retired from the NAACP, succeeded by Benjamin Hooks. He died in 1981.

KEY DATES	
1901	Born in St. Louis, Missouri, on August 30.
1934 in 1949.	Begins editing NAACP magazine *Crisis*; retired
1955	Named executive secretary of the NAACP, until 1977.
1963	Helps organize the historic March on Washington.
1967	Receives Presidential Medal of Freedom.
1981	Dies in New York City on September 8.

See also: DuBois, W. E. B.; Hooks, Benjamin; White, Walter

Further reading: Wilkins, Roy. *Standing Fast: The Autobiography of Roy Wilkins.* New York, NY: Viking Press, 1982.

WILLIAMS, Bert
Entertainer

Comedian Bert Williams was a vaudeville star, who became renowned for his act with fellow entertainer George Walker (1873–1911). Popular with audiences, Williams was also respected by fellow entertainers. The actor and comedian W. C. Fields once called Bert Williams "the funniest man I ever saw, and the saddest."

Early life

Born in Nassau, the Bahamas, on November 12, 1874, Egbert Austin Williams was the son of Frederick Williams, Jr., and Julia Monceur. From an early age Williams showed a talent for comedy and mimicry; he was also a gifted musician. When Williams was a child his family moved to New York, settling in California in 1886. Owing to his father's poor health, Williams gave up his idea of studying engineering and took to playing in minstrel shows to earn money for the family. Minstrel shows began in the 1830s, when white performers blackened their faces with burnt cork or greasepaint to perform African American songs and dances. After the Civil War (1861–1865) blacks were also allowed to join minstrel shows.

Walker and Williams

In 1893 Williams met Walker while both men were performing as part of Martin and Selig's Minstrels in San Francisco. The two men joined forces and began to perform together. Competing with white blackface performers, they subtitled their act "the Two Real Coons." Williams, who was light-skinned, used blackface makeup and developed the persona of "Mr. Nobody," a slow, illiterate black, while Walker played a fast-talking hustler.

▲ *Entertainer Bert Williams in a publicity still for the Ziegfeld Follies of 1910.*

In 1896 the duo went to New York City, where they became extremely successful. Two years later composer Will Marion Cook and poet Paul Laurence Dunbar collaborated to create the *Senegambian Carnival* for the two men. Signed to the Victor label, the pair also began to record songs from their shows from 1901. In 1903 they appeared in the all-black Broadway show, *In Dahomey*. Other shows included *Abyssinia* (1906) and the *Bandanna Land* (1907). After Walker was diagnosed with syphilis he retired in 1909.

From 1910 to 1920 Williams played in the Ziegfeld Follies. The only black cast member of *Under the Bamboo Tree* (1921), he collapsed on tour and died a month later.

See also: Black Identity and Popular Culture; Dunbar, Paul Laurence

Further reading: http://www.pbs.org/wnet/broadway/stars/williams_b.html (Biography).

KEY DATES

1874	Born in Nassau, the Bahamas, on November 12.
1886	Moves to California with his family.
1893	Meets George Walker in San Francisco, California.
1898	Composer Will Marion Cook and poet Paul Laurence Dunbar create *Senegambian Carnival* for Williams and Walker.
1910	Joins the Ziegfeld *Follies*.
1921	Appears in *Under the Bamboo Tree*.
1922	Died in New York City on March 4.

WILLIAMS, Cathay
Soldier

Cathay Williams was the first female Buffalo Soldier (the nickname given to the first all-black regiments). She enlisted in the Army after the end of the Civil War (1861–1865) and served in the U.S. Regulars as William Cathey. She is immortalized in poetry: "Cathay Williams became William Cathay/And no one was to know/The secret of her identity/As a soldier she did grow."

Early life

She was born into slavery in Independence, Missouri, in about 1844, but very little else is known about Williams's early life. Her mother was a slave belonging to a wealthy farmer, William Johnson, and her father was a freeman. As a child Williams moved with her mother and their master to Jefferson City, Missouri, where Williams worked as a house slave until the outbreak of the Civil War in 1861.

Civil War

When war broke out Williams was about 17 years old. She was taken by Colonel Benton of the 13th Army Corps to Little Rock, Arkansas, where she was told to cook for the soldiers. Cathay traveled with the corps through Arkansas, Louisiana, Virginia, and Iowa. She witnessed several battles and the burning of cotton fields. After the end of the war in 1865, Williams was able to travel back to Missouri to her family.

Enlisting in the Army

Women were not allowed to enlist in the Army, but on November 15, 1866, Williams, disguised as a man, managed to join the 38th U.S. Infantry. The 38th was a newly formed designated, segregated black American regiment led by white officers, housed in Jefferson Barracks, Missouri.

Described as 5 feet 9 inches (1.79m) tall, with black hair, black eyes, and black face, Williams gave her name as William Cathay, which was written down as "Cathey," and her profession as cook. Either any medical examination must have been cursory or the medical examiner, for whatever reason, chose to ignore the fact that Williams was a woman. Although Williams was not the first woman to disguise herself as a man and serve in the Army, she was the first to have been documented as doing so. Her motivation may have been financial. Williams's job prospects as an illiterate black woman would have been slim, but as a black man in the Army, she would earn much more money.

According to records "William Cathey" spent much of his service in ill health. By April 1867 Company A of the regiment to which Williams belonged was situated in Fort Riley, Kansas. Williams became ill shortly after arriving in Kansas and did not return to her post until May 14. It is unlikely that she was faking: Sick soldiers had their pay docked at $10 per month. By October the unit had marched to Fort Cummings, New Mexico, where it remained until June 1868. By January Williams was ill again. She was finally diagnosed with neuralgia, a name then given to any acute pain thought to do with the nervous system. No one is believed to have found out that William Cathey was a woman. She was discharged on October 14, 1868, along with two other privates, on the grounds of disability. In 1869 the 38th U.S. Infantry was consolidated, along with the 39th, 40th, and 41st to form the African American 24th and 25th Infantries.

Life as a civilian

Williams went on to work as a cook in Fort Union, New Mexico Territory. She then moved to Pueblo, Colorado, where she worked in a laundry, before moving to Las Animas, Colorado, where she stayed for a year. She told her story to a journalist in 1875. By 1889 she was living in Trinidad, Colorado. She died sometime before 1900.

KEY DATES	
1844	Born in Independence, Missouri, at about this time.
1861	Taken by Colonel Benton to work as a cook and laundress, most probably for the Eighth Indiana Regiment.
1866	Enlists as William Cathey; becomes first female Buffalo Soldier.
1900	Believed to have died before this date.

Further reading: Tucker, Philip Thomas. *Cathay Williams: From Slave to Female Buffalo Soldier.* Mechanicsburg, PA: Stackpole Books, 2002.
http://www.gallerychuma.com/female_buffalo_soldier.htm (Biography and Williams's account of her life).

WILLIAMS, Chancellor
Intellectual, Scholar

Chancellor Williams was a black American historian, intellectual, and writer. He documented African history and civilization and received great acclaim for his 1971 book, *The Destruction of Black Civilization—Great Issues of a Race from 4500 B.C. to 2000 A.D.*

Early life
Born in Bennettsville, South Carolina, on November 22, 1898, Chancellor James Williams was the youngest child of a former slave and a cook. He became curious about race and how black people fitted into society while at school. Williams went on to gain a BA and an MA in history from Howard University, Washington, D.C. An excellent student, he was a visiting research scholar at the University of Oxford and the University of London, both in England.

An African focus
Williams began writing in the 1940s, publishing *The Raven* in 1943. He was particularly interested in black issues, particularly black history. In 1956 he traveled to University

▼ *In addition to his acclaimed scholarly works, Chancellor Williams wrote several novels.*

College, Ghana, to conduct field research, examining African civilizations before colonization. He published many articles on the subject and was a meticulous researcher, conducting a study in 1964 that involved analyzing more than 26 countries and 100 languages.

Black civilization
In 1971 Williams received critical acclaim for his work *The Destruction of Black Civilization: Great Issues of a Race from 4500 BC to 2000 A.D.* The 21st Century Foundation awarded Williams its first Clarence L. Holte International Biennial Prize. The book established his position as a leading black scholar and became central to Afrocentric thought. John Henrik Clarke claimed that Williams's book was "a foundation and new approach to the history of our race."

Williams always advocated independent research by black scholars into black studies. He said: "As long as we rely on white historians to write black history for us, we should keep silent about what they produce."

Williams was also a novelist and editor of a newsletter, the *New Challenge*. The father of 14 children, Williams suffered ill health and was blind before his death in 1992.

See also: Clarke, John Henrik

Further reading: Williams, Chancellor. *The Destruction of Black Civilization: Great Issues of a Race from 4500 BC to 2000 A.D.* Chicago, IL: Third World Press, 1987.
http://www.aaregistry.com/african_american_history/1813/A_supporter_of_the_Motherland__Dr_Chancellor_Williams (Biography).

WILLIAMS, Cootie
Musician, Bandleader

Cootie Williams was a trumpeter with several important jazz bands, most famously the Duke Ellington Orchestra. He developed a distinctive style of swing trumpet with a wide range of tones and expressions that fostered later more experimental forms of jazz.

Early life

Born in Mobile, Alabama, on July 10, 1911, Charles Melvin Williams could already play the drums, trombone, and tuba while still at school, and toured as a drummer with saxophonist Lester Young's family band before teaching himself how to play the trumpet. He toured in the South, ending up in New York City in 1928. There he made his first recording and played in bands, including the Fletcher Henderson Orchestra. His playing brought him to the attention of Duke Ellington, who in 1929 invited Williams to join his orchestra to replace Bubber Miley.

A brilliant musician

Williams refined Miley's style, using a variety of mutes and plungers to extend the tonal range of the trumpet. He caused such an impact that Ellington wrote two compositions to showcase his playing, "Echoes of Harlem" (1936) and "Concerto for Cootie" (1940). During this time Williams also made several recordings as a backing musician for Billie Holiday. Williams left the Duke Ellington Orchestra in 1940, playing briefly with the Benny Goodman Orchestra before forming his own band, Cootie Williams and his Rug Cutters, which included Charlie Parker, Thelonious Monk, and Bud Powell, then developing the bebop style of jazz. Williams contributed some material to Monk's "Round Midnight," but his contribution was not included in the standard version.

In the late 1940s and 1950s swing declined in popularity. Williams reduced his band in size and

▲ *Cootie Williams plays with the Duke Ellington Orchestra in Paris, France, in February 1963.*

eventually turned to rhythm and blues rather than swing. He re-formed his band in 1955 for a residency at the Savoy Ballroom, and made several new recordings, including *The Big Challenge* (1957) and *Cootie in Hi-Fi* (1958). After a brief stay with Benny Goodman in 1962, he returned to the Duke Ellington Orchestra. After Ellington's death Williams played with the Mercer Ellington band in the 1970s. He died in New York City in 1985.

See also: Ellington, Duke; Holiday, Billie; Monk, Thelonious; Parker, Charlie; Young, Lester

Further reading: Dance, Stanley. *The World of Duke Ellington.* New York, NY: Da Capo Press, 1981.
http://www.aaregistry.com/african_american_history/1021/An_innovator_on_Trumpet_Cootie_Williams (Biography).

KEY DATES	
1911	Born in Mobile, Alabama, on July 10.
1929	Joins the Duke Ellington Orchestra
1940	Forms his own band, Cootie Williams and his Rug Cutters.
1985	Dies in New York City on September 15.

WILLIAMS, Daniel Hale
Surgeon

A distinguished surgeon and influential medical teacher, Daniel Hale Williams, or "Dr. Dan" as he was known to patients and friends, dedicated his life to improving health care and increasing medical professional opportunities for African Americans. Williams founded Provident Hospital in Chicago, Illinois, the first black-owned hospital in the United States. It provided training for black medical interns and nurses as well as first-class medical care for African Americans in Chicago. Williams is also credited with having performed the first successful open-heart surgery (*see box*).

Early life

Williams was born in Hollidaysburg, Pennsylvania, on January 18, 1856, into a large free family. One of eight children of barber Daniel Williams and Sarah Price, Williams and his siblings were of mixed black, Native American, and European heritage. Williams was a fair-skinned, red-haired boy, who was often mistaken for being white.

When Williams was 11 his father died. He was sent to Baltimore, Maryland, to become an apprentice shoemaker. Williams disliked the trade, and after three years moved with his sister Sally to Janesville, Wisconsin, where he learned to be a barber, working at Harry Anderson's Tonsorial Parlor and Bathing Rooms. Anderson took the Williamses into his home, treating them as part of his family. He helped Williams financially while the young man attended high school. Williams graduated from Hare's Classical Academy in 1877.

A medical profession

While in Janesville Williams met white surgeon Henry Palmer (1827–1895). Known as the "fighting surgeon" for his work during the Civil War (1861–1865) as regimental surgeon with the 7th Wisconsin Infantry Palmer agreed to take Williams on as a medical apprentice. In 1880 Williams passed the entrance exams to the illustrious Chicago Medical School (now Northwestern University Medical School). He was an exemplary student, paying for his tuition by playing music for tourists on boat excursions on Lake Michigan.

After graduating in 1883, Williams began to practice as a physician and surgeon, working briefly in Washington, D.C., before settling on Chicago's South Side, where he was one of only four African American physicians in the whole of the Chicago area. Williams worked as a surgeon at the South Side Dispensary (1884–1892) and the Protestant Orphan Asylum (1884–1893).

Creating adequate medical care

Williams was appalled by the poor medical care available to Chicago's black inhabitants, who were barred from admission to the city's white hospitals and often had to undergo surgery at home. He was aware of the lack of training on offer to young African American physicians and nurses, who were unable to attend Chicago's segregated teaching hospitals. In 1890 the Reverend Louis Reynolds, pastor of St. Stephen's African Methodist Episcopal (AME) Church, asked Williams for professional advice regarding his sister Emma, who had been turned down by several nursing schools on the grounds of her race. Infuriated by this prejudice Williams decided to establish an interracial hospital with a nursing school for black women. Williams's plan received support from several black and white philanthropists, including Chicago-based publisher and restaurant-owner Herman H. Kohlsaat (1853–1924). Williams was able to buy a three-story building at Dearborn and Twenty-Ninth Street, which was renovated into a hospital. The Provident Hospital and Training School Association was incorporated in January 1891: It officially opened four months later, staffed by some white and black doctors from Williams's old school. Emma Reynolds was one of the eight students in Provident's first nursing class.

The hospital opened with just 12 beds and quickly became oversubscribed. However, with the help of more

KEY DATES	
1856	Born in Hollidaysburg, Pennsylvania, on January 18.
1883	Receives MD from Chicago Medical College.
1884	Becomes surgeon at Chicago's South Side Dispensary (until 1892) and the Protestant Orphan Asylum (until 1893).
1891	Founds Provident Hospital and Training School in Chicago, Illinois; it opens on May 4.
1893	Performs successful open-heart surgery on James Cornish, a stabbing victim, on July 10.
1895	Helps found the National Medical Association.
1931	Dies in Idlewild, Michigan, on August 4.

INFLUENCES AND INSPIRATION

Williams inspired many black and white doctors and nurses, both as a teacher and as a physician and surgeon. He is believed to be the first surgeon to perform open-heart surgery.

In July 9, 1893, a young African American named James Cornish was stabbed in the chest during a bar brawl. He was taken to the Provident Hospital but had lost a great deal of blood by the time Williams attended to him.

Williams searched through various journals and books to find information about performing surgery on the area, but he could not find anything relevant. Williams knew that he had to cut open the man's chest and operate on him internally to give Cornish any chance of survival. Surgeons tended to steer away from this kind of operation because of the risk of infection, but Williams decided to go ahead.

He cut open Cornish's chest and was able to find and suture the damage made to the pericardium, the sac surrounding the heart. He was careful to apply antiseptic procedures before closing Cornish's chest. The operation was a success and the wound remained free of infection. In only two months Cornish made a complete recovery, living 20 more years.

charitable donations from wealthy city philanthropists, Williams was able to add an additional 65 beds through the construction of a new building at Dearborn and Thirty Sixth streets. Abolitionist and activist Frederick Douglass, Williams's friend, donated the proceeds from his lecture at the World's Columbian Exposition, held in Chicago in 1893, to the hospital. The Provident prospered to become the country's leading black-controlled hospital.

Saving lives

In 1893 Williams achieved national fame when he successfully saved the life of a stabbing victim by sewing up a tear in the tissue around his heart. He was the first man to perform open heart surgery and also the first to open a chest successfully without having the patient die of infection (*see box*).

Making a difference

In 1893 Williams's friend, Judge Walter Q. Gresham (1832–1895), who was secretary of state to President Grover Cleveland (1885–1889, 1893–1897), also asked Williams to apply for the position of surgeon in chief at Freedmen's Hospital, the federally funded hospital for black patients in Washington, D.C. Although Williams initially refused, he accepted the post in the following year. Under Williams the Freedmen was revolutionized: It became an interracial hospital, opened a nursing school, and established a board of experts from which staff could seek advice.

In 1895 Williams was also instrumental in founding the National Medical Association (NMA), a national organization for black physicians. It was a significant step because the American Medical Association did not accept African Americans. The NMA was important in the provision of education for black medical staff. Williams became its vice president in the same year.

In 1898 Williams married and returned to Chicago, devoting the rest of his career to the teaching and practice of medicine. In 1912 Williams was appointed associate attending surgeon at St. Luke's and worked there until his retirement from medicine. In accepting the position Williams was forced to resign from Provident, the hospital that he had worked so hard to establish, after accusations that he was being disloyal in accepting a post at a rival hospital, even though Williams had patients in some five different hospitals in the city.

Last years

Williams received many awards during his lifetime. In 1913 he became the only African American among the 100 charter (founding) members of the American College of Surgeons (ACS). He also wrote many articles that were published in medical journals.

Williams retired after suffering a stroke in 1926, and died in Idlewild, Michigan, in 1931. Provident Hospital, now part of Cook County Bureau of Health Services, continues to flourish as a teaching and community hospital. In 1970 the U.S. Congress passed a bill issuing a commemorative stamp in Williams's honor.

See also: Douglass, Frederick

Further reading: Kay, Judith. *The Life of Daniel Hale Williams.* Breckenridge, CO: Twenty First Century Books, 1993. http://www.gibbsmagazine.com/DrWilliams.htm (Biography).

WILLIAMS, Fannie Barrier
Social Activist

Fannie Barrier Williams was a social activist who anticipated modern feminism. She was one of the many women in the late 19th century who worked to improve the position of African Americans. Williams believed passionately in the need to end racism and sexism. She lectured widely about both issues around the United States.

Early life

Williams was born Fannie Barrier in Brockport, New York, on February 12, 1855. Her parents were freed slaves. In 1870 she graduated from the State Normal School in Brockport (now the State University of New York at Brockport). She attended the New England Conservatory of Music in Boston, Massachusetts, and the School of Fine Arts in Washington, D.C. She then started to teach school in the South and in Washington, D.C. Her contact with racism in the South focused her attention on the need to work toward ridding the country of racism.

Chicago

In 1887 she married S. Laing Willliams, a prominent lawyer. They settled in Chicago, Illinois, and she retired from teaching. Williams helped her husband establish a law practice with his partner, activist Ferdinand L. Barnett, the husband of journalist Ida B. Wells-Barnett.

Williams became known for her public speaking. She helped raise funds for Daniel Hale Williams's Provident Hospital and Training School Association, which established the Provident Hospital in 1891.

Activism

Williams was influenced by the abolitionist Frederick Douglass, who supported women's equality and promoted political activism and moral persuasion as ways to help end slavery. Williams later embraced the ideas of Booker T. Washington, agreeing with his emphasis on practical skills and industrial education for African Americans; she also supported Washington's accommodationist stance, unlike many other black civil and social activists.

In 1893 Williams persuaded the Board of Control of the World's Columbian Exposition, held in Chicago, to include black people in the exhibits planned for the celebration. At the exposition itself Williams gave a well-received address about black American women.

Williams also protested against unfair practices, once fooling the inspector on a train by traveling in the whites-only section of a southern train, although her pale skin allowed her to get away with the trick.

Pioneer

In 1896, after having been rejected once, Williams became the first black woman to be admitted to the Woman's Club of Chicago. She was also the first African American woman to serve on the Chicago Library Board (1924–1926). Williams was active in many different civic and community organizations. She was a founding member of the National League of Colored Women in 1893. Two years later she served as state representative at the National Colored Women's Congress. Williams believed that black women needed education to enable them to move out of domestic employment; she also lobbied for voting rights and equal opportunities. Following the death of her husband in 1921, Williams retired from public life. She moved back to Brockport, where she lived with her sister until her death on March 4, 1944.

See also: Douglass, Frederick; Washington, Booker T.; Wells-Barnett, Ida B.; Williams, Daniel Hale

Further reading: Brown, Elsa Barkley, et al. (eds). *Black Women in America: An Historical Encyclopedia*. Volume 2. Bloomington, IN: Indiana University Press, 1994.
www.africanamericans.com/FannieBarrierWilliams.htm (Biography of Williams).

WILLIAMS, George Washington
Historian, Clergyman

George Washington Williams gained prominence during the latter half of the 19th century as a journalist, minister, lawyer, politician, and author. His work charting the history of black people in America ensured Williams a permanent place in furthering the cause of black history.

Early life

Williams was born in Bedford Springs, Pennsylvania, in 1849. His father was an itinerant laborer and Williams traveled around a lot as a child, and received no formal education. During the Civil War (1861–1865) Williams enlisted in the Union Army, at age 14.

Religious life

Williams remained in the army until 1868. He later entered the Newton Theological Seminary in Cambridge, Massachusetts, graduating in 1874 as the first African American to be ordained there. As a minister and student in Boston, Massachusetts, Williams became engaged in debates about race and democracy. His short-lived journal, the *Commoner* appeared in 1875 to provide a voice for the black community. The journal went bankrupt, and in early 1876 Williams took a position in Cincinnati, Ohio, as pastor of the Union Baptist Church.

Williams's interest in politics led him three years later to become the first black congressman elected to Ohio's state legislature, but he left after one term to write the *History of the Negro Race in America from 1619–1880*.

Published in 1882, the book set a standard for the objective writing of African American history. Twentieth-

▲ *George Washington Williams was the first black American to write a history of his people.*

century scholars continued to elaborate on many of the issues Williams first discussed. Many of Williams's opinions were controversial: He concluded, for example, that the fabric of the American republic had been corrupted by slavery since its inception, and that the Constitution provided a protective device for slavery and laid the foundation for the massive conflict that would tear the nation apart in the 1860s.

Williams's other major work, *A History of the Negro Troops in the War of the Rebellion* (1888), combines interviews with black Civil War veterans with extensive research into newspapers and other primary sources. In his last years Williams traveled widely and campaigned against the atrocities of the Belgian colonial regime in the Congo until his death in 1891.

Further reading: Franklin, John Hope. *George Washington Williams: A Biography*. Chicago, IL: University of Chicago Press, 1985.
http://www.factmonster.com/ipka/A0878504.html (Biography).

KEY DATES

1849 Born in Bedford Springs, Pennsylvania, on October 16.

1863 Enlists in the Union Army at age 14 to fight in the Civil War.

1874 Is first African American to be ordained by the Newton Theological Seminary, Cambridge, Massachusetts.

1879 Elected to the Ohio House of Representatives.

1882 Publishes *History of the Negro Race in America from 1619–1880*.

1891 Dies in Blackpool, England, on August 2.

WILLIAMS, Joe
Singer

Joe Williams was a popular singer whose smooth baritone is widely regarded as one of the finest and most memorable voices in the history of jazz. In his long career he made 48 albums; he is best remembered for his vocals on "Everyday I Have the Blues," a 1955 hit for the Count Basie Orchestra.

Early life
Born in Cordele, Georgia, on December 12, 1918, Joseph Goreed Williams was raised in Chicago, Illinois, by his mother and grandmother. As a child he sang hymns and spirituals in gospel choirs at the Methodist Church where his mother was the organist. In his teens Williams started performing jazz and blues in South Side nightclubs, where he was originally employed as a bouncer. He made his professional stage debut in 1937 with Jimmy Noone.

A successful musical career
In 1943, on the recommendation of the manager of Chicago's Regal Theater, Williams made the journey to Boston, Massachusetts, where he was hired to front the Lionel Hampton Orchestra after Dinah Washington left. Over the next 11 years Williams went on numerous tours with Hampton, but took time out to work with other jazz legends including Red Saunders, Johnny Long, Erskine Tate, and Coleman Hawkins. In 1954 Williams got an even bigger break when he became the singer with Count Basie: They played together regularly for the next seven years.

In 1961 Williams went solo with his own backing combo, but he always remained on good terms with Basie, who called him his "Number One Son." The two men had several subsequent on-stage reunions, and whenever Williams sang "You Are So Beautiful" he dedicated it to Basie. Later in life Williams found a different kind of fame,

▲ *Joe Williams sings on the opening night of the Newport Jazz Festival in 1965.*

this time as an actor in the role of Grandpa Al Hanks in the long-running 1980s TV sitcom *The Cosby Show*: He and Bill Cosby were old friends.

Remarkably Williams lost little of his vocal power in old age, and kept working as a singer for an average of 40 weeks a year, mainly on cruise liners and in top hotels and clubs. He died from a respiratory infection at age 80 in 1999. Williams influenced many jazz and blues musicians, including Tony Bennett, who said that Williams defined who he was and recalled that Williams once told him: "It's not that you want to sing, it's that you have to sing."

See also: Basie, Count; Cosby, Bill; Hawkins, Coleman; Washington, Dinah

Further reading: Kliment, Bud. *Count Basie*. Los Angeles, CA: Melrose Square Publishing Co., 1994.
www.riverwalk.org/profiles/williams.htm (Profile).

KEY DATES

1918	Born in Cordele, Georgia, on December 12.
1943	Joins the Lionel Hampton Orchestra.
1954	Joins the Count Basie Orchestra.
1955	Records "Everyday I Have the Blues" with Count Basie.
1999	Dies in Las Vegas, Nevada, on March 29.

WILLIAMS, Paul Revere
Architect

Paul Revere Williams had a prolific career as an architect in Los Angeles, California. He specialized in domestic buildings, including many luxury homes for Hollywood stars. He used a relaxed and eclectic style.

Early life

Born in Los Angeles, California, on February 18, 1894, Williams was the son of Chester Stanley Williams and Lila Wright Churchill. Orphaned at age four, Williams was raised by foster parents. Williams was one of a handful of black students who attended Sentous Elementary High School, before going on to study at Los Angeles Polytechnic High School.

Becoming an architect

Williams worked for several architects in Los Angeles after graduating from school in 1912. He attended the University of Southern California in Los Angeles from 1916 to 1919, but did not graduate. His main training came from the Beaux-Arts Institute of Design, where he attended night classes from 1915 to 1920. Three years later Williams became a licensed architect in the state of California and a member of the American Institute of Architects, the first African American to become so, after which he set up his own practice.

Williams had to overcome racial prejudice and a lack of social connections to establish his career. His breakthrough came in 1930, when he designed a mansion for the automobile manufacturer Everett Lobban Card in Beverley Hills. This led to further commissions from Hollywood stars such as Lon Chaney (1930), Barbara Stanwyck (1936), and Frank Sinatra (1950). Williams established a multiracial practice, employing Chinese and German architects. In an autobiographical article, "I am a Negro," published in 1937, he described how he worked

▲ *Paul Revere Williams (right), when he was president of the Municipal Art Commission, at a 1959 Toulouse-Lautrec exhibition in Los Angeles.*

hard to win clients attracted by his casual and stylish designs. His association with African American businesses also led to commissions for the Second Baptist Church (1924), the First African Methodist Episcopal Church (1925), YMCAs at 28th Street, New York (1925), and in Hollywood (1926), and the headquarters of the Golden State Mutual Life Assurance Company (1949). While his links with Hollywood kept his practice secure during the Great Depression of the 1930s, Williams extended his work to include federal public housing projects. His association with other architectural practices led to his involvement in such projects as the "Theme" Building at the Los Angeles International Airport (1964). His public commissions included the Grave of the Unknown Soldier in Pearl Harbor, Hawaii (1953). He died in 1980.

Further reading: Hudson, Karen E. *Paul Revere Williams: A Legacy of Style.* New York, NY: Rizzoli, 1993.
http://www.knpb.org/productions/house/garvey_williams.asp (Biography).

KEY DATES

1894	Born in Los Angeles, California, on February 18.
1930	Receives first major commission for Card Mansion, Beverley Hills.
1949	Designes the Golden State Mutual Life Assurance Company headquarters in Los Angeles.
1980	Dies in Los Angeles, California, on January 23.

WILLIAMS, Peter
Religious Leader

Peter Williams was the cofounder of New York City's first independent black church, which would later become the African Methodist Episcopal (AME) Zion Church. In so doing, he set a powerful example for thousands of other African Americans who during the early 19th century left their white-run congregations to form their own Methodist, Episcopal, Baptist, and Presbyterian churches.

Early life
Williams was born into slavery in New York City in 1749. His owner was a white tobacconist named Aymar, who taught Williams his trade. In 1778 Williams also began to work as a sexton, a minor church official, for the John Street Methodist Episcopal Church.

Achieving freedom
During the American Revolution (1775–1783), Aymar supported the British cause. Williams's son, who was very proud of his father, often related how during the war his father had refused to reveal to a British officer the whereabouts of a prominent American rebel, even though he was threatened with death if he did not do so. At the end of the war Williams's master, Aymar, left the United States; he sold Williams to the John Street church for $40.

Williams worked hard for the church and by 1796 had saved enough money to purchase his own freedom. He subsequently set up his own store on New York's William Street and became a prosperous, well-respected member of the city's growing free-black community.

Dissatisfaction
By this time the congregation of the John Street Church was almost 40 percent black. Williams, along with other black church members, had grown dissatisfied with the way in which African Americans were treated by the church; for instance, they could only take communion after the white members of the congregation had done so and a black American could not become a minister.

In 1796 Williams and a group of black Methodists—Francis Jacobs, William Brown, Abraham Thompson, June Scott, Samuel Pontier, Thomas Miller, William Miller, James Varick, and William Hamilton—petitioned and were granted permission by Francis Asbury (1745–1816), the first bishop of the Methodist Church in the United States, to hold meetings of their own in the church premises, although they continued to be a part of the Methodist Episcopal Church.

Breaking away
By 1799 the congregation had grown and the group began to plan to build a separate building of worship. They purchased a site on the corner of Church and Leonard streets, fronting onto Church Street, where they began to build a church. Finished in 1800, the church opened its doors to the congregation, but it soon became apparent that the group wanted to become a separate religious body.

Advised by the Reverend John McClaskey, a church elder, they proceeded to draw up the articles of government. In 1801 Williams and Jacobs signed a charter incorporating the "African Methodist Episcopal Church [called Zion] of the City of New York." Williams became a regular preacher at the new church.

The AME Zion Church broke with the Methodist Episcopal Church in 1824, a year after Williams's death. In the 21st century the AME Zion Church is the second-largest of the black Methodist denominations.

KEY DATES	
1749	Born into slavery in New York City.
1778	Begins work as a sexton.
1783	Sold for $40 to the church.
1796	Purchases his freedom.
1800	Builds the first AME Zion church.
1801	Incorporation of the African Methodist Episcopal Church [called Zion] of the City of New York.
1823	Dies in New York City.

See also: Religion and African Americans; Williams, Peter, Jr.

Further reading: Lincoln, C. Eric, and Lawrence H. Mamiya. *The Black Church in the African-American Experience.* Durham, NC: Duke University Press, 1990.
www.infoplease.com/ipa/A0878506.html (Short biography).
http://www.varickmemorialamezion.org/Main/zionhistory.htm (History of the AME Zion Church).

WILLIAMS, Peter, Jr.
Religious Leader, Abolitionist

Peter Williams, Jr., was an important figure in the early 19th-century antislavery movement, as well as the first African American to be ordained as an Episcopal minister in New York State. His father was Peter Williams, one of the founders of the African Methodist Episcopal (AME) Church.

Early life
Williams was born into slavery in New Brunswick, New Jersey, in about 1780. His father purchased his family's freedom in 1796 and set up a successful tobacconist store on Williams Street in New York City. The young Williams went to school at the African Free School, just a few doors away.

Williams followed his father into preaching. Unlike his father, however, who made the first steps toward founding an independent black church, he chose to remain within a white-controlled church. In 1812 he became a licensed lay

▼ **This etching of Peter Williams, Jr., is thought to date from the 1820s.**

preacher in the Episcopal Church, and in 1820 was appointed minister of the newly consecrated St. Philip's African Church in Manhattan. He led a large and influential black congregation that included the future priest and missionary Alexander Crummell.

A crisis of conscience
By the 1820s Williams had already developed a reputation as one of the country's most powerful advocates of black rights. He vigorously opposed the slave trade, denounced the activities of the American Colonization Society, which sought to resettle black Americans in Africa, and drew attention to the paradoxical and indefensible situation of African American slaves— "slaves in the midst of freedom; slaves to those who boast that freedom is the unalienable right of all."

In 1827 Williams helped set up the first black-edited newspaper, *Freedom's Journal*. In 1833 he became a member of the board of managers of the New York Anti-Slavery Society. In 1834 Williams's white bishop ordered him to resign his position in the society and to preach only the Christian gospel from his pulpit. Williams, forced to chose between his loyalty to his church and his political conscience, chose the former. He died in 1840.

See also: Crummell, Alexander; Religion and African Americans; Williams, Peter

Further reading: Hewitt, John H. "Peter Williams, Jr.: New York's First African American Episcopal Priest." *New York History,* 79 (April 1998), 101–29.
www.infoplease.com/ipa/A0878505.html (Short biography).

WILLIAMS, Serena
Tennis Player

As the younger half of a dynamic sibling tennis duo, Serena Williams burst onto the tennis scene in the late 1990s and proceeded to capture a slew of Grand Slam titles. Combining power and grace, the gifted right-hander won four Grand Slam titles in a row in 2002 and 2003, as well as numerous doubles championships with her equally talented sister, Venus. The Williams sisters emerged as significant and influential African American celebrities both on and off the court. Despite being the younger sibling, Serena Williams's success on the court often entailed defeating her older sister. In 2002, for example, she defeated Venus in the finals of the French Open, Wimbledon (England), and the U.S. Open.

Early life
Born in Saginaw, Michigan, on September 26, 1981, Williams was the youngest of five children. She began to develop her talent, at age five, on the public courts of Compton, California, a violent and often dangerous district of Los Angeles. Coached by their father Richard, both Serena and Venus demonstrated a clear early aptitude for the game. Such promise prompted their father to move them to Palm Beach Gardens, Florida, to train with Rick Macci, the former coach of teen-tennis sensations Jennifer Capriati and Mary Pierce.

A professional player
In 1995, at age 14, Williams turned professional, a move that brought criticism particularly because the World Tennis Association (WTA) did not recognize players that young. She played in her first professional, non-WTA tournament, the Bell Challenge in Quebec, Canada, in October 1995. In 1997 she began playing in WTA events, achieving upset victories over Mary Pierce (ranked No. 7 in the world) and Monica Seles (ranked No. 4) at the Ameritech Cup in Chicago. She finished her first WTA year ranked No. 100. In 1998 Williams was ranked WTA No. 21, the first female to rise so quickly in the rankings. Her

▲ **Serena Williams plays at the NASDAQ 100 Open Tennis Match, Key Biscane, on March 29, 2005.**

first Grand Slam title came in September 1999, when she defeated Martina Hingis at the U.S. Open. She was the lowest seeded player ever to win the title and only the second black American woman (after Althea Gibson) to win a Grand Slam title.

Plagued by health problems, Williams was forced to slow down. She did, however, compete in the 2000 Olympic Summer Games in Sydney, Australia, where she teamed up with Venus to win the doubles gold medal. In 2002 Williams had a breakthrough year. She won the French Open, Wimbledon, and the U.S. Open, defeating her sister in the finals of all three Grand Slam events. In January 2003 she captured her fourth Grand Slam victory in a row at the Australian Open; later that year she captured her second Wimbledon title. Williams has also turned her hand to acting and fashion design.

KEY DATES	
1981	Born in Saginaw, Michigan, on September 26.
1999	Wins U.S. Open on September 12.
2003	Wins fourth Grand Slam victory in a row.

See also: Gibson, Althea; Williams, Venus

Further reading: Stewart, Mark. *Venus & Serena Williams: Sisters in Arms*. Brookfield, CT: Millbrook Press, 2000. http://www.venusandserena.homestead.com/ SerenaBiography.html (Biography).

WILLIAMS, Vanessa
Singer, Actor, Model

Multimillion record-selling artist Vanessa Williams is also a successful actor and model. Known for her good looks, Williams was the first black woman to win the Miss America title.

Early life
Born in Millwood, New York, on March 18, 1963, Vanessa Lynn Williams was one of the two children of Milton and Helen Williams. Both of Williams's parents had music degrees and introduced their daughter to music from a young age. Williams went on to study theater at Syracuse University. Her beauty made it easy for her to get modeling jobs. Williams also entered beauty pageants. After being crowned Miss New York, Williams entered the Miss America competition in 1983 and became the first black Miss America. Her reign was not to last, however. Before she had entered the competition, Williams had posed nude for *Penthouse*. Williams resigned as Miss America in July 1984 and the photographs were published in September.

▼ **A talented musician, Vanessa Williams is known for her smooth and sophisticated style.**

KEY DATES	
1963	Born in Millwood, New York, on March 18.
1983	Wins the Miss America title; resigns 11 months later, following a scandal involving nude photographs.
1988	Releases the album *The Right Stuff* to critical acclaim; receives three Grammy nominations.
1997	Appears in *Soul Food*; wins the NAACP Image Award for Best Actress.
2005	Releases *Everlasting Love*.

Singer and actor
Williams did not let the scandal keep her down. She concentrated instead on her singing career, performing background vocals for established artists; she was featured on George Clinton's 1986 album *Skeletons in the Closet*.

Signed in 1986 by Wing, a subsidiary of Mercury and Polygram Records, Williams began work on her first album. Two years later she released *The Right Stuff*, which spawned the Top 10 pop chart hit and No. 1 rhythm-and-blues single "Dreaming." The album established Williams as a serious singer and earned three Grammy nominations. Her second album, *The Comfort Zone,* (1991) was equally successful and the song "Save the Best for Last" was No. 1 on the pop charts for several weeks. Her 1995 album, *The Sweetest Days*, featuring Sting and Kenneth "Babyface" Edmonds, went platinum, helping consolidate Williams's reputation as a star musician.

In the 1990s Williams guest-starred on popular TV shows including *The Prince of Bel Air, Ally McBeal*, and *Boomtown.* Her movie roles included *Eraser (1996), Soul Food* (1997), for which she won an NAACP Image Award, and the remake of the cult movie *Shaft* (2000). Williams also appeared in theater and musical productions including *Kiss of the Spiderwoman* (1994) and the revival of Stephen Sondheim's musical *Into the Woods* (2002), for which she received a Tony nomination. Williams has won three NAACP Image Awards and a Billboard Music Award.

See also: Clinton, George; Edmonds, Kenneth "Babyface"

Further reading: http://www.vanessawilliamsmusic.com (Official site).

WILLIAMS, Venus
Tennis Player

Venus Williams has consistently exhibited her dominance on the court against many of the world's best tennis players. From an early age she demonstrated the tremendous potential of her game, which was rooted in her powerful groundstrokes and daunting serve. With dominant wins at Wimbledon (England), the U.S. Open, and the Sydney Olympics, 2000 was the highlight of Williams's career, prompting her to say, "I guess I've graduated to a different level where I can be like some of the greats."

Early life

Born in Lynwood, California, on June 17, 1980, Williams was encouraged to play tennis from an early age by her father Richard, who had dreams of raising a tennis champion. She perfected her game on the courts of the tough Los Angeles district of Compton, California. Williams's father began coaching her at age four; he also coached Serena. In an effort to develop their skills, Williams moved his talented daughters to Florida in 1991 to train with one of the game's top coaches, Rick Macci.

Professional career

Williams turned pro at age 14, just before the new World Tennis Association (WTA) rule banning 14-year-olds from playing in tour events. Williams entered her first tournament in October—the Bank of the West Classic in Oakland—where she lost to the then-No. 2 player in the world, Arantxa Sanchez Vicario. Williams did not compete in a Grand Slam tournament until the 1997 French Open.

At the 1997 U.S. Open Williams became the first unseeded player to reach the final and the first black American to do so since Althea Gibson's wins in 1957 and 1958. Although Williams lost, her ranking shot up from No. 66 to No. 25. She won her first WTA singles title at the IGA Tennis Classic in Oklahoma City in March 1998, and later that year entered the WTA Top 10 player list.

In July 2000 Williams won her first Grand Slam title at Wimbledon, following it up with victories at the U.S. Open and the Sydney Olympics in September. She teamed up with her sister Serena to capture a second gold medal at the Olympic games in doubles. Her victories prompted *Sports Illustrated* to name Williams "Sportswoman of the Year." In 2001 she successfully defended her Wimbledon title and defeated Serena to win the U.S. Open singles

▲ *Venus Williams plays in the Wimbledon Tennis Championships Ladies' Final on July 2, 2005; Williams unexpectedly beat the No. 1 seed and favorite Lindsay Davenport.*

title, confirming her status as the top ladies tennis player in the world.

In 2002, however, Williams was defeated in three grand slam finals by Serena. Despite accruing a number of doubles championships and being a finalist in several tournaments, Williams did not win another Grand Slam title until her dramatic Wimbledon victory over No. 1 seed Lindsay Davenport in July 2005.

KEY DATES	
1980	Born in Lynwood, California, on June 17.
1998	Takes first professional title, the IGA Tennis Classic
2000	Wins first Grand Slam title at Wimbledon on July 8.
2005	Beats the No. 1 seed Lindsay Davenport in the Wimbledon Tennis Championships Ladies Final.

See also: Gibson, Althea; Williams, Serena

Further reading: Stewart, Mark. *Venus & Serena Williams: Sisters in Arms.* Brookfield, CT: Millbrook Press, 2000. http://www.venuswilliams.com (Official site).

WILLIAMSON, John Lee
Musician

John Lee "Sonny Boy" Williamson was responsible for creating the blues harmonica style and bridging country and electric blues. He developed blues harmonica playing from the simple country style of the South in the early 1930s to becoming an integral part of the electric dance bands of Chicago in the early 1940s. After Williamson's murder in 1948, "Rice Miller" Williamson (1899–1965), who appeared on a radio show from 1941 to 1945 billed as Sonny Boy Williamson, claimed to be the original "Sonny Boy"; as a result John Lee Williamson is sometimes referred to as Sonny Boy 1.

Early life
Born in southwest Madison County, near Jackson, Mississippi, on March 30, 1914, Williamson taught himself to play the blues harp as a child and could play it well enough by the time he was in his teens to perform in juke joints in Tennessee and Arkansas with guitarist Sleepy John Estes.

Making a career of music
In 1934 Williamson settled in Chicago, Illinois, where he played in bands with blues guitarists Big Bill Broonzy and Big Joe Williams. There his style matured from the country blues approach associated with Estes to what became regarded as the peak of electric blues harmonica playing: Drawing rather than blowing notes, slurred and bent notes, and hand, tongue, and breath control effects. Williamson also sang, often mixing vocal and harmonica lines in the same piece. Like other musicians associated with the Chicago sound in the 1930s and 1940s, Williamson combined hard electric dance rhythms with the emotional intensity of the original blues.

KEY DATES	
1914	Born in Jackson, Tennessee, on March 30.
1937	Has first hit with "Good Morning School Girl."
1940	Releases "I Been Dealing With the Devil."
1941	Releases "My Black Name."
1947	Releases "Mellow Chick Swing."
1948	Dies in Chicago, Illinois, on June 1.

▲ *John Lee Williamson was inducted into the W. C. Handy Blues Hall of Fame in 1980.*

Recording star
Williamson recorded with the Bluebird label and RCA in the late 1930s and 1940s and many songs became hits. He had his first success with "Good Morning School Girl" in 1937, followed by "I Been Dealing With the Devil" (1940), "My Black Name" (1941), "Elevator Woman" (1945), and "Mellow Chick Swing" (1947).

Williamson had a reputation for violence when drunk, but he was was liked and respected among his fellow musicians. In 1948 he was murdered outside a nightclub. For many years his grave lay unmarked, but in 1990 a historical marker was revealed in his honor. On it were the words: "In his mouth and hands the harmonica learned to wail and chirp, laugh and cry, in spanking new rhythms and to daring new beats." His influence can be seen on later blues harmonica players such as Walter Horton, Junior Wells, and Forrest City Joe.

See also: Wells, Junior

Further reading: http://physics.lunet.edu/blues/ John_Lee_Williamson.html (Biography and links).

WILSON, August
Playwright

The Pulitzer Prize-winning writer August Wilson was one of the United States's most important playwrights and the most influential African American dramatist of his generation.

Early life

Wilson was born Frederick August Kittel on April 27, 1945, in Pittsburgh, Pennsylvania, the fourth of six children and the eldest son of German baker Frederick Kittel and cleaner Daisy Wilson. After Wilson's parents separated when he was a young boy, his mother remarried. Wilson had little contact with his father. In 1959 Wilson's stepfather, David Bedford, moved the family to the white suburb of Hazelwood. Wilson found the move difficult: His family was subjected to racial abuse from neighbors and

▼ *August Wilson was one of only seven U.S. playwrights and the first black writer to win the Pulitzer Prize twice—in 1987 and 1990.*

they had bricks thrown through their windows. Wilson was bullied and taunted at school. He was also accused of cheating after he submitted an essay on the French leader Napoleon Bonaparte (1769–1821) that was thought to be too literate for a black boy to have written. Disillusioned, Wilson dropped out of school at age 15. He continued his education at the local library, reading widely, particularly the work of black writers such as Ralph Ellison and Richard Wright, and that of the Welsh writer Dylan Thomas (1914–1953).

A literary career

In 1965, following Frederick Kittel's death, Wilson took his mother's last name and became known as August Wilson. He also bought a typewriter and began writing poems, submitting them to local black magazines. In that same year Wilson started listening to the blues, especially recordings by Bessie Smith (*see box*). In 1967 Wilson joined the Army for a year, after which he returned to Pittsburgh.

INFLUENCES AND INSPIRATION

August Wilson claimed that he was influenced by the "four Bs" —blues music, experimental Argentinian writer Jorge Luis Borges (1899–1986), black arts movement poet Amiri Baraka, and artist Romare Bearden.

Wilson realized the importance of the blues while listening to Bessie Smith's "Nobody in Town Can Bake a Sweet Jelly Roll Like Mine." It made him realize that he wanted to write in the street vernacular that he heard every day rather than in the English of white writers such as Dylan Thomas. He said after hearing Smith, "The universe stuttered, and everything fell into place."

Wilson claimed that Borges's short stories made him realize that "you can be specific as to a time and place and culture and still have the work resonate with the universal themes of love, honor, duty, betrayal, etc."

Baraka's work showed Wilson that all art was political, and it inspired him to set up the Black Horizons Theater Group.

Wilson said that he saw Bearden's collages as depicting black life "on a grand and epic scale ... in a language that was vibrant and ... affirmed its value, and exalted its presence." Wilson compared his artistic process to that of Bearden who as a collagist pieced things together so that they made sense, just as Wilson did in his plays.

Wilson became involved in the black arts movement and was particularly influenced by the poet Amiri Baraka. In 1968 he cofounded the Black Horizons Theater with Rob Penny; he also began publishing poetry on black subjects such as Muhammad Ali and Malcolm X.

Wilson considered himself to be a poet. In 1973, however, he wrote his first play, *Recycle*. He wrote several plays during this time including *Jitney*, which he revised in the 1980s. In 1977 Wilson moved to St. Paul, Minnesota, where he supported himself by writing educational dramas for the Minnesota Science Center. In 1982 Wilson received critical acclaim for the revised version of *Jitney*, a play set in a Pittsburgh taxi station. He decided to embark on an ambitious 10-play cycle in which each piece would be set in a different decade of the 20th century and confront a different issue facing African Americans. *Gem of the Ocean* was set in the 1900s, *Joe Turner's Come and Gone* in the 1910s, *Ma Rainey's Black Bottom* in the 1920s, *The Piano Lesson* in the 1930s, *Seven Guitars* in the 1940s, *Fences* in the 1950s, *Two Trains Running* in the 1960s, *Jitney* in the 1970s, *King Hedley II* in the 1980s, and *Radio Golf* in the 1990s.

Critical acclaim

In 1982 *Ma Rainey's Black Bottom* was accepted by the Eugene O'Neill Theater Center's National Playwrights Conference in Waterford, Connecticut. Wilson met Lloyd Richards at the conference. Richards, who was dean of Yale drama school, directed the play when it debuted at the university in 1984, before it transferred to Broadway in October, winning three New York Drama Critics' Circle Awards. The play established Wilson as a leading playwright and was the first of many such collaborations with Richards. They included *Fences* (1985), a play about a one-time baseball star, which won the Pulitzer Prize for Drama. Wilson won a second Pulitzer for *The Piano Lesson* (1990). In August 2005 Wilson announced that he had terminal liver cancer. He died on October 2.

KEY DATES

1945   Born in Pittsburgh, Pennsylvania, on April 27.

1965   Hears Bessie Smith's "Nobody in Town Can Bake a Sweet Jelly Roll Like Mine"; changes name to August Wilson.

1968   Cofounds Black Horizons Theater with Rob Penny.

1982   National Playwrights Conference at O'Neill Theater Center accepts *Ma Rainey's Black Bottom*; meets director Lloyd Richards who goes on to direct several of his plays.

1984   *Ma Rainey's Black Bottom* opens on Broadway.

1987   Wins Pulitzer Prize for Drama for *Fences*.

1990   Wins second Pulitzer Prize for *The Piano Lesson.*

2005   Dies in Seattle, Washington, on October 2.

See also: Baraka, Amiri; Bearden, Romare; Ellison, Ralph; Richards, Lloyd; Smith, Bessie; Wright, Richard

Further reading: Shannon, Sandra G. *The Dramatic Vision of August Wilson.* Washington, D.C.: Howard University Press, 1995.
http://www.nytimes.com/pages/theater/theaterspecial (Obituary).

WILSON, Cassandra
Musician

One of the most exciting and acclaimed singers of the contemporary jazz scene, Cassandra Wilson artfully blends jazz, blues, rhythm and blues (R&B), country, folk, and even rock in her music. Wilson is profoundly aware of and deeply connected to her blues, jazz, and folk heritage, and each of her albums pays deep respect to her favorite influences. Like the jazz and blues legends who came before her, Wilson is an original.

Early life
Born in Jackson, Mississippi, on December 4, 1955, Wilson was the daughter of a bass guitarist and a schoolteacher. Her musician father taught her to love jazz when she was a child. Wilson first performed in public at age five, when she sang at her brother's kindergarten graduation. She began playing the guitar and piano at age nine. After attending public schools in Mississippi and forming a

▼ *Cassandra Wilson performs at the Royal Festival Hall, London, England, in April 2004.*

KEY DATES	
1955	Born in Jackson, Mississippi, on December 4.
1964	Starts piano and guitar lessons.
1985	Releases debut album as solo vocalist and band leader, *Point of View.*
1988	*Billboard* magazine names *Blue Skies* jazz album of the year.
2001	Named "America's Best Singer" by *Time* magazine.

band with two white schoolmates, Wilson studied at Jackson State University. She emerged as a gifted jazz vocalist while singing with the Black Arts Music Society.

Musical career
In the early 1980s Wilson moved to New Orleans, where she studied with saxophonist Earl Turbinton. In 1982 she moved to New York City to work with David Holland and Abbey Lincoln. After recording with Steve Coleman's Motherland's Pulse record label, Wilson signed to JMT. She released her debut solo album, *Point of View,* in 1985. Three years later *Billboard* magazine named Wilson's *Blue Skies* jazz album of the year.

After Wilson moved from JMT to the Blue Note label in the early 1990s, she won over new audiences with lush and sophisticated tributes to a diverse group of legendary songwriters from Robert Johnson and Hank Williams to Miles Davis. She has covered the songs of popular artists like Bob Dylan and U2 and has won a corps of devotees with amazing interpretations of great jazz standards. With her popularity reaching new heights Wilson toured with Wynton Marsalis in 1997. Two years later she released *Traveling Miles,* her homage to the jazz musician Miles Davis. In 2001 *Time* magazine named Wilson America's Best Singer. For her 14th solo album, *Glamored,* Wilson returned home to Jackson, Mississippi.

See also: Davis, Miles; Johnson, Robert; Marsalis, Wynton

Further reading: Giddens, Gary. "Cassandra Wilson—A Different Songbook." *Visions of Jazz.* New York, NY: Oxford University Press, 1998.
http://www.cassandrawilson.com/ (Official site).

WILSON, "Flip" Clerow
Comedian, Actor, TV Producer

Despite a difficult childhood "Flip" Clerow Wilson lived the American dream, rising from poverty to great success as a comedian, actor, and producer. Wilson was influenced by comics such as Redd Foxx, Bill Cosby, and Charlie Chaplin. He is best remembered for his TV series the *Flip Wilson Show.*

Early life
Born to a poor family in Jersey City, New Jersey, in 1933, Wilson was one of 17 children. For much of his early childhood he found his way into trouble, and ended up spending much of his youth in foster homes. After running away from several homes, Wilson was sent to reform school, but he learned his lesson early. At age 16 he changed his life by enlisting in the Air Force; he lied to his recruiter about his age.

His Air Force colleagues gave Wilson the name "Flip" because he had such a "flipped out" sense of humor. Wilson's hilarious impressions, comedic talent, and amiable spirit won him many friends and fans, even among officers. Wilson was so popular that the Air Force sent him on a comedy tour of military bases to boost morale.

The emergence of the comedian
In 1954 Wilson left the Air Force and moved to San Francisco, where he worked various day jobs while refining his comedy routines. In the late 1950s Wilson started touring the country, barely scraping by as a comic. His fortune changed in 1959, however, when an audience member began sponsoring him to the tune of $50 a week.

Wilson blossomed as a comic in the 1960s, with regular appearances at Harlem's Apollo Theater. From 1965 he also began to appear on television, making his first appearance on Johnny Carson's *Tonight Show,* followed by others such as *The Ed Sullivan Show* and *Love, American Style.*

▲ **Flip Wilson's success was the result of hard work. He insisted on artistic control over his material, a first for a black American comedian.**

In 1970 Wilson was given his own show, *The Flip Wilson Show,* becoming the first black American to take a leading role in the writing and production of the weekly show. In its prime, *The Flip Wilson Show* was the second most popular TV show in America: Wilson entertained audiences with character sketches that bravely parodied and contradicted prevailing racial stereotypes. In 1974 *The Flip Wilson Show* was canceled. In that same year Wilson won custody of his children after his divorce, and he dedicated himself to being a father. Despite several film and TV roles, he was never able to make a major comeback before his death from liver cancer in 1998.

KEY DATES	
1933	Born in Jersey City, New Jersey, on December 8.
1950	Enlists in the Air Force.
1970	Debut of the TV series, *The Flip Wilson Show.*
1998	Dies in Malibu, California, on November 25.

See also: Cosby, Bill; Foxx, Redd

Further reading: http://www.imdb.com/name/nm0933400 (Biography).

WILSON, Harriet E.
Writer

Harriet E Wilson published one book, *Our Nig,* during her lifetime, thought to be largely autobiographical. Although largely overlooked for more than 100 years after Wilson's death, the novel is thought to be the first written by an African American woman, as well as the first black American novel published in America.

Early life

Very little is known for certain about the life of Harriet E Wilson. Much of what is thought to be accurate comes from the records of the New Hampshire census and from her novel. The exact place and time of her birth are not known. However, the 1850 federal census for New Hampshire lists her as Harriet Adams and her birth date as either 1827 or 1828. Another census, however, this time in Boston in 1860, suggests that she was born in Fredericksburg, Virginia, in 1807 or 1808.

Service

Some sources believe that Wilson was in service to the Nehemiah Hayward family until her adolescence. The quality of her writing makes it clear that she must have at some time received some level of schooling. In about 1847 the family moved to Baltimore but Wilson stayed behind, eking out a living. It is almost certain that in 1850 Wilson was living with the Boyles, a white family, in Milford, New Hampshire.

Family

In 1851 Wilson is believed to have been working as a straw-hat maker in Milford. She met and married Thomas Wilson, who claimed to be a fugitive slave. Their son, George Mason Wilson, was born the following May or June by which time Thomas Wilson had already abandoned his wife. He left her in poverty and she was forced to find work and rely on the kindness of friends. The Milford charity records in 1855 and 1856 indicate that Wilson and her son spent a month on a county poor farm in 1855. A white family eventually took Wilson and her son into their home. City directories also show that Wilson lived in Boston, Massachusetts, during the 1850s.

Wilson suffered from ill health and she turned to writing to try to support herself and her son, as she explains in the preface to *Our Nig, or, Sketches from the Life of a Free Black, in a Two-Story White House, North.*

KEY DATES	
1827	Born in New Hampshire at about this time.
1851	Marries Thomas Wilson.
1852	Gives birth to son, George Mason Wilson.
1859	Publishes *Our Nig* on August 18.
1960	George Mason Wilson dies.
1860s	Dies at about this time.

Showing that Slavery's Shadows Fall Even There, By "Our Nig." She wrote: "Deserted by kindred, disabled by failing health, I am forced to some experiment which shall aid me in maintaining me and my child."

Our Nig was published on August 18, 1959, by G. C. Rand and Avery in Boston. It follows Wilson's own life by telling the story of Frado, the protagonist. An indentured servant to the Bellmonts until she is 18, Frado suffers greatly at the hands of Mrs. Bellmont and her daughter. She marries a fugitive slave, who deserts her, and gives birth to their son on a poor county farm. Frado suffers greatly before a kind white woman gives her a recipe for a patent remedy that Frado begins to sell for money.

Rediscovery

Wilson failed in her aim to provide for her son. He died in 1860, less than six months after the book's publication. Wilson also succumbed to ill health sometime in the 1860s, although her precise place and time of death are not known. For a long time Wilson remained in obscurity, especially since *Our Nig* was often listed as having been written by a white male. The scholar Henry Louis Gates, Jr., bought her book in a charity shop and began to investigate it. He edited an edition, published in 2002.

See also: Gates, Henry Louis, Jr.; Slavery

Further reading: Wilson, Harriet E. *Our Nig, or Sketches from the Life of a Free Black, in a Two-Story White House, North, Showing That Slavery's Shadows Fall Even There.* New York, NY: Vintage, 2002.
www.litencyc.com/php/speople.php?rec=true&UID=5038 (Detailed biography of Wilson).

WINFIELD, Dave
Baseball Player

At an imposing 6 feet 6 inches (2m) tall and weighing more than 200 pounds (90 kg), Dave Winfield established himself as one of the best all-around athletes to play baseball. Drafted to play professional basketball and a talented football player, he lasted in the majors for more than two decades. In 2001 Winfield was inducted into the Baseball Hall of Fame.

Early life
Born in St. Paul, Minnesota, on October 3, 1951, David Mark Winfield was the younger of two brothers. Growing up in one of the city's poorer neighborhoods, Winfield learned to play baseball on local playgrounds. In 1969 he was initially selected by the Baltimore Orioles, but instead chose to attend the University of Minnesota on a baseball scholarship where he majored in political science.

The man in the golden glove
At Minnesota Winfield excelled at both basketball and baseball, where he was the best pitcher on the Gophers team. He led the team to the semifinals of the College World Series, earning himself the Series Most Valuable Player award.

After his four-year college career Winfield made the rare move from amateur baseball directly to the major leagues, choosing to join the San Diego Padres in 1973. He soon proved his prowess, finishing with 20 home runs and 75 RBI in his first season.

In 1979 Winfield earned the first of his seven Gold Glove awards. Further proving his extraordinary talents he stole 20 or more bases five times during his first eight seasons. In 1980 Winfield signed a record-setting 10-year, $23 million contract with the New York Yankees. He

▲ *Winfield played in more than 1,100 games during his time with the Padres and the Yankees.*

became the first Yankee since the legendary Joe DiMaggio to drive in 100 or more runs in five consecutive seasons, and earned four straight Gold Gloves (1982–1985). Due to illness, Winfield missed the 1989 season. In 1990 he joined the California Angels and two years later the Toronto Blue Jays, where he showed no signs of slowing down. In 1995, following two years with the Minnesota Twins, Winfield retired and finished his career with the Cleveland Indians.

In 2000 Winfield was elected into the Padres Hall of Fame and had his jersey number (31) retired by them. Off the field Winfield established the David M. Winfield Foundation, a charitable organization helping underprivileged youth and families in need.

Further reading: Winfield, Dave, and Tom Parker. *Winfield: A Player's Life*. New York, NY: Avon Books, 1989.
http://www.thebaseballpage.com/past/pp/winfielddave (Biography).

KEY DATES	
1951	Born in St. Paul, Minnesota, on October 3.
1973	Joins the San Diego Padres.
1979	Wins the first of his seven Gold Glove awards; signs a $23 million contract with the New York Yankees in the following year.
1990	Is traded to the California Angels.
1995	Retires from professional baseball.

WINFIELD, Paul
Actor

Award-winning actor Paul Winfield was a versatile and imposing figure on stage, screen, and television. His acting ability made his wide-ranging performances—from a sharecropper to Martin Luther King, Jr.—believable. Winfield was the third black actor to be nominated for an Academy Award for Best Actor (1972).

Early life
Born in Los Angeles, California, on May 22, 1941, Winfield proved his acting mettle relatively young when he became the first black actor to win Best Actor in the annual Speech and Drama Teachers Association Drama Festival while attending the Manual Arts High School. He became the first person to win the same honor three years running. Winfield secured a two-year scholarship to the University of Portland in Oregon and was subsequently awarded scholarships to study at Stanford University and Los Angeles City College. He finally earned a BA degree from the University of California, Los Angeles (UCLA).

A good judge of character
After a spell on the stage Winfield had a Hollywood break playing Paul Cameron, actor Diahann Carroll's boyfriend in the TV sitcom *Julia* (1968–1971). He made his film debut in *The Lost Man* (1969), and received an Academy Award nomination for Best Actor for his role in *Sounder* (1972). He played former Brooklyn Dodger catcher Roy Campanella in *It's Good To Be Alive* (1974), and earned Emmy nominations for his interpretation of Martin Luther King, Jr., in the 1978 TV miniseries *King* and as the character Dr. Huguley in *Roots: The Next Generation* (1979). Winfield also portrayed Captain Clark Terrell in *Star Trek II: The Wrath of Khan* in 1982. Naturally authoritative, Winfield played several judges, and won a 1994 Emmy for his performance as a judge in the TV series *Picket Fences*.

Winfield also had recurring roles in the TV series *227* (1989–1990) and *Wiseguy* (1987–1991). He was also a

▲ *Winfield's natural gravitas meant that he was often cast as a member of the military, a judge, an ambassador, or a special agent.*

versatile stage actor, appearing in works by Anton Chekhov, William Shakespeare, and many modern playwrights. Winfield was honored by the California Federation of Black Leadership, the Black Publishers of America, and the Black Child Development Institution of Washington, D.C. He received the NAACP Image Award for Best Actor and was inducted into the Black Filmmakers Hall of Fame. In 2004, not long after playing a small role in a remake of *Sounder*, Winfield died of a heart attack at age 62.

See also: Campanella, Roy; Carroll, Diahann; King, Martin Luther, Jr.

Further reading: http://www.aaregistry.com/african_american_history/2451/Paul_Winfield_an_actor_with_great_style (Biography).

KEY DATES

1941   Born in Los Angeles, California, on May 22.

1972   Receives an Academy Award nomination for Best Actor for his performance in *Sounder*.

2004   Dies in Los Angeles, California, on March 7.

WINFREY, Oprah
Talk Show Host, Actor, Businesswoman, Activist

Named by *Time* magazine as one of the most important people of the 20th century, and ranked No. 9 on *Forbes* magazine's 2005 list of the 100 most powerful women, Oprah Winfrey single-handedly revolutionized the television talk-show format and became the host of the most watched daytime show in television history.

A smart businesswoman, Winfrey is the wealthiest female entertainer in the world, the first African American woman to own her own production company, Harpo, and the first black female to be listed on *Forbes* magazine's annual list of billionaires. A committed activist and philanthropist, Winfrey has also had a significant social and economic effect on the lives of many disenfranchised groups, including black people, women, and children.

From humble beginnings to a media empire
Oprah Gail Winfrey was born on January 29, 1954, on a farm in Kosciusko, Mississippi. Her parents were unmarried and separated soon after her birth, leaving Winfrey in the care of her maternal grandmother. At age six, Winfrey moved to Milwaukee to live with her mother, and by age 13 she had been sexually abused by male relatives. Winfrey said later, "I was, and am, severely damaged by the experience. All the years I convinced myself I was healed. I wasn't … I still carried the shame, and I unconsciously blamed myself for those men's acts."

Winfrey soon began to act out as a way of dealing with the abuse and to get attention from her mother. In one instance she faked a robbery in her house and stole her

▲ **Oprah Winfrey has helped millions of people around the world through her TV talk shows.**

mother's purse in order to buy more fashionable glasses. After she ran away from home at age 13, her mother sent her to live with her father in Nashville, Tennessee. His strict discipline and guidance saved her life (*see box*). In a safer and much calmer household, Winfrey quickly began to excell. She joined the school's drama club and won a $1000 college scholarship for a short speech entitled "The Negro, the Constitution, and the United States." Soon after she was the first black woman to win Nashville's Miss Fire Prevention title, and was crowned Miss Black Tennessee after her first and only foray into beauty pageants. In 1976 she graduated from Tennessee State University with a degree in speech communications and theater.

While still in college, Winfrey landed a job as a coanchor for the evening news. After graduation she joined the ABC-affiliated station in Baltimore, Maryland,

KEY DATES	
1954	Born in Kosciusko, Mississippi, on January 29.
1976	Graduates from Tennessee State University.
1984	Moves to Chicago to take over the ailing talk show, *A.M. Chicago*.
1985	*A.M. Chicago* becomes *The Oprah Winfrey Show*; makes acting debut in *The Color Purple*.
1991	Lobbies for federal child protection legislation; the "Oprah Bill" is signed into law by President Clinton in 1993.
1996	Starts Oprah's Book Club.
2000	Launches *O, The Oprah Magazine*.

INFLUENCES AND INSPIRATION

Winfrey frequently credits her father, Vernon Winfrey, as being the strongest influence in her life. Little is known about Vernon Winfrey's personal life except that at age 21, while on leave from military duty, he fathered Oprah but did not know about his daughter until some time later. Although Winfrey's parents did not stay together, she was sent to live with her father at the age of 13 when she ran away from home. Seeing that his daughter was heading down the wrong path, Vernon Winfrey imposed a strict discipline that transformed her life. Providing her with rules, and structure, he required that she read a book a week and write a report on it and that she learn five new vocabulary words every day. Vernon instilled in Winfrey a sense of character, responsibility, and purpose, as well as a passion for reading that Winfrey later brought to wide attention with her book club. Winfrey commented that her father was always concerned that she made the best of her life and expected nothing less "than what he thought was my best."

---

as a reporter and coanchor. In 1978 she became the cohost of the station's *People are Talking* show, and six years later left Baltimore to work for WLS–TV in Chicago, Illinois.

Hired as the anchor of *A.M. Chicago*, a morning talk program with the station's lowest ratings, she transformed the show in just one month by changing its focus to current and often controversial topics. Within three months the show out-ranked the popular *Phil Donahue Show*: in September 1985 it was renamed *The Oprah Winfrey Show*. A year later it made its national debut and became the third most popular show in syndication with 10 million daily viewers in 192 cities. This was largely because of Winfrey's unique, empowering communication style, one that blended public and private to reveal personal intimacies and attract a die-hard female following that felt they were watching a close friend and not a talk-show host.

The show's prodigious success soon brought Winfrey other opportunities. After seeing her on TV for the first time in 1985, Quincy Jones cast Winfrey in *The Color Purple*, a film he was producing with Steven Spielberg. Based on Alice Walker's novel of the same name, the film was Winfrey's acting debut. She received critical praise and an Academy Award nomination for her performance. Emboldened by this success Winfrey soon formed Harpo, her own production company, to bring to life stories written by black authors.

As *The Oprah Winfrey Show* continued to grow in popularity, to consistently outperform every other syndicated show in TV history, and to earn revenues of $300 million per year, Winfrey further diversified her business. In 1998 she became a partner in Oxygen Media, a cable TV station aimed at women. In 2000 she launched *O*, a lifestyle magazine for women. Although most successful magazines take five years to generate a profit, *O* developed a base of 2.5 million readers and posted a revenue of $140 million in just one year, making it the most successful debut magazine in the industry.

Giving back

Winfrey has used her success to make things better for other people. Motivated by the case of a four-year-old girl who was molested and murdered in Chicago, Winfrey used her popularity to campaign for federal child protection legislation designed to keep nationwide records on convicted abusers. Signed into law by President Clinton in 1993, the "Oprah Bill," as it became known, allows child-care providers to check the backgrounds of prospective employees.

In 1996 Winfrey embarked on one of her most successful projects, promoting literacy by forming an on-air reading club. Oprah's Book Club boosted book sales dramatically, frequently turning the books that she selected into instant bestsellers and bringing fame to authors who had often languished in obscurity.

Oprah's Angel Network, started a year after the book club to help raise money for college students in financial need, raised $3.5 million in its first year. In addition to these personal, philanthropic projects, Winfrey has made generous contributions to Morehouse College, the Harold Washington Library, and the United Negro College Fund, and funded the building of a girls' school in South Africa.

See also: Jones, Quincy; Walker, Alice

Further reading: Winfrey, Oprah, with Bill Adler. *The Uncommon Wisdom of Oprah Winfrey: A Portrait in Her Own Words*. New York, NY: Carol Publishing Corporation, 1997. http://www.oprah.com (Official site).

WINKFIELD, Jimmy
Jockey

Jimmy Winkfield was, in the early years of the 20th century, one of the most renowned horse jockeys in the United States before moving to Europe in 1904. One of only four jockeys to win back-to-back Kentucky Derbys, Winkfield enjoyed enormous success and popularity in both America and Europe.

Early life

Born in Chilesburg, Kentucky, on April 2, 1880, Winkfield was drawn from an early age to the rich horse-racing tradition in his native state of Kentucky. He worked in stables as a boy exercising horses, and was eventually able to race in 1898. He was a talented jockey: Within two years he finished third in his first Kentucky Derby, before

▼ **Despite his race, Jimmy Winkfield managed to reach the top of his field.**

KEY DATES	
1880	Born in Chilesburg, Kentucky, on April 12.
1901	Wins first of two consecutive Kentucky Derbys.
1904	Leaves the United States to race in Europe and Russia; becomes the Russian national riding champion that year.
1974	Dies in Maisons-Laffitte, France, on March 23.

winning the race for two consecutive years and finishing second in 1903, an outstanding record in such a prestigious race.

A change in circumstances

Winkfield and other African American jockeys were threatened by white supremacists and white jockeys vying for first place. In 1904 Winkfield left the United States; he never raced in his native country again.

Winkfield went first to Russia, where he was an immediate sensation. He won the All-Russian Derby and the Czar's Prize in 1904, the first of dozens of prizes he would take in Russia and Europe. He gained considerable wealth, married a Russian heiress, and lived a privileged life in Moscow until the Russian Revolution in 1917 forced Winkfield, along with the entire aristocratic racing community, south to Odessa. The following year, as the revolutionary Red Army approached Odessa, Winkfield led several trainers, jockeys, and owners, along with 200 thoroughbreds, overland to Poland, a hazardous journey that the group survived only by eating horse flesh.

By 1920 Winkfield had moved to Paris, France, where he continued to race: He had more than 2,500 lifetime wins in America and abroad. Winkfield retired from riding in 1930, turning his hand to breeding and training. The last time he visited the United States was in 1961, when he and his daughter went to a ceremony at the Kentucky Derby to honor former jockeys. The Winkfields were not allowed to enter the front door of the banquet room. He died in 1974.

Further reading: Hotaling, Edward. *Wink: The Incredible Life and Epic Journey of Jimmy Winkfield.* New York, NY: McGraw Hill, 2004.
http://www.racingmuseum.org/hall/nrm-hall.asp?varPage=19 (House resolution honoring Winkfield).

WONDER, Stevie
Musician, Composer, Activist

Music legend Stevie Wonder has had a long and distinguished career. Apart from his chart hits, his music has been enormously influential and continues to be sampled by artists such as the Wu-Tang Clan and Tupac Shakur. Wonder has collaborated with many of the big names in the music business, including Paul McCartney. He has also scored films, including Spike Lee's *Jungle Fever.*

Early life
Born in Saginaw, Michigan, on May 13, 1950, Steveland Judkins was the son of Lula Mae Hardaway and Calvin Judkins. Wonder, who was renamed by Clarence Paul when he was 10 (*see box*), was born premature and spent the first six weeks of his life in an incubator. His low birth

▼ *Stevie Wonder has dedicated many songs to people who have influenced him and to people he has loved: "Isn't She Lovely?" is about his daughter, Aisha.*

weight and poor health resulted in his loss of sight. The Judkins moved to Detroit, Michigan, when Wonder was a baby and his parents separated shortly afterward. He was brought up by his mother in Detroit's Brewster Housing Projects.

From a very young age Wonder showed a unique aptitude for music. By age eight he could imitate singers whom he heard on the radio and could play the piano and harmonica without having received any formal training. He sang in the Whitestone Baptist Church and busked on the streets.

A musical prodigy
At age 10 Wonder was introduced to Berry Gordy, the owner of Motown Records, by Ronnie White of Smokey Robinson and the Miracles; White's brother was a friend of the young boy. Gordy recognized Wonder's talent and signed him to Motown in 1961. He put the musician,

INFLUENCES AND INSPIRATION

Stevie Wonder was influenced by a wide range of artists, including Sam Cooke, Ray Charles (to whom he dedicated *A Tribute to Uncle Ray*), Duke Ellington ("Sir Duke"), and Bob Marley ("Jamming") but Wonder owes his name and early career to his mentor, Clarence Paul.

In 1961, after Wonder was signed by Berry Gordy, the head of the Detroit-based black label Motown, he was introduced to Paul, a staff producer and songwriter at the label. Paul

became Wonder's mentor and producer and treated the young boy like a son. He renamed him "Wonder," after saying "We can't keep introducing him as the eighth wonder of the world."

Paul himself was a singer and songwriter. Influenced by gospel and big band music, he taught the young Wonder vocal techniques. He produced Wonder's first hit "Thank You (for Loving Me All the Way)" (1962), and wrote several of Wonder's hits, such as "Fingertips—Part 2,"

"Hey Love," and "I'm Wonderin'." Paul also convinced Motown to release Wonder's version of Bob Dylan's song, "Blowin' in the Wind," which was a rhythm-and-blues No. 1 and a No. 9 pop hit in 1966. Paul also wrote songs for other artists at Motown, including Marvin Gaye and Mary Wells, and he nurtured young talent. The two men remained close throughout Wonder's career. When Paul died in 1995, Wonder was at his side.

producer, and songwriter Clarence Paul in charge of the young boy. Paul renamed him Little Stevie Wonder and produced some of Wonder's major hits. Two years later Wonder released the instrumental album *The Jazz Soul of Little Stevie Wonder* and also *A Tribute to Uncle Ray* (Ray Charles).

Part of Wonder's success lay in his remarkable, often improvised performances. His first No.1 single, "Fingertips—Part 2" was a live recording that showcases his improvisational skill. The album from which it was released, *The 12 Year Old Genius*, went to No. 1 on the charts. His career was placed on hold until his voice broke, but in 1965 Wonder re-emerged and continued to build his career, with hits such as a cover of Bob Dylan's "Blowin' in the Wind" and "I Was Made to Love Her."

The summer of 1967 saw race riots in various cities, including New York, Chicago, and Detroit. Wonder became increasingly politicized, and Martin Luther King, Jr.'s, assassination in 1968 led him to participate directly in the civil rights movement, playing at benefits organized by rights organizations such as the Southern Christian Leadership Conference (SCLC).

Musically, Wonder could do very little wrong, with hits such as "My Cherie Amour" and "Signed, Sealed, Delivered, I'm Yours." In 1971 Wonder's Motown contract expired and he negotiated a new deal in which he had complete artistic control over his music and held the music rights in his own company, Black Bull Music. Over the next years Wonder produced several groundbreaking albums, including *Music of My Mind* and *Talking Book* (both 1972), *Songs in the Key of Life* (1976), and *Hotter than July* (1980), which featured "Happy Birthday," a tribute to Martin Luther King, Jr., and "Jamming," a tribute to Bob Marley.

The recipient of many awards, including several Grammys, Wonder was inducted into the Rock and Roll Hall of Fame in 1989. In 1995 he released the album *Conversation Peace* and in 2005 he released his first new album in 10 years, *A Time 2 Love*.

KEY DATES	
1950	Born in Saginaw, Michigan, on May 13.
1961	Signs to Berry Gordy's Motown label.
1963	Releases *The Jazz Soul of Little Stevie Wonder* and *A Tribute to Uncle Ray*.
1971	Records *Where I'm Coming From*; contract with Motown ends.
1976	Releases *Songs in the Key of Life*.
1989	Inducted into the Rock and Roll Hall of Fame.
1995	Releases Grammy-winning album, *Conversation Peace*.

See also: Cooke, Sam; Charles, Ray; Ellington, Duke; Gordy, Berry; King, Martin Luther, Jr.; Robinson, Smokey; Shakur, Tupac

Further reading: Troupe, Quincy. *Little Stevie Wonder*. New York, NY: Harcourt Mifflin, 2005.
http://www.stevie-wonder.com/ (Official site).

WOODARD, Alfre
Actor, Producer

▲ *Alfre Woodard has played many diverse roles, from an aide to a disabled woman in the movie* **Passion Fish** *to a police woman in the* **The Forgotten.**

Alfre Woodard is a successful, award-winning movie and television actor and film producer. She was named one of the Most Beautiful People in America by *People* magazine. Woodard, who has appeared in such films as *Passion Fish* (1992), *The Singing Detective* (2003), and *The Forgotten* (2004), is known to many audiences as Betty Applewhite in the hit TV-show *Desperate Housewives*.

Born the youngest of three children in Tulsa, Oklahoma, on November 8, 1952, Woodard was named by her godmother, who reportedly said that she saw a vision of the name "Alfre" written in gold letters. At high school Woodard excelled as a track star. Her introduction to acting came after a nun persuaded her to audition for a school play. Woodard went on to attend Boston University, Massachusetts, then made her professional theater debut in 1974 with Washington, D.C.'s, Arena Stage.

Making a name
Woodard spent some time on Broadway before moving to Los Angeles, California, where she got her first big break in *Remember My Name* (1978) alongside actor Jeff Goldblum. She was nominated for an Academy Award for her performance in *Cross Creek* (1983), and went on to excel in many unconventional roles. After a memorable appearance in *Miss Firecracker* (1989), Woodard appeared in *Grand Canyon* (1991) and *Passion Fish* (1992), for which she won a Golden Globe nomination. *Rich in Love* (1993), *Crooklyn* (1994), and *Down in the Delta* (1998), which she also coproduced, were among Woodard's other notable film appearances.

Achieving recognition
Woodard continued to show her versatility in a number of well-regarded television roles, winning Emmys for her recurring roles on *Hill Street Blues* (1984) and *L.A. Law* (1987), and an ACE award for the made-for-cable series *Mandela* (1987). She also won an Emmy nomination and a Screen Actors Guild Best Actress Award for her performance in the *The Piano Lesson* (1995). She later won an Emmy, a Golden Globe, and a SAG Award for her performance in *Miss Evers' Boys* (1997): Woodard played a nurse who treated many of the subjects of the infamous 1930s Tuskegee Study of Untreated Blacks with Syphilis. Woodard won another Emmy for *The Practice* in 2003. She also won a role in the acclaimed series *Desperate*

Housewives (2005). Although the creators were originally looking for a white actor, Woodard persuaded them otherwise. She has also appeared in the movies *Something New* and *Take the Lead* (both 2006).

KEY DATES	
1952	Born in Tulsa, Oklahoma, on November 8.
1983	Receives an Academy Award nomination for her role in *Cross Creek*.
1992	Nominated for a Golden Globe for *Passion Fish*.
1997	Wins several major TV awards for her role as a nurse in *Miss Evers' Boys*.
2005	Stars as Betty Applewhite on the hit TV show *Desperate Housewives*.

Further reading: http://www.tv.com/paul-winfield/person/1647/biography.html (Winfield biography on TV.com)
http://www.imdb.com/name/nm0005569/ (Biography).

WOODS, Granville T.
Inventor

One of the most prolific inventors of the late 19th century, Granville T. Woods was granted at least 45 patents during his lifetime, mostly in the fields of railroad technology and telecommunication systems. Woods and his inventions became so famous that he was sometimes referred to as the "Black Edison," after Thomas Alva Edison (1847–1931), the famous white inventor.

Early life
Born in Columbus, Ohio on April 23, 1856, Woods is believed to have been the son of Tailer and Martha Woods. He left school at age 10 and became an apprentice in a workshop repairing railroad machinery.

Wright was passionate about steam locomotives, and used part of his wages to pay colleagues to teach him about railroad engineering. Numerous new railroads were being built across the United States, and ambitious young engineers everywhere were vying to come up with new ways to improve their efficiency and safety.

Becoming the Black Edison
From 1872 Wright took up various engineering jobs in the railroad industry. Although he was quickly promoted because of his ingenuity and hard work, he repeatedly found that more senior positions were barred to him because of his skin color. Finally Woods decided that his best option was to set up his own business. He and his brother Lyates set up a workshop in Cincinnati, Ohio, in 1880, the beginnings of what would eventually become the Woods Electrical Company in 1887. They developed and made locomotion machinery and built communications equipment.

Wright registered his first patent, for an improved steam boiler furnace, in 1884. Over the following decades numerous other patented inventions followed. In 1887, for example, he patented the "Synchronous Multiplex Railway Telegraph," which helped prevent accidents by allowing

▲ *Granville T. Woods invented the "third rail" that carries power to electric-powered trains.*

moving trains to communicate with each other. Woods also developed technology for the electric railroad and played an important role in the development of elevated and underground transit systems in major U.S. cities.

Woods's high profile led to challenges from other inventors. Edison sued him twice, claiming that Woods had stolen his ideas. Woods won both cases in court and eventually Edison tried to woo him with the offer of a job in his company. Woods refused, preferring to remain independent. However, Woods found himself marginalized in what was becoming an increasingly segregated society, and his business declined, closing in 1893. Woods died impoverished on January 30, 1910, in New York City. In 2004 New York City Transit issued four million MetroCards commemorating Woods.

Further reading: Fouche, Lewis. *Black Inventors in the Age of Segregation: Granville T. Woods, Lewis H. Latimer, and Shelby J. Davidson.* Baltimore, ML: The John Hopkins Press, 2003.
www.enquirer.com/editions/1997/02/14/loc_blackhistory.html
(Biography)

KEY DATES	
1856	Born in Columbus, Ohio, on April 23.
1887	Founds the Woods Electrical Company.; patents the Synchronous Multiplex Railway Telegraph.
1910	Dies in New York City on January 30.

WOODS, Tiger
Golfer

Tiger Woods is one of the greatest golfers of modern times, and possibly of all time. Woods, who is of mixed black, white, Native American, and Asian origin, has broken down racial barriers in what was seen as a predominantly white sport, making it possible for players from ethnic minorities to be taken seriously.

Early life

Eldrick Woods, nicknamed "Tiger" after an army friend of his father's, was born in Cyprus, California, on December 30, 1975. His father, Lieutenant Colonel Earl Woods, was a Vietnam War veteran who met Woods's mother, Kultida Punsawad, an Army secretary of mixed Thai and Chinese origin, while he was stationed in Vietnam. Earl Woods started teaching his son golf at age three, making every effort to instill in the child a liking for the sport.

Several black Americans had become prominent in golf, including John Shippen, the first black golf professional; dentist George Grant, who patented the first golf tee; and tennis player Althea Gibson, who played the sport after she retired from tennis. In general, however, golf was seen as a white sport. This did not put off either Earl or his son, who showed a remarkable talent from an early age. He was featured in *Golf Digest* when he was five and at age eight won the Optimist International Junior Championship. He repeated this win at age 9, 12, 13, 14, and 15.

In 1991 Woods became the youngest U.S. Junior Amateur Champion in golf history. In 1994, the year he graduated from high school, Woods became the youngest person to win the U.S. Amateur Championship. Later that year he went to Stanford University on a golf scholarship, but majored in economics. By his sophomore year Woods had won three U.S. Amateur Championships and was winning tournaments all over the country. He dropped out of college in 1996 to turn professional.

A professional career

From the start Woods dominated the game. He won his first major title in 1997, the Masters at the Augusta National Golf Club, winning by 12 strokes, the widest ever margin of victory in the tournament. Woods continued to win major tournaments, easily beating established pros. By September 2005 Woods had won 10 major championships:

▼ *Tiger Woods is one of golf's greatest ambassadors; his foundation makes it possible for young people from all backgrounds to play the sport.*

KEY DATES	
1975	Born in Cypress, California, on December 30.
1984	Wins Optimist International Junior Championship.
1994	Becomes the youngest player to win a U.S. Amateur Championship; enrolls at Stanford University on a golf scholarship.
1996	Turns professional.
1997	Wins the Masters at the Augusta National Golf Club.
2001	Becomes the first person to have won all the major modern golf championships at the same time.
2004	Marries model Elin Norgren.

INFLUENCES AND INSPIRATION

While most African Americans celebrated the fact that a black player had reached the top of the predominantly white golf profession, Woods offended some of them when he stated that he was not purely black. His father, Earl Woods, is of mixed black, Native American, and white ancestry, while his mother, Kutilda, is half Thai and half Chinese. Kutilda made sure that her son was aware of his non-African heritage, taking him to Thailand when he was a child.

On an Oprah Winfrey show, Woods said that as a child he had invented the term "Cablinasian" to describe himself—Caucasian, black, Indian, and Asian. He said, "I'm just who I am, whoever you see in front of you."

Woods's remarks offended some black people. In 1997, however, some members of Congress put forward the "Tiger Woods Bill" to change the classifications on the Census to include a "multiracial" category. As a compromise the administration provided respondents with a "check all that apply" category.

the Masters in 1997, 2001, 2002, and 2005; the British Open in 2000 and 2005; the U.S. Open in 2000 and 2002; and the PGA (Professional Golfers' Association) Championship in 1999 and 2000. The year 2000 was the best of Woods's career so far: He won 11 tournaments, including the U.S. Open, the British Open, and the PGA Championship, becoming the first person to do so in the same year. When he won the Masters again Woods became the first player to hold all the four major titles of modern golf at the same time.

As one of the most successful golfers of his time, Woods became a national celebrity. His victories also brought him considerable financial wealth: In 2002, for example, he was the PGA's leading money winner for the fourth year running with $6,912,625.

Woods has won numerous honors: He was selected as PGA Tour Player of the Year in 1997, 1999, 2000, 2001, 2002, and 2003; Associated Press named him Male Athlete of the Year in 1997, 1999, and 2000; *Sports Illustrated* chose him as Sportsman of the Year in 1996 and 2000; and the World Sports Academy selected him as World Sportsman of the Year in 1999 and 2000.

Criticism

With such success it is perhaps inevitable that Woods has attracted criticism. Early in his career some people were dissatisfied that he had abandoned his studies in order to pursue money, arguing that he served as a poor model for America's youth.

Woods's race and his attitude toward it have also caused controversy. Some members of the golfing establishment did not welcome the prospect of a black American dominating the sport that had been traditionally the domain of affluent white people. In addition some African Americans were upset by the fact that Woods

refused to be classified as an African American (*see box*). He was also criticized by some of the black community when he married Swedish model Elin Norgren at the Sandy Lane Hotel in Barbados on October 5, 2004.

Within the game, Woods has upset fellow golfers because of his negative stance toward the admittance of female players into the PGA. He was also reticent about repealing the male-only membership rule at Augusta, an attitude that some young golfers criticize as old fashioned and surprising.

A generous man

Woods has been very generous with his wealth, establishing several charitable foundations. Influenced by the South African activist Nelson Mandela, who urged Woods to do something good with his celebrity, in 1996 the golfer established the Tiger Woods Foundation (TWF). It provides scholarships, grants, and golf clinics for youngsters and has various off-shoot organizations. Start Something encourages 8- to 17-year-olds to work toward a specific aim or dream. The Tiger Woods Learning Center (TWLC), located in Anaheim, California, provides all kinds of education programs for children. Each year celebrities take part in Tiger Jam, a fund-raising concert that raises millions of dollars for charity, and professional golfers take part in the Target World Challenge to raise money for the foundation.

See also: Gibson, Althea; Grant, George

Further reading: Callahan, Tom. *In Search of Tiger.* New York, NY: Random House, 2003.
http://www.tigerwoods.com/splash/splash.sps (Official site).
http://www.twfound.org/ (Tiger Woods Foundation site).

WOODSON, Carter G.
Academic, Intellectual

Known as the "Father of Negro History," Carter G. Woodson is almost solely responsible for founding the academic discipline of black studies. Woodson insisted that people of African descent were not only worthy of study, but that they had a great history and were vital to the development of the United States.

Early life
Born in New Canton, Virginia, on December 19, 1875, Carter Godwin Woodson was the son of James Henry Woodson and Anne Eliza Riddle. Woodson's parents were former slaves and were poor and illiterate sharecroppers, but they taught their nine children to respect themselves and to insist on respect from others. Although Woodson desperately wanted to get an education, he had little formal schooling since he had to help his family.

The importance of education
At age 17 Woodson left home to work in coal mines to earn money to attend high school in West Virginia. He graduated from high school at age 22 and went on to study at West Virginia's Berea College, graduating in 1900. After several years of teaching, both in West Virginia and in the Philippines, Woodson resumed his studies. In 1908 he earned an MA in history from the University of Chicago, and in 1912 he became only the second black person to earn a doctorate from Harvard.

Woodson devoted his career to studying and documenting the contributions of Africans and black Americans to world civilization. He firmly believed that black Americans needed to learn about and celebrate

▲ **Carter G. Woodson, photographed here in the 1910s, initiated Negro History Week, the precursor of today's Black History Month.**

their own past in order to build race pride and be useful citizens. When Woodson began his teaching and research career in 1909, however, few people saw black studies as a legitimate area of study. There were almost no outlets for scholars to publish work in this area.

Woodson set out to change that: In 1915 he founded the Association for the Study of Negro Life and History, an organization devoted to black studies. A year later he began publishing the *Journal of Negro History*; he served as its editor for 35 years. Woodson wrote 18 books and published hundreds of articles and book reviews. *The Negro in Our History* (1922) and *The Mis-Education of the Negro* (1933) urged black people to take pride in their African heritage. Woodson died in 1950, but his legacy lives on in such events as Black History Month.

Further reading: Goggin, Jacqueline. *Carter G. Woodson: A Life in Black History.* Baton Rouge, LA: Louisiana State University Press, 1997.
http://www.africawithin.com/woodson/woodson_bio2.htm (Biography).

KEY DATES

1875 Born in New Canton, Virginia, on December 19.

1915 Founds the Association for the Study of Negro Life and History (now known as the Association for the Study of Afro-American Life and History).

1916 Founds the first scholarly journal devoted to black studies, the *Journal of Negro History*.

1926 Begins Negro History Week in February to bring national attention to the contributions of black people thoughout American history.

1950 Dies in Washington, D.C., on April 3.

WOODSON, Robert L.
Community Activist

Founder of the National Center for Neighborhood Enterprise (NCNE), Robert L. "Bob" Woodson, Sr., has helped empower numerous African American neighborhood-based organizations.

Early life
Born in Philadelphia, Pennsylvania, on April 8, 1937, Woodson was raised in a poor district of the city. After the death of his father in 1946 he became estranged from his mother; he dropped out of high school at 17 and joined the Air Force. After leaving the service he studied mathematics at Cheyney University, Pennsylvania, and on graduating began work in a juvenile jail. His experiences and observations there inspired him to take a masters degree in social work at the University of Pennsylvania.

Civil rights
In the 1960s Woodson became a civil rights activist, using his experience to help develop community programs locally and nationally; in the 1970s he worked in the administration of Justice Division of the National

▼ *Robert L. Woodson is sometimes referred to as the godfather of the movement to empower neighborhood civil organizations.*

KEY DATES

1937	Born in Philadelphia, Pennsylvania, on April 8.
1954	Joins the Air Force.
1981	Founds the NCNE.
1990	Awarded a fellowship by the MacArthur Foundation.

Urban League (NUL) and was a resident fellow at the American Enterprise Institute. Woodson became frustrated with working for the organization, which he regarded as hogtied by bureaucracy and overly theoretical in its approach. He left it in 1981 to take practical action of his own.

The NCNE
Woodson founded the NCNE, which originally worked with community and faith-based organizations to combat a whole range of social problems from youth violence, drug abuse, teenage pregnancy, and homelessness to unemployment, poor education, and deteriorating neighborhoods. One of the NCNE's early successes was the creation of the House of Umoja, a violence-free zone that greatly reduced gang warfare in Woodson's native Philadelphia. The project was later used as a model for a similar initiatives in Atlanta, Georgia; Baltimore, Maryland; Dallas, Texas; Milwaukee, Wisconsin; and in the Benning Terrace neighborhood of Washington, D.C. The NCNE now has a major input into the formulation of public policy.

Woodson has written several books, including *The Triumphs of Joseph: How Today's Community Healers are Reviving Our Streets and Neighborhoods* (1998). He worked as a consultant for the 104th Congress and for grassroots organizations all over the world. Woodson lives in Silver Spring, Maryland.

See also: National Organizations

Further reading: Woodson, Robert L. *The Triumphs of Joseph: How Today's Community Healers are Reviving Our Streets and Neighborhoods.* New York, NY: The Free Press, 1998.
http://www.ncne.com/showpage.cfm?category_id=3&showpage=1 (Biography).

WORK, Monroe Nathan
Scholar

Scholar Monroe Nathan Work is best known for his 1928 book *A Bibliography of the Negro in Africa and America*, a comprehensive list of some 17,000 books and other materials relating to African and African American history and culture that is still widely used by researchers today. Like his contemporary and fellow book lover Arthur Schomburg, Work helped create a body of material that celebrated the heritage of black Americans.

Early life
The son of former slaves, Work was born in 1866. He grew up first in Cairo, Illinois, and then Summer County, Kansas. He was fond of learning, but after completing his elementary education left school to help on his father's farm. Work was 23 years old before he was able to continue his education. After graduating from high school in Arkansas City, Work intended to become a minister and enrolled at the Chicago Theological Seminary in Illinois. However, in 1898 his rigorous intellectual curiosity led him to study at the University of Chicago, from which he earned an MA in sociology and psychology in 1903.

The plight of black Americans
In 1903 Work began teaching at the Georgia State Industrial College in Savannah, where he stayed for five years. Work was fascinated by black history and how it had shaped the way African Americans lived in his times. He began to collect books by black writers that had long been forgotten, and called upon black historians to research their race's African past. As a sociologist he wrote about racial discrimination and violence, as well as a groundbreaking essay on black crime.

In 1904 Work attended a series of meetings with W. E. B. DuBois and other leading black intellectuals opposed to Booker T. Washington's accommodationist approach to black advancement. Out of these meetings the Niagara movement was established, the precursor of the National Association for the Advancement of Colored People (NAACP). While supporting the Niagara movement, Work also established the Savannah Men's Sunday Club, a lobbying and civic group that petitioned government on such issues as organizing youth activities and improving black health education. Work became a member of Savannah's black elite; he also married Florence E. Henrson in 1904.

Tuskegee and research
Despite his support for the Niagara movement, in 1908 Work accepted a job at Tuskegee Institute in Alabama, the pioneering black college headed by Booker T. Washington. Working closely with Washington as his researcher and record keeper, Work gradually moved away from the Niagara movement and the idea that protest could achieve change for black Americans. Instead, he advocated education as a way to fight prejudice, believing that ignorance created racism and discrimination.

At Tuskegee Work was at what he called "the center of things relating to the Negro" and he dedicated much of his time to expanding the Department of Records and Research. He compiled and cataloged research materials relating to black life, and from 1912 published the *Negro Yearbook*, an annual listing of contemporary events, organizations, resources, and books. He also compiled *Lynching Reports,* in which he sought to record the racial violence endemic in the South. In 1928 Walker published *A Bibliography of the Negro in Africa and America*, the fruit of his decades-long research and the first bibliography of its kind. In addition Work published more than 70 articles and pamphlets on African American culture and life. He worked at Tuskegee until his death in 1945.

See also: DuBois, W. E. B.; Schomburg, Arturo; Washington, Booker T.

Further reading: McMurray, Linda O. *Recorder of the Black Experience: A Biography of Monroe Nathan Work*. Baton Rouge, LA: Louisiana State University Press, 1985. www.nathanielturner.com/monroenwork.htm (Biography).

WRIGHT, Jeremiah A.
Religious Leader, Activist

Jeremiah A. Wright is the pastor of the Trinity United Church of Christ in Chicago, Illinois. A well-known activist, he began to preach Africentric Christianity, an approach that identifies an African presence in the Bible and teaches followers that there is an African heritage in the context of Christianity. Wright, who was named 15th in *Ebony* magazine's list of top preachers, has campaigned on such issues as tolerance of AIDS sufferers. He has written many articles and books on theological issues.

Early life
Born in Philadelphia, Pennsylvania, on September 22, 1941, Wright was the son of the Reverend Jeremiah Wright and academic and musician Mary Henderson Wright. His parents instilled in him a sense of civic duty and community.

▼ *As senior pastor of the Trinity United Church of Christ, Jeremiah A. Wright has a congregation of more than 8,000 people.*

Educated in the city's public school system, Wright studied for a BA at Howard University, Washington, D.C., and for an MA at the University of Chicago. He received his doctorate in divinity from United Theological College, Dayton, Ohio, where he studied under Samuel DeWitt Proctor, the influential civil rights and religious leader, whose work also inspired Martin Luther King, Jr., and Jesse Jackson.

Reclaiming Christianity
In 1972 Wright was appointed pastor of the Trinity United Church of Christ. Under his direction the church began to operate under the motto "Unashamedly Black and Unapologetically Christian." He wanted to create an environment in which it was possible for members of his congregation to be Christian without having to give up their cultural diversity. Wright went out of his way to make the black community central to the church's activities and focused his preaching on reclaiming Christianity for Africans. He took members of his congregation to Africa, saying that he wanted them to learn that Africa and Christianity had been connected for a long time.

Wright increased the church membership of the Trinity United Church of Christ: In 2005 it comprised more than 8,000 people. Wright also helped establish a fund to aid black seminary students with their tuition. Having struggled financially himself Wright said, "I swore if I ever got to a position to do so, I'd help make things easier on seminary students." The recipient of many awards, Wright is also the spiritual adviser to Senator Barack Obama.

KEY DATES	
1941	Born in Philadelphia, Pennsylvania, on September 22.
1972	Becomes pastor of Chicago's Trinity United Church of Christ, rising to become senior pastor.
1990s	Becomes a spiritual adviser to Senator Barack Obama.

See also: Jackson, Jesse; King, Martin Luther, Jr.; Obama, Barack; Religion and African Americans

Further reading: http://www.tucc.org/pastor.htm (Biography on United Trinity Church of Christ site).

WRIGHT, Richard
Writer

One of the great American writers of the 20th century, Richard Wright is best known for his 1940 novel *Native Son*, the brutal story of a 19-year-old black Chicago man named Bigger Thomas who accidentally kills a white woman, is hunted down, tried, and finally executed. The book marked a milestone in African American literature, and was heralded as both a powerful outburst of black protest and a masterful work of art. Wright had a great influence on the generation of black writers that followed in his wake, including James Baldwin and Ralph Ellison.

A native son

Born near Natchez, Mississippi, on September 8, 1908, Wright was the son of Nathan Wright, an illiterate sharecropper, and Ella Wilson, a schoolteacher. Wright's father deserted the family home when Wright was very young. His mother struggled to support Wright and his brother, but she suffered a stroke when Wright was age 10. Ella and her sons were forced to live with her parents in Jackson, Mississippi. Margaret Wilson, Wright's grandmother, was deeply religious and refused to allow any books in her house except the Bible. Despite this Wright read as much as he could, and he began to write short stories from an early age. Wright's grandmother resented his independent spirit and tried to force it out of him, advocating religion as a way to instill discipline in the young boy. Wright was an atheist for most of his life.

Wright's childhood was marred by poverty, racism, and violence. His uncle was murdered by a lynch mob simply because he was a successful businessman. Nonetheless, Wright did well at school, graduating from Smith Robertson Junior High School as his class valedictorian in 1925. However, Wright quickly dropped out of senior high school and went out to work. He later wrote about his childhood in another of his bestselling books, *Black Boy* (1945).

With few prospects in his hometown, Wright joined the many impoverished African Americans then migrating northward, and in 1927, at age 19, he settled in Chicago. There he worked as a post office clerk and hospital orderly while continuing to read widely (*see box*). In 1932 Wright joined the Communist Party; he saw it as fighting to improve the lives of ordinary working people, both black and white. He continued to write, publishing

▲ *After Richard Wright moved to France, his work was largely overlooked in America until the 1960s, when civil rights activists recognized its importance.*

his first story, "Superstition," in *Abbott's Monthly Magazine*; he also worked as a journalist for radical magazines. He became impatient with the attempts of the Communist Party to direct what and how he should write.

An independent career

In 1937 Wright decided to move to New York City to pursue an independent literary career. He rapidly established himself as an important new figure in black literature, befriending other black writers, including Ralph Ellison, James Baldwin, and Gwendolyn Brooks. He was the Harlem correspondent of the communist paper the *Daily Worker*, before he joined the New York Writers' Project. In the following year his career began to take off when he won a national competition of Works Progress Administration writers for the collection of short stories, *Uncle Tom's Children* (1938).

In 1940 Wright published *Native Son*, a novel born of his determination to write something "so hard and deep that [readers] would have to face it without the consolation of tears." Wright was able to complete it with the aid of a Guggenheim Fellowship. The book was an instant bestseller, making Wright not only the best known

---

INFLUENCES AND INSPIRATION

Richard Wright was a voracious reader. Prominent among the books he read as a young man were the established classics of white American literature. Wright was especially inspired by the novels of "naturalist" writers such as Theodore Dreiser (1871–1945). The naturalists sought to show how individuals and their actions were shaped by heredity and environment, and were often accused of over-emphasizing the seamier aspects of American life in their work. Dreiser's *American Tragedy* (1925)—the story of a white man who accidentally kills his pregnant girlfriend and is executed for her murder—was a direct influence on *Native Son*.

Wright paid scant attention to early black writers, however, despite the existence of a rich tradition of African American literature. In a 1937 essay titled "Blueprint for Negro Writing," Wright described his African American literary predecessors as "prim and decorous ambassadors who went a-begging to white America." He said that their "humble" works failed either to portray or challenge the racism and violence faced by ordinary African Americans. In the essay Wright signaled his determination to set up a new model of what black literature should be—one that allowed the black writer "the maximum degree of freedom in thought and feeling." Wright believed that such literature, like that of the naturalists, should give an unflinching portrayal of black American life and challenge readers' perceptions in order to bring about change.

---

but the wealthiest black writer in the United States. A powerful exposure of the realities of white racism in contemporary America, *Native Son* suggested that Biggar's crimes were inevitable in a society that refused to recognize his humanity and were an apocalyptic warning of the violence that would engulf the United States if things did not change. Many African Americans felt uneasy with the novel's bleak portrayal of black urban life, however, especially its emphasis on race hatred.

The writer in exile

In 1941 Wright married Ellen Poplar, a white fellow member of the Communist Party, and the couple began to raise a family. Despite the success of *Native Son* and the autobiographical *Black Boy* (1945), which sold half a million copies, Wright increasingly felt that the United States no longer offered him or his family a future. In 1947 he decided to settle permanently in Paris, France, where he hoped they would live free from racism. By then a writer of international standing, Wright was lionized by the leading French writers of the day, including Jean-Paul Sartre, and found himself at the center of a community of expatriate African American writers that included, at various times, Ellison, Baldwin, and Chester Himes.

Wright continued to write, publishing such books as *The Outsider* (1953) and *Savage Holiday* (1954), but none of these works attracted the acclaim of *Native Son* or *Black Boy* in the United States. Some critics even suggested that the "exiled" Wright had lost contact with the realities of U.S. race relations.

Wright traveled widely in Africa, Asia, and Europe, and wrote about the problems facing nonwhite peoples all over the world as their countries ceased to be European colonies. His activities attracted the interest of the CIA, and some commentators believe that Wright was investigated for being involved in communist activities. In 1960 Wright died suddenly, apparently of a heart attack. After his death, his wife published more of his works, including *Eight Men* (1961), a collection of short stories, and a further volume of autobiography. During the 1960s many activists praised Wright's work for bringing out into the open the hatred, fear, and violence that crippled U.S. culture.

See also: Baldwin, James; Brooks, Gwendolyn; Ellison, Ralph; Himes, Chester

Further reading: Fabre, Michel. *The Unfinished Quest of Richard Wright*. New York, NY: Morrow, 1973.
www.olemiss.edu/depts/english/ms-writers/dir/wright_richard/ (Biography, including useful bibliography).

KEY DATES

1908	Born near Natchez, Mississippi, on September 8.
1940	Publishes *Native Son*.
1945	Publishes *Black Boy*.
1947	Settles in Paris, France.
1960	Dies in Paris, France, on November 28.

WYATT, Addie L.
Labor Leader, Civil Rights Activist

Addie L. Wyatt is a well-respected civil and labor activist. A close friend and associate of Martin Luther King, Jr., Wyatt together with her husband Claude Wyatt, Jr., worked with King and Jesse Jackson in the early 1960s on Operation Breadbasket. Addie L. and Claude Wyatt are copastors of the Vernon Park Church of God in Chicago, Illinois.

Early life
Born in Brookhaven, Mississippi, on March 8, 1924, Wyatt was the oldest girl of eight children. She attended church from an early age and became a fearless public speaker. From her mother, Maggie Cameron, the church, and her community, Wyatt learned the importance of human dignity and equality. In 1940 she married Claude Wyatt, Jr.

A labor unionist and civil rights activist
In 1941 Wyatt began working in meatpacking plants, where she joined the Amalgamated Meat Cutters and Butcher Workmen of North America. Wyatt quickly became known as a strident labor activist, campaigning for better rights for minority groups. In 1953 she became the vice president of the United Packinghouse and Food and Alliance Workers Union Local 26, a position in which she remained until 1984. In 1955 she was ordained and went on to preach at the Vernon Park Church of God.

In the early 1950s the Wyatts became involved in the Chicago Freedom movement, working closely with Martin Luther King, Jr. Wyatt was one of the few women on the Action Committee that organized protests and demonstrations for the civil rights movement. In 1962 Wyatt also helped found Operation Breadbasket along with

▲ **Addie L. Wyatt was one of the most important U.S. female labor leaders of the 20th century.**

Jesse Jackson, whom she later worked with in his activist organization the Rainbow/PUSH Coalition. In the early 1960s Wyatt served on the Labor Legislation Committee of the Commission on the Status of Women. She was a founding member of the National Organization for Women in 1966.

Wyatt has received many honors and awards. In 1975 *Time* magazine featured Wyatt on its cover as Woman of the Year. From 1980 to 1984 Wyatt also appeared in *Ebony* magazine's top 100 most influential black Americans' list.

See also: Civil Rights; Jackson, Jesse; King, Martin Luther, Jr.

Further reading: http://www.cfm40.org/node/215 (Biography).

KEY DATES	
1924	Born in Brookhaven, Mississippi, on March 8.
1941	Joins the Amalgamated Meat Cutters and Butcher Workmen of North America.
1956	Begins working with Martin Luther King, Jr.
1962	Helps establish Operation Breadbasket.
1975	Appears on the cover of *Time* as Woman of the Year.
1980	Named by *Ebony* magazine as one of the 100 most influential black Americans for four years running.

YORK
Slave

The first African American to travel the continent north of Mexico, York was a member of Meriwether Lewis (1774–1809) and William Clark's (1770–1838) expedition to the Pacific Ocean (1804–1806). The slave or "man servant" of Clark, York proved to be an invaluable member of the Corp of Discovery, as the group became known; York's strength, ingenuity, and loyalty often safeguarded the lives of his fellow explorers.

Early life
Born into slavery in Caroline County, Virginia, probably on November 17, 1770, what is known of York's life has been gathered from Clark's journals and letters. Owned by Clark's father, York and Clark, who were roughly about the same age, were childhood companions. York moved with the family to Kentucky in the late 1780s and was bequeathed to Clark by his father.in 1799. Although believed to have been treated better than most slaves, York still suffered beatings at his master's hand. He was also not allowed to live with his wife.

Lewis and Clark
In 1801 Lewis, who was a young Army captain, became the secretary-aide of the soon-to-be-inaugurated president Thomas Jefferson, who asked Lewis to undertake an expedition to explore the western continent. Jefferson appropriated money from Congress to pay for the journey and Lewis invited his friend and former commanding officer, Clark, to be the joint leader.

The Corps of Discovery was made up of nine Kentuckians; it aimed to establish a route from the Mississippi Valley to the Pacific Coast while developing relations with Native Americans. York accompanied Clark as his manservant, first in the training phase at Camp Dubois, Illinois, from December 1803 to May 1804, and then on the two-year expedition itself.

Quickly proving his worth, York helped paddle boats, tend the sick, and hunt for food. He rescued Clark, who had been swept away during a flash flood on the Missouri River near Great Falls. Unlike other slaves, York was allowed to carry a firearm and his opinion was taken into account when key decisions were made by the team.

Native Americans were fascinated by York's color; they initially tried to rub it away with handfuls of dirt. York's spectacular height and muscular build also impressed

KEY DATES	
1770	Born in Caroline County, Virginia, probably on November 17.
1780s	Moves with the Clark family to Kentucky in the late 1780s.
1799	Bequeathed to William Clark by his father.
1803	Begins training with Clark as part of the Corps of Discovery.
1804	Is a member of the two year Corps of Discovery expedition.
1811	Between 1811 and 1815 is granted freedom.
1822	Dies of cholera between 1822 and 1832.

Native Americans, such as the Shoshone, and he was able to help the expedition members to form relationships that might otherwise not have been possible. He was also given the trusted task of trading goods with the native groups. At other times York was reminded of his slave status, however. Clark wrote that he ordered his "black Servent to Dance which amused the Croud verry much [sic]."

Reality
York's return to slavery in 1806 brought home the reality of his situation. While the other explorers were rewarded with double pay and plots of land, York received nothing. He repeatedly petitioned Clark for his freedom, or asked to be sold to the Louisville family who owned his wife, but Clark refused on the grounds that York was still "serviceable to me at this place"; Clark even threatened to hire York to a harsh master to teach him a lesson. Sometime after 1811 York was freed and Clark provided him with the resources to set up a haulage business. It was not successful and it is believed that York died in the cholera epidemic of 1822–1832. His achievements were ignored for many years, but in 2001 a statue of him was erected in Louisville, Kentucky.

Further reading: Betts, Robert B. *In Search of York: The Slave Who Went to the Pacific With Lewis and Clark.* Boulder, CO: University Press of Colorado, 2002.
http://lewisandclarktrail.com/york.htm (Online resource with biography for York).

YOUNG, Andrew Jackson, Jr.
Activist, Politician, Diplomat

Andrew Jackson Young, Jr., was a preacher, civil rights activist, and politician. He served as a leader of the Southern Christian Leadership Conference (SCLC), a U.S. congressman, a U.S. ambassador to the United Nations, and as mayor of Atlanta, Georgia.

Early life
Born in New Orleans, Louisiana, on March 12, 1932, Jackson was the elder of the two sons of Andrew J. Young, a dentist, and Daisy Fuller, a teacher. He and his brother were the only black children in a white, middle-class neighborhood in New Orleans. In 1947 Young graduated from Gilbert Academy, a private high school, and entered Dillard University. Intending to become a dentist, he transferred to Howard University, Washington, D.C., the following year. However, after graduating with a BS degree in 1951, Young decided to enroll in the Hartford Theological Seminary in Connecticut. He completed a divinity degree in 1955, the year in which he was ordained into the United Church of Christ.

Civil rights and politics
A pastor at several black churches in the South, Young became active in the civil rights movement, specifically voter registration drives. His work brought him into contact with Martin Luther King, Jr., and Young became King's administrative assistant, helping lead the SCLC. He served as executive director of the organization in 1964; three years later he became executive vice president. Following King's assassination in 1968, Young worked

▲ **Andrew Jackson Young worked closely with leading civil rights activist Martin Luther King, Jr.**

with Ralph Abernathy, the new president of the SCLC. Young resigned in 1970 to run for Congress but was defeated. He ran again in 1972 and won. Young was reelected in 1974 and 1976.

Young was appointed U.S. ambassador to the UN after Jimmy Carter's 1976 victory in the presidential election. Young focused on the developing countries and caused controversy when it was discovered that he had met with the Palestinian Liberation Organization (PLO), which was believed to sponsor terrorism in Israel. In 1981 several leaders of the black community, including Coretta Scott King, persuaded Young to run in the mayoral elections in Atlanta. He won and was reelected in 1985. He served from January 1982 until January 1990. Young launched an unsuccessful candidacy for governor of Georgia in 1990. In 1999 he was elected to a two-year term of the National Council of Churches. In 2004 Young briefly considered running for the U.S. Senate.

See also: Abernathy, Ralph; Civil Rights; King, Coretta Scott; King, Martin Luther, Jr.; National Organizations

---

Further reading: http://www.infoplease.com/biography/us/congress/young-andrew-jackson-jr.html (Biography).

KEY DATES	
1932	Born in New Orleans, Louisiana, on March 12.
1955	Ordained as a minister in the United Church of Christ.
1962	Becomes administrative assistant to Martin Luther King, Jr.
1972	Becomes the first black congressman from Georgia since Reconstruction.
1977	Appointed by Jimmy Carter as U.S. ambassador to the United Nations.
1981	Becomes mayor of Atlanta, Georgia.

YOUNG, Coleman
Politician

Coleman Young was the first African American to become mayor of a major city. He was a leading voice for a generation of black political leaders during the 1970s.

Early years

Born in Tuscaloosa, Alabama, on May 24, 1918, Coleman Alexander Young was the oldest of five children of William Coleman Young and Ida Reese. In 1923 Young's father moved the family to Detroit. They settled in a racially diverse area of the city called Black Bottom. Although Young received excellent grades at St. Mary's Catholic School, three high schools refused him scholarships because of his color. He eventually attended Eastern High School and graduated second in his class, but racism prevented him from being awarded academic scholarships by two universities. Young attended a technical school briefly before looking for a full-time job.

Fighting for equality

Young began working at the Ford Motor Company, where he became involved in labor issues. During World War II (1939–1945) Young served with the Tuskegee Airmen, the first black flying unit in the U.S. military. Toward the end of his service he was briefly imprisoned for protesting segregation. Returning to Detroit, in 1951 he helped found the National Negro Labor Council, which campaigned for better African American labor rights.

In 1952 Young was called before the House Committee on Un-American Activities, the organization investigating communist activity in the United States. When asked to name associates he suspected of holding communist beliefs, Young said: "I am no stool pigeon. I consider it an un-American activity to pry into a person's private thoughts, to pry into a person's associates. I consider that an un-American activity." Young was subsequently blacklisted by several unions and labor groups. He was forced to take a series of menial jobs in order to survive.

KEY DATES	
1918	Born in Tuscaloosa, Alabama, on May 24.
1973	Elected mayor of Detroit, Michigan; reelected four times.
1997	Dies in Detroit on November 29.

▲ *Coleman Young during his 1977 campaign for reelection as mayor.*

In the 1960s Young turned his attention toward politics. He believed that he could be more effective in fighting discrimination if he held office. In 1961 he was elected to the Michigan Constitutional Convention, and after unsuccessfully running for a seat in the Michigan Senate in 1961 was elected to the House in 1964. Four years later he became the first black member of the Democratic National Committee. He campaigned for integration in the state police force. Following the 1967 Detroit race riots, Young fought hard to bring peace to the city.

In 1973 Young became the first black mayor of Detroit. In that position he revitalized the city, working hard with business, labor, and civic leaders to keep the city from bankruptcy. He brought greater numbers of black people into the police to better represent the city's population and brought in effective law enforcement policies. He also appointed people from ethnic minorities and women to his staff. Reelected an unprecedented four times, Young was particularly popular with black voters, but his outspoken and often controversial views alienated some people. From 1993 he suffered ill health; he died in 1997.

See also: Political Representation

Further reading: Rich, Wilbur C. *Coleman Young and Detroit Politics: From Social Activist to Power Broker.* Detroit, MI: Wayne State University Press, 1999.
http://www.freep.com/news/young/index.htm (Biography).

YOUNG, Lester
Musician

Lester Willis Young was an influential tenor saxophonist of the swing era, who was probably best known for his collaboration with Count Basie. Singer Billie Holiday gave Young the name "Pres" for being president of the tenor saxophone. Young's playing had a soft, velvety tone and was full of cool, melodic improvisations. It was the basis of that of many other musicians ranging from Charlie Parker to white musicians of the "cool" school of jazz such as Stan Getz.

Early life

Born in Woodville, Mississippi, in 1909, Young was the eldest child of Lizetta and Willis Handy Young. Young and his two siblings learned to play several instruments from an early age, performing with their father in a band at carnivals and shows around the country. Young played the violin, trumpet, and drums before finally settling on the alto saxophone as his primary instrument in 1923.

At age 19 Young quit the family band after an argument; he then played tenor sax with Art Bronson's Bostonians. In 1930 Young returned to Minneapolis, where he played with a variety of performers including Frank Hines. Impressed with Young, Hines signed Young as one of the Thirteen Original Blue Devils. In 1933 Young relocated to Kansas City with several of the band's members to play with the Bennie Moten–George E. Lee band, King Oliver, and Fletcher Henderson.

Musical genius

In 1934 Young joined the Count Basie Orchestra, but he left to join Fletcher Henderson's orchestra later that year. Henderson resisted Young's experimental style, however, and Young left just a few months later. Over the next two years he played with Andy Kirk, Boyd Atkins, and Rook

KEY DATES	
1909	Born in Woodville, Mississippi, on August 27.
1934	Joins the Count Basie Orchestra
1936	Makes first recording with Basie, "Oh, Lady Be Good!"
1944	Drafted into military service during World War II.
1959	Dies in New York City on March 15.

▲ *Lester Young played with some of the leading musicians of his day, including Count Basie, Fletcher Henderson, and Billie Holiday.*

Ganz before rejoining Basie in 1936. He made his first recording with Basie, "Oh, Lady Be Good!" later that year. Young became more famous as Basie's popularity increased. During this period Young also collaborated with Billie Holiday on legendary performances like "The Man I Love (1939)" and "All of Me" (1941). While Holiday referred to young as "Pres," Young named the singer "Lady Day."

In the early 1940s Young played in small bands in the Los Angeles area with musicians such as Dizzy Gillespie. In 1944 Young was conscripted into the Army until the end of World War II in 1945, after which he worked as a performer and bandleader and toured with Miles Davis. In the late 1950s Young suffered from depression. In 1957 he was admitted to the hospital for malnutrition and cirrhosis of the liver. He toured again briefly before his death in 1959.

See also: Basie, Count; Davis, Miles; Henderson, Fletcher; Gillespie, Dizzy; Holiday, Billie; Oliver, Joe "King"; Parker, Charlie

Further reading: Daniels, Douglass H. *Lester Leaps In: the Life and Times of Lester "Pres." Young.* Boston, MA: Beacon Press, 2002.
http://www.starpulse.com/Music/Young,_Lester (Biography).

YOUNG, Roger Arliner
Zoologist

In 1940 Roger Arliner Young became the first African American woman to be awarded a PhD in zoology. Like her mentor, the outstanding black scientist Ernest Everett Just, she made important discoveries in the field of marine biology. Her career was hampered by having to care for her invalid mother, by her own mental ill-health, and, above all, by the discrimination and lack of collegiate support faced by many women scientists at the time.

Early life
Young was born in Clifton Forge, Virginia, on May 19, 1899. Her family moved when she was very young, and she grew up in Burgettstown, Pennsylvania. She showed early academic promise, but her family was poor and her mother was often ill.

In 1916 Young began studying at Howard University, in Washington, D.C. Beginning her first scientific studies in 1921, Young initially achieved poor grades but she began to study under the personal tutelage of the head of zoology, Ernest Everett Just, who saw great promise in the young woman. She graduated with a BS degree in 1923.

An influential mentor
Just also helped Young in finding funding for graduate studies at the prestigious University of Chicago. She studied under Frank Lillie, an embryologist who had helped develop the Marine Biological Institute and the Oceanographic Institute at Woods Hole, Massachusetts, one of the leading research establishments in the United States. In 1924 Young published her first research paper, ""On the Excretory Apparatus in Paramecium," in *Science* magazine. Two years later she was awarded a

master's degree in zoology. In 1927 Just invited her to work with him during the summer at the Woods Hole Marine Biological Laboratory.

Triumph and decline
In 1929 Young taught Just's classes while he was traveling; she did this on several occasions. Rumors began to circulate that they were having an affair.

Later that year Young began studying for her doctorate; she failed the qualifying exams in 1930 when she suffered a deep bout of depression. Despite this setback she returned to Howard, where she took up a position as a junior professor. Just had become disillusioned with his former student, meanwhile, and tension between the two grew. Finally, Young was fired in 1936, ostensibly for missing classes and misusing equipment.

Research
Undeterred, Young continued her research, focusing her work on the effects of radiation on sea urchin eggs. She published several notable research papers, and from 1937 to 1940 successfully completed her doctoral studies at the University of Pennsylvania under Lewis Victor Heilbrunn, a general physiologist who was a friend of Just's. Young was the first black woman to gain a doctorate in the field.

Young subsequently taught at various black colleges, including North Carolina College for Negroes and Shaw University, North Carolina, as well as at colleges in Texas, Louisiana, and Mississippi, but poor mental health, along with the lack of opportunities open to women scientists, prevented her from developing her career. In the late 1950s and early 1960s Young spent several years in a state mental asylum. She was discharged in 1962, and took up another teaching post in New Orleans, but lived only another two years. She died destitute in New Orleans in 1965.

See also: Just, Ernest Everett

Further reading: Sullivan, Richard, and James Haskins. *African American Women Scientists and Inventors.* New York, NY: Wiley, 2002.
www.sdsc.edu/ScienceWomen/young.html (Biography)
http://www2.lhric.org/pocantico/womenenc/young.htm (Biography).

KEY DATES	
1899	Born in Clifton Forge, Virginia, on May 19.
1916	Attends Howard University.
1921	Begins to study with Ernest Everett Just.
1923	Receives BS from Howard University.
1940	Becomes the first African American woman to be awarded a PhD in zoology
1964	Dies in New Orleans, Louisiana, on November 9.

YOUNG, Whitney M., Jr.
Civil Rights Activist, Social Worker

Whitney M. Young, Jr., was executive director of the National Urban League (NUL). An influential civil rights activist, Young was awarded the Presidential Medal of Freedom by Lyndon B. Johnson in 1969 for his work in that field.

Early life

Born in Lincoln Ridge, Kentucky, on July 31, 1921, Young was the son of Whitney Moore Young, the president of a private black American college, and Laura Ray, a schoolteacher. He lived until 1936 in a simple two-story wooden house on the campus of the Lincoln Institute of Kentucky, where his father taught.

After attending Kentucky State College, Young joined the Army Specialist Training program. During World War II (1939–1945) he served in an antiaircraft company of African American soldiers commanded by white officers. After just three weeks he was promoted from private to first sergeant, creating hostility among both black and white soldiers. This experience of racism increased Young's interest in civil rights and propelled him into a career in race relations.

Civil rights

In the 1940s Young became president of the National Urban League's Omaha, Nebraska, branch and helped get black workers into jobs previously reserved for whites. In the process he more than tripled the organization's paid membership. In 1947 Young earned a master's in social work at the University of Minnesota. He became a university lecturer and by 1954 was dean of the School of Social Work at Atlanta University, Georgia. In that position Young supported alumni in their boycott of the Georgia Conference of Social Welfare, which had a poor record of

▲ **Whitney M. Young in 1963, the year in which he helped lead the March on Washington.**

placing African Americans in good jobs. He also joined the National Association for the Advancement of Colored People (NAACP) and rose to become state president.

In 1961 Young became executive director of the NUL. By 1964 he had expanded the organization from 38 to 1,600 employees and increased the annual budget from $325,000 to $6.1 million creating thousands of new jobs for African Americans. During his 10-year tenure at the NUL, he initiated programs such as "Street Academy," an alternative education system to prepare high school dropouts for college. Young also participated in the 1963 March on Washington. From 1966 he was president of the National Association of Social Workers. He was against the Vietnam War, claiming that it diverted funds from domestic programs. Young died in 1971.

KEY DATES	
1921	Born in Lincoln Ridge, Kentucky, on July 31.
1961	Becomes executive director of the NUL.
1963	Is one of the leaders in the March on Washington.
1969	Awarded the Presidential Medal of Freedom.
1971	Dies in Lagos, Nigeria, on March 11.

See also: Civil Rights; National Organizations

Further reading: http://www.naswdc.org/diversity/black_history/young.asp (Biography).

YOUNGBLOOD, Shay
Writer, Teacher

The recipient of many awards, including the New York Foundation for the Arts' Sustained Achievement Award (2004–2005), novelist, playwright, poet, and teacher Shay Youngblood writes about the experiences of African American people and the importance of family bonds.

Early life

Born in Columbus, Georgia, in 1959, Youngblood was raised by her grandmother and aunts following the death of her mother. A voracious reader, Youngblood often dreamed that she lived in a library. She also enjoyed listening to the stories of her extended family, particularly those of her female relatives, who inspired in her a love of storytelling and encouraged her to be "an independent free-thinking person."

Graduating with a BA in mass communications from Clark–Atlanta University in 1981, Youngblood joined the Peace Corps and served as an agricultural information officer in the Dominican Republic. While there Youngblood published her first short story, "In a House of Wooden Monkies."

▼ *Like Shay Youngblood herself, several of her heroines are orphaned at a young age.*

KEY DATES	
1959	Born in Columbus, Georgia.
1988	The play *Shakin' the Mess Outta Misery* opens at the Horizon Theater, Atlanta.
1989	Publishes *The Big Mama Stories*.
1991	Wins the NAACP Theater Award for best playwright.
1997	Publishes debut novel *Soul Kiss*.
2000	Publishes *Black Girl in Paris*.

Creative experience

Inspired by the stories and people of her childhood, Youngblood's first play, *Shakin' the Mess Outta Misery*, was performed at the Horizon Theater in Atlanta in 1988. Youngblood was subsequently named Susan Smith Blackburn Playwrighting Prize finalist in 1989; two years later she won the NAACP theater award for best playwright. Her childhood memories provided material for her first collection of short stories, *The Big Mama Stories*, published in 1989.

While writing plays such as *Communism Killed My Dog* (1991) and *Black Power Barbie in Hotel de Dream* (1992), Youngblood worked several different jobs to earn a living, including as an artist's model and a cleaner. A friend persuaded her to apply for a master's in fine arts creative writing course at Brown University, Rhode Island, from which she graduated in 1993. Youngblood then returned to playwriting, producing such works as *Amazing Grace* (1995). Finding play scripts too restrictive in terms of plot, in the mid-1990s Youngblood turned to writing novels. She published *Soul Kiss* in 1997 and *Black Girl in Paris* in 2000.

Youngblood has received numerous awards for her playwriting, including the Lorraine Hansberry Playwriting Award and several NAACP writers awards. She has also taught many writing courses, including creative writing at the Syracuse Community Writer's Project and playwriting at Brown University. She was also writer-in-residence at the University of Mississippi.

Further reading: Youngblood, Shay. *The Big Mama Stories.* Ann Arbor, MI: Firebrand Books, 1989.
http://www.shayyoungblood.com (Official site).

ZOLLAR, Doris
Activist

An elegant and charming person with a deep-rooted sense of philanthropy, Doris Zollar served as the first African American chair of the Chicago chapter of the United Nations Children's Fund and sat on the board of several prestigious Chicago community organizations.

Early life
Born in Little Rock, Arkansas, on December 7, 1931, Zollar had a comfortable and happy childhood surrounded by family. Her grandfather had defeated attempts made by neighboring white people to take his valuable farmland. Zollar grew up in a supportive environment and her parents emphasized the value of both education and philanthropy.

Following her parents' lead, Zollar graduated from Little Rock's Dunbar High School in 1947. Four years later she earned a BA from Talladega College, Alabama, and went on to earn an MA from the Univesity of California, Los Angeles (UCLA). In 1954 she married Lowell Zollar, a pediatrician and medical director. The couple settled in Chicago, Illinois, where Zollar first worked as a public schoolteacher.

Making a difference
In 1974 Zollar became the executive assistant to the director of the Woodlawn Organization. The historic community group has worked to better the social environment of the predominantly black Chicago neighborhood of Woodlawn by protesting unjust education and unfair housing conditions. Two years later Zollar became the director of development for the organization, and a year later established Triad Consulting, a business focused on contracting and vending ventures.

Committed philanthropists, Zollar and her husband have contributed their family funds to various groups. Zollar has helped raise money for the high-profile

▲ **Doris Zollar has dedicated her life to helping improve the lives of vulnerable people.**

organizations on whose boards she has served, including the Chicago chapter of Jesse Jackson's Rainbow/PUSH Coalition—of which Zollar was a founding member—the United Negro College Fund, the United Nations Children Fund, the World Service Council of the YWCA, the Chicago Heart Association, the Chicago Academy of Performing Arts, and the Chicago Port Authority. In addition Zollar set up a scholarship in her husband's name that gives funds to a college-bound senior graduating from Lowell Zollar's alma mater, DuSable High School. Zollar has lived her life honoring the simple advice that her beloved mother gave her during childhood: "A closed fist will not let anything out, but it can't accept anything either. You must always give."

Further reading: http://www.thehistorymakers.com/biography/biography.asp?bioindex=275&category=civicMakers (Biography).

KEY DATES

1931	Born in Little Rock, Arkansas, on December 7.
1954	Marries Lowell Zollar and moves to Chicago.
1976	Becomes the director of development for the Woodlawn Organization.

SET INDEX

Set Index

Set Index

Set Index